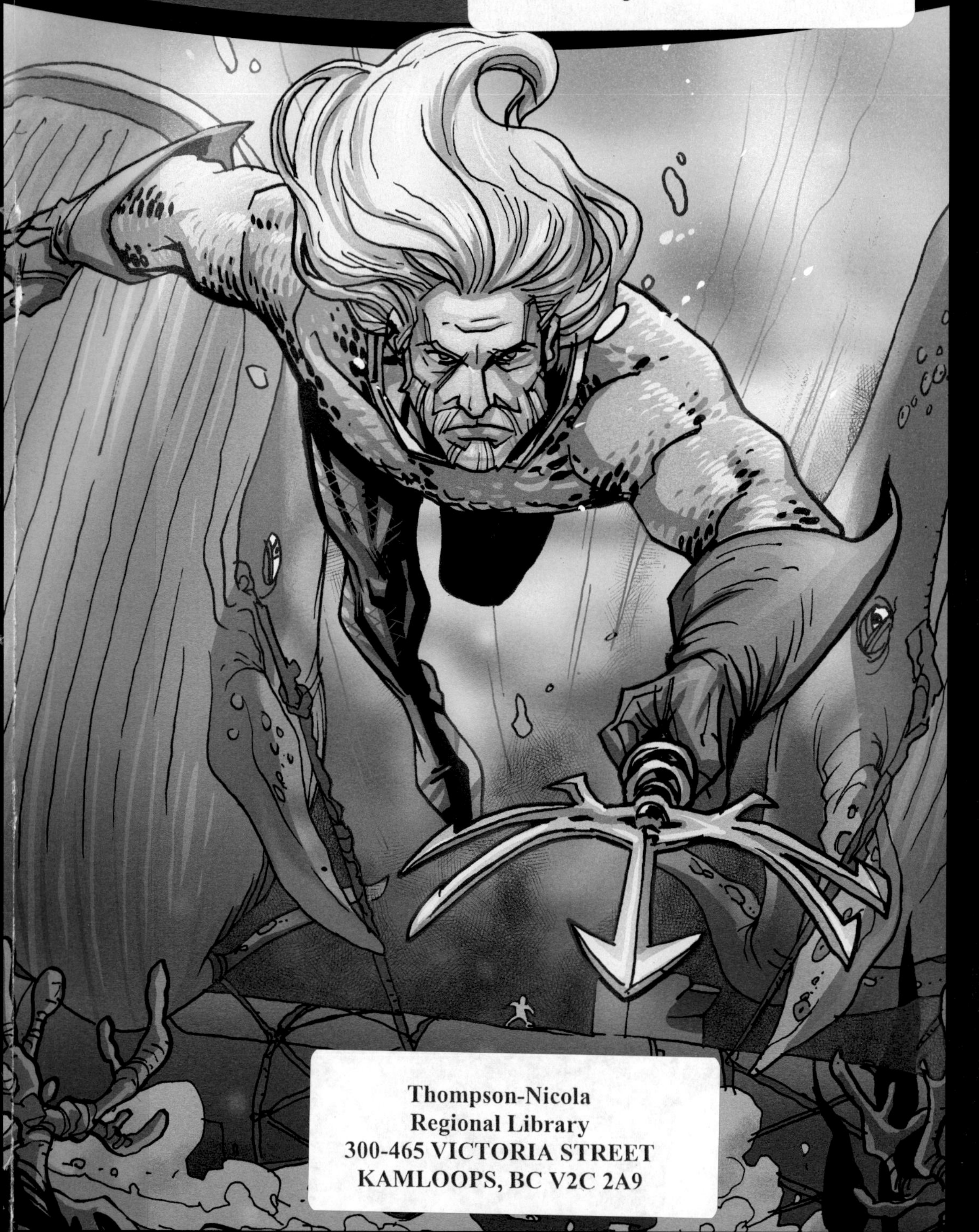

JUSTICE LEAGUE

VOL.6 THE PEOPLE VS. THE JUSTICE LEAGUE

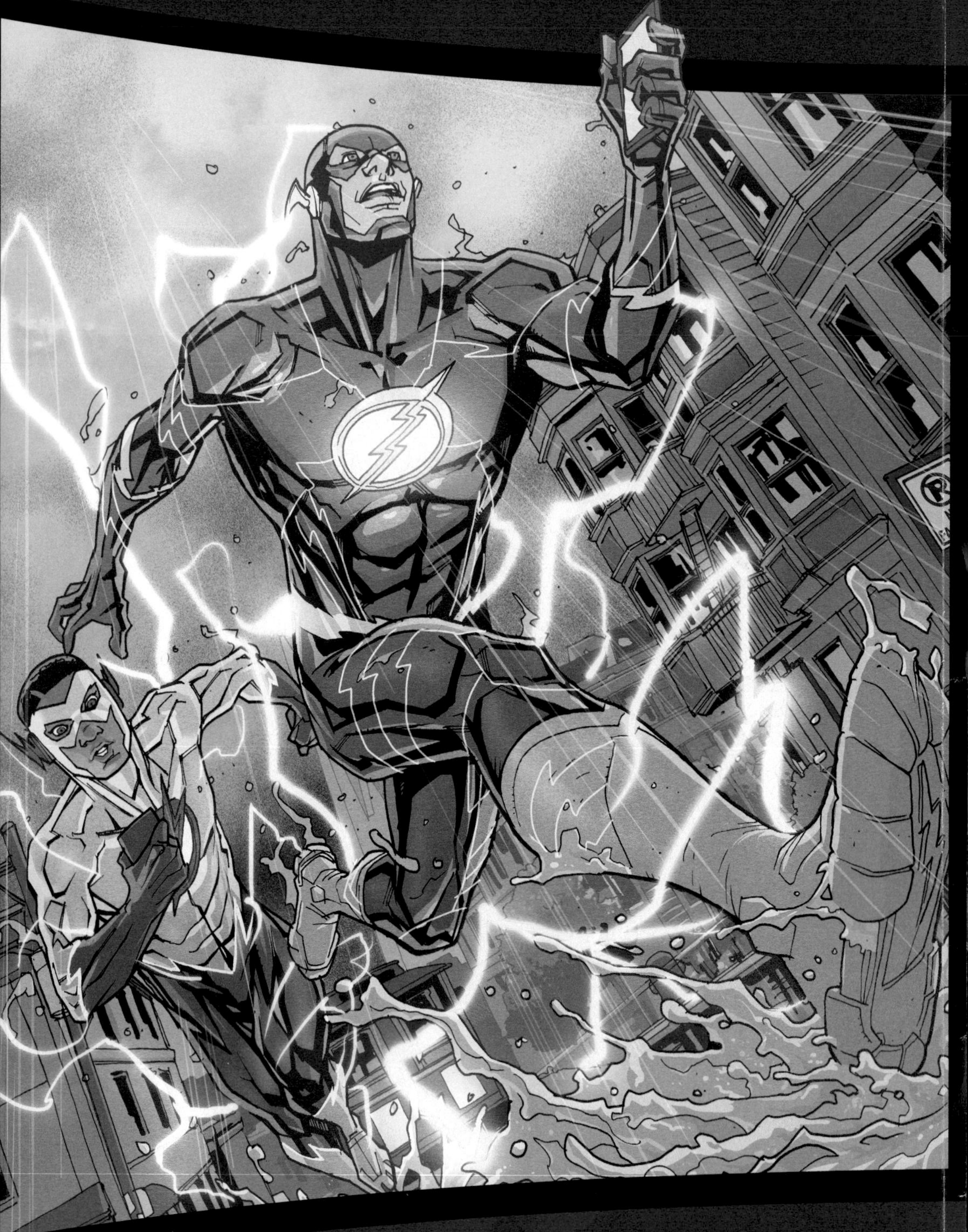

JUSTICE LEAGUE
VOL.6 THE PEOPLE VS. THE JUSTICE LEAGUE

CHRISTOPHER PRIEST
writer

PETE WOODS
PHILIPPE BRIONES * **MARCO SANTUCCI**
artists

PETE WOODS
GABE ELTAEB * **ALEX SOLLAZZO**
colorists

WILLIE SCHU
letterer

PETE WOODS
collection cover artist

SUPERMAN created by **JERRY SIEGEL** and **JOE SHUSTER**
By special arrangement with the Jerry Siegel family

BRIAN CUNNINGHAM ✳ REBECCA TAYLOR Editors - Original Series
JEB WOODARD Group Editor - Collected Editions ✳ ROBIN WILDMAN Editor - Collected Edition
STEVE COOK Design Director - Books ✳ MEGEN BELLERSEN Publication Design

BOB HARRAS Senior VP - Editor-in-Chief, DC Comics
PAT McCALLUM Executive Editor, DC Comics

DIANE NELSON President ✳ DAN DiDIO Publisher ✳ JIM LEE Publisher ✳ GEOFF JOHNS President & Chief Creative Officer
AMIT DESAI Executive VP - Business & Marketing Strategy, Direct to Consumer & Global Franchise Management
SAM ADES Senior VP & General Manager, Digital Services ✳ BOBBIE CHASE VP & Executive Editor, Young Reader & Talent Development
MARK CHIARELLO Senior VP - Art, Design & Collected Editions ✳ JOHN CUNNINGHAM Senior VP - Sales & Trade Marketing
ANNE DePIES Senior VP - Business Strategy, Finance & Administration ✳ DON FALLETTI VP - Manufacturing Operations
LAWRENCE GANEM VP - Editorial Administration & Talent Relations ✳ ALISON GILL Senior VP - Manufacturing & Operations
HANK KANALZ Senior VP - Editorial Strategy & Administration ✳ JAY KOGAN VP - Legal Affairs ✳ JACK MAHAN VP - Business Affairs
NICK J. NAPOLITANO VP - Manufacturing Administration ✳ EDDIE SCANNELL VP - Consumer Marketing
COURTNEY SIMMONS Senior VP - Publicity & Communications ✳ JIM (SKI) SOKOLOWSKI VP - Comic Book Specialty Sales & Trade Marketing
NANCY SPEARS VP - Mass, Book, Digital Sales & Trade Marketing ✳ MICHELE R. WELLS VP – Content Strategy

JUSTICE LEAGUE VOL. 6: THE PEOPLE VS. THE JUSTICE LEAGUE

DC Comics, 2900 West Alameda Ave., Burbank, CA 91505
Printed by LSC Communications, Kendallville, IN, USA. 5/18/18. First Printing.
ISBN: 978-1-4012-8076-5

Library of Congress Cataloging-in-Publication Data is available.

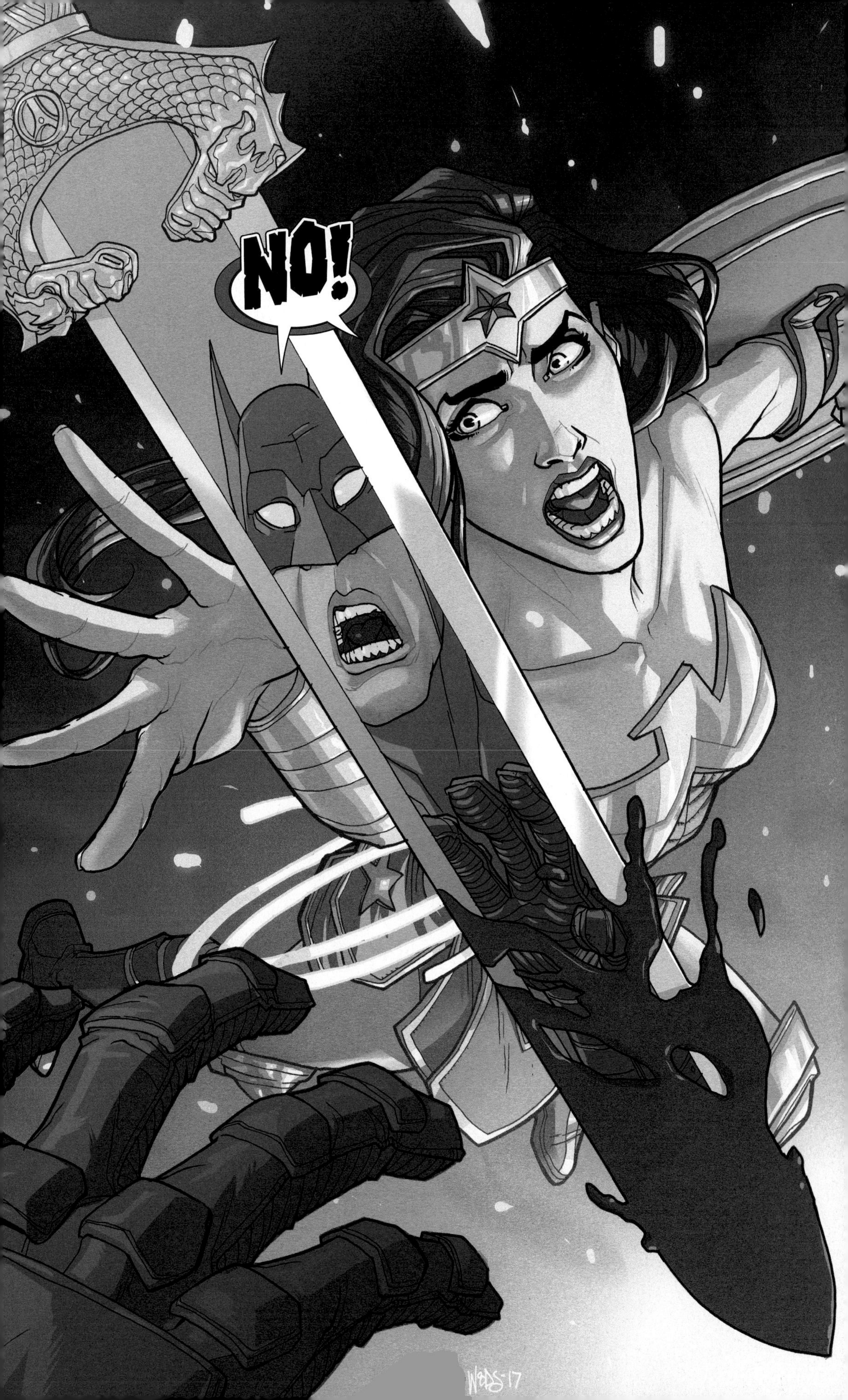
NO!

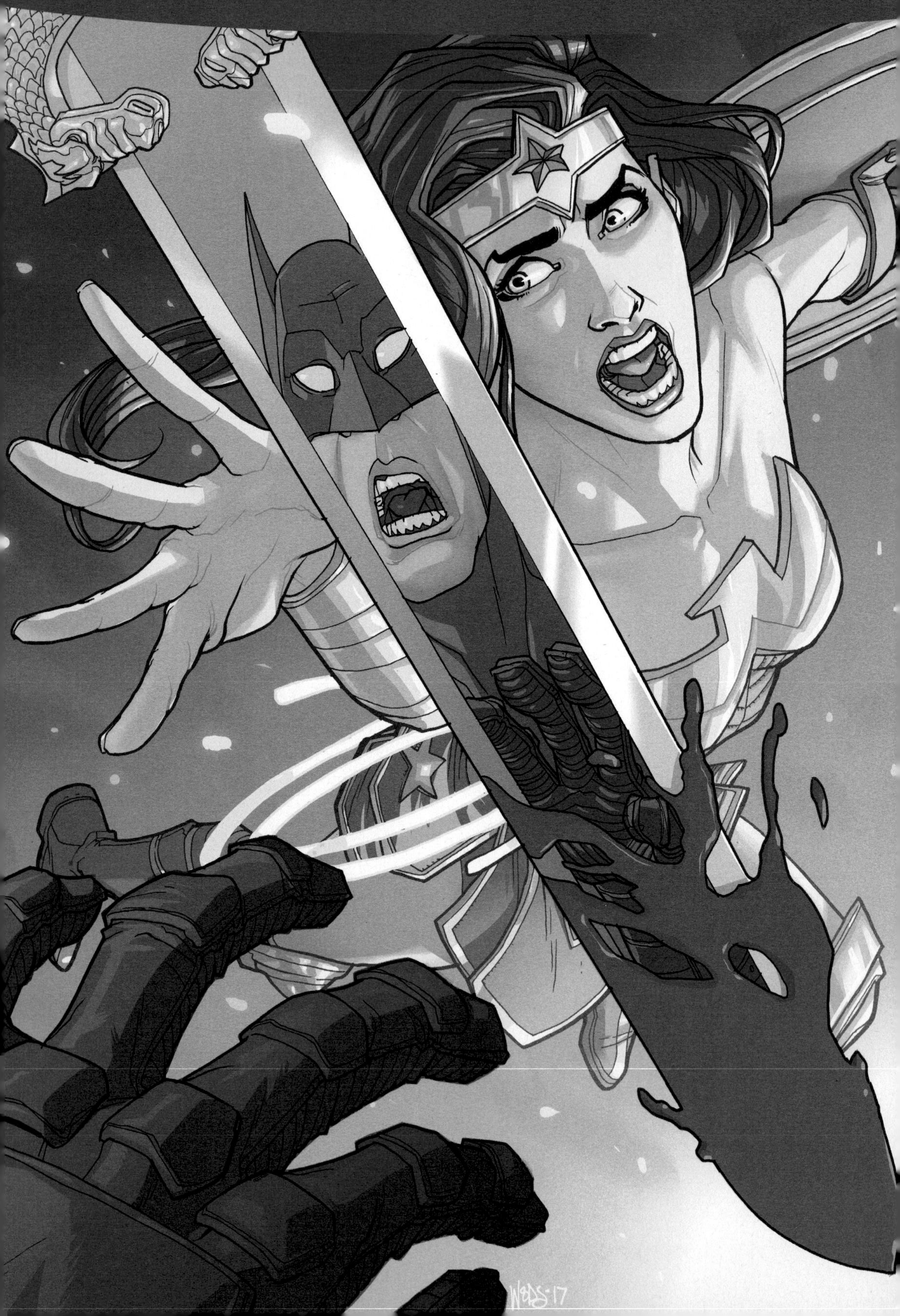

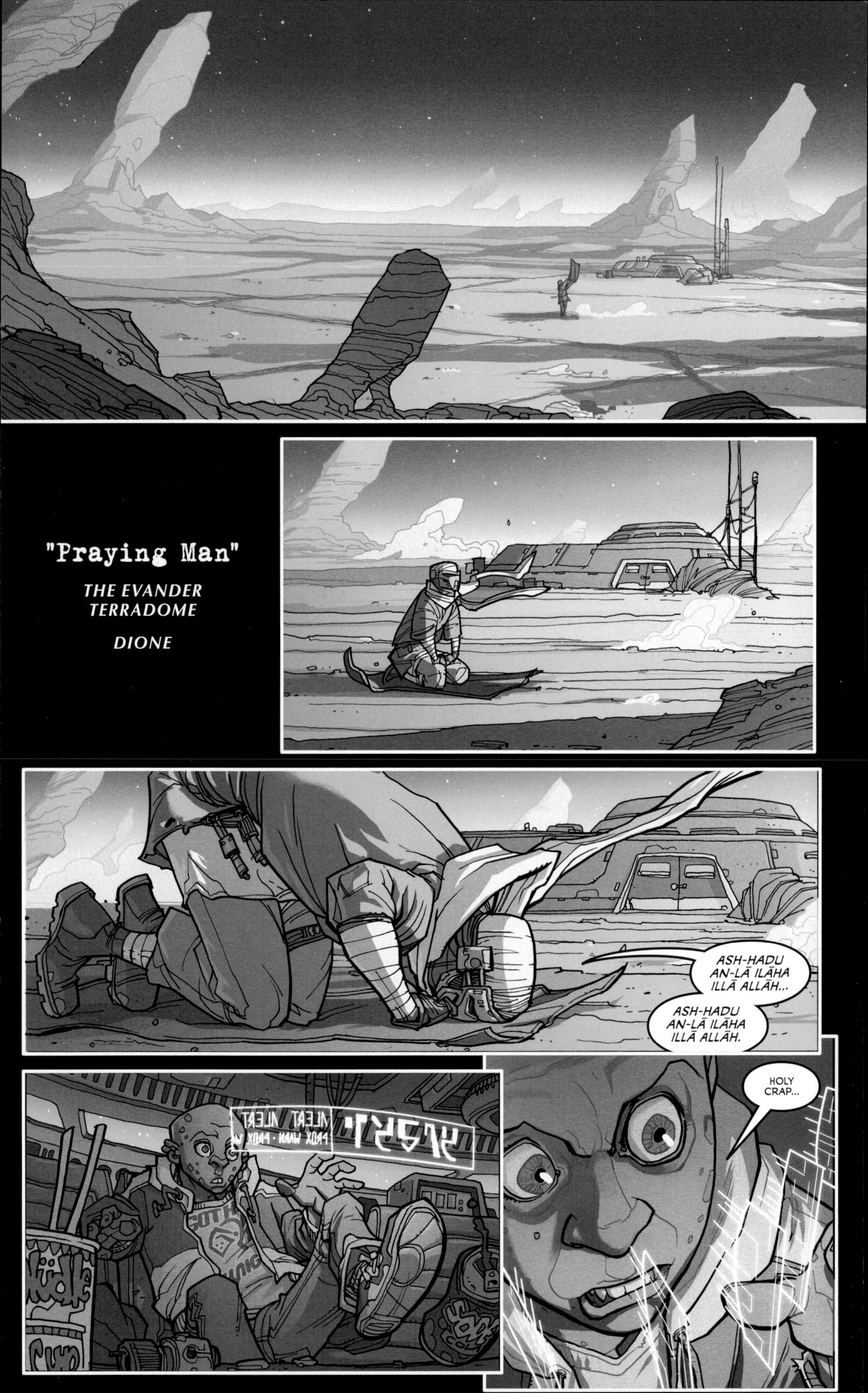
"Praying Man"
THE EVANDER TERRADOME
DIONE
ASH-HADU AN-LĀ ILĀHA ILLĀ ALLĀH...
ASH-HADU AN-LĀ ILĀHA ILLĀ ALLĀH.
HOLY CRAP...

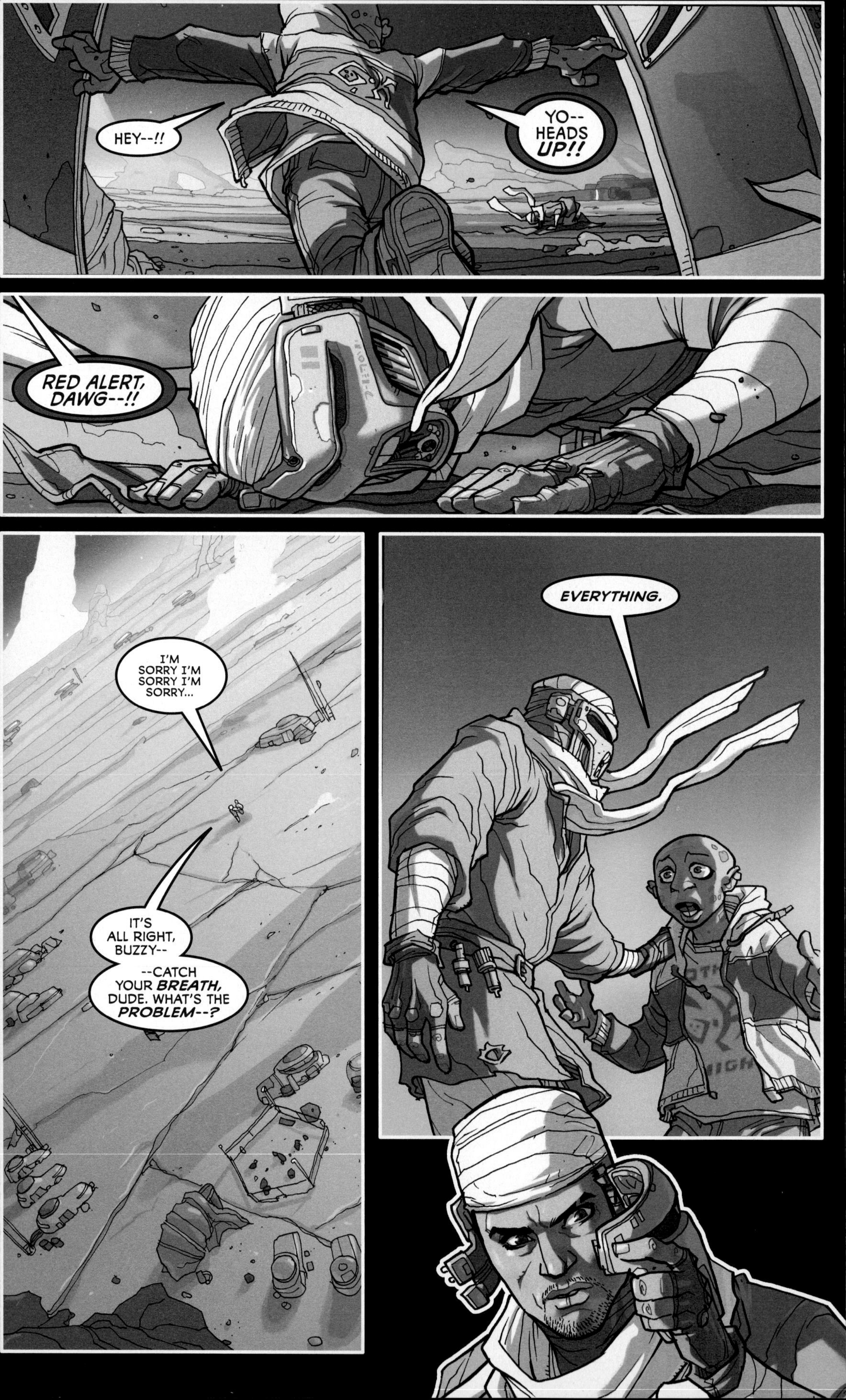
HEY--!!
YO-- HEADS UP!!
RED ALERT, DAWG--!!
I'M SORRY I'M SORRY I'M SORRY...
IT'S ALL RIGHT, BUZZY--
--CATCH YOUR BREATH, DUDE. WHAT'S THE PROBLEM--?
EVERYTHING.

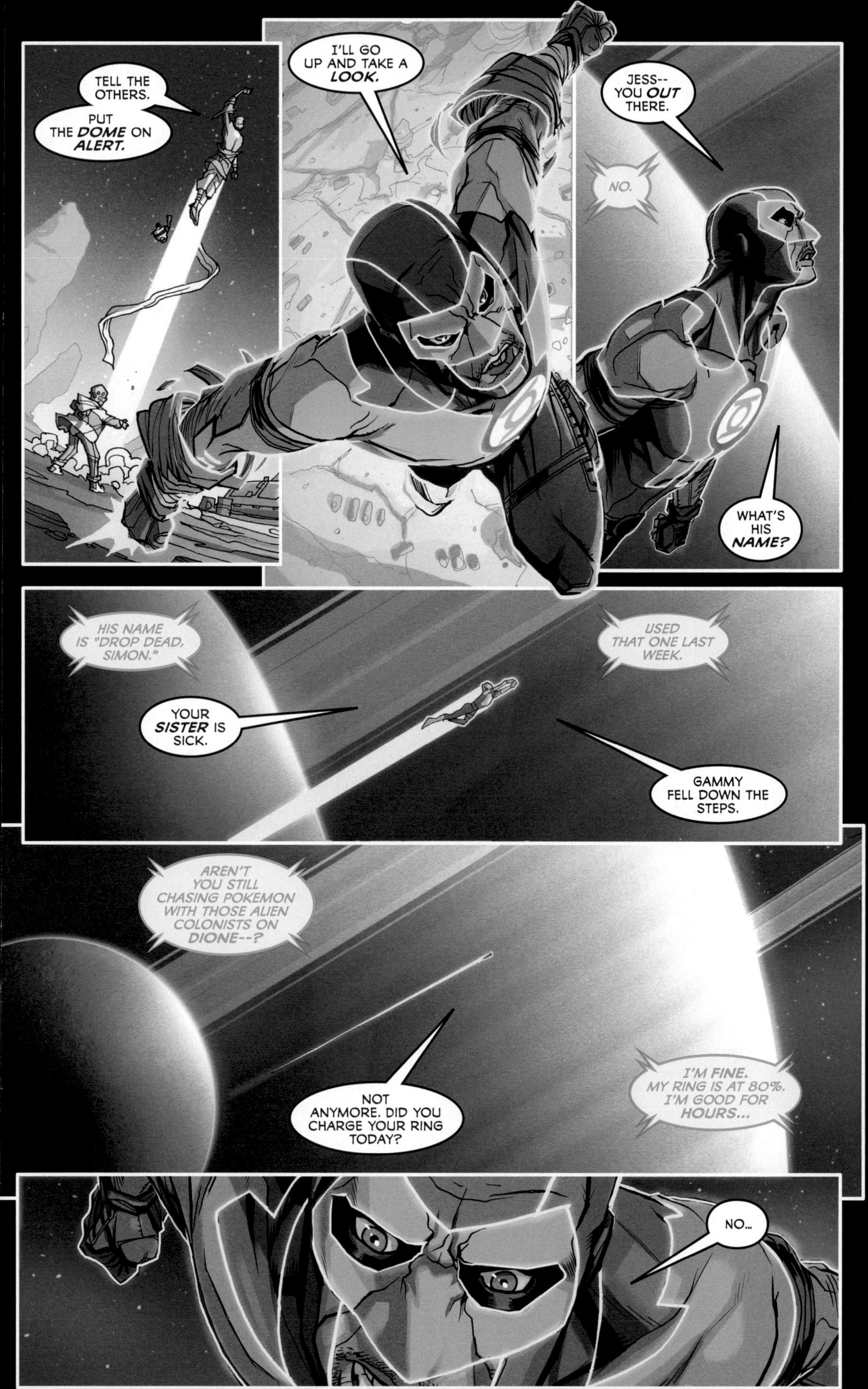
TELL THE OTHERS.
PUT THE DOME ON ALERT.
I'LL GO UP AND TAKE A LOOK.
JESS-- YOU OUT THERE.
NO.
WHAT'S HIS NAME?
HIS NAME IS "DROP DEAD, SIMON."
USED THAT ONE LAST WEEK.
YOUR SISTER IS SICK.
GAMMY FELL DOWN THE STEPS.
AREN'T YOU STILL CHASING POKEMON WITH THOSE ALIEN COLONISTS ON DIONE--?
NOT ANYMORE. DID YOU CHARGE YOUR RING TODAY?
I'M FINE. MY RING IS AT 80%. I'M GOOD FOR HOURS...
NO...

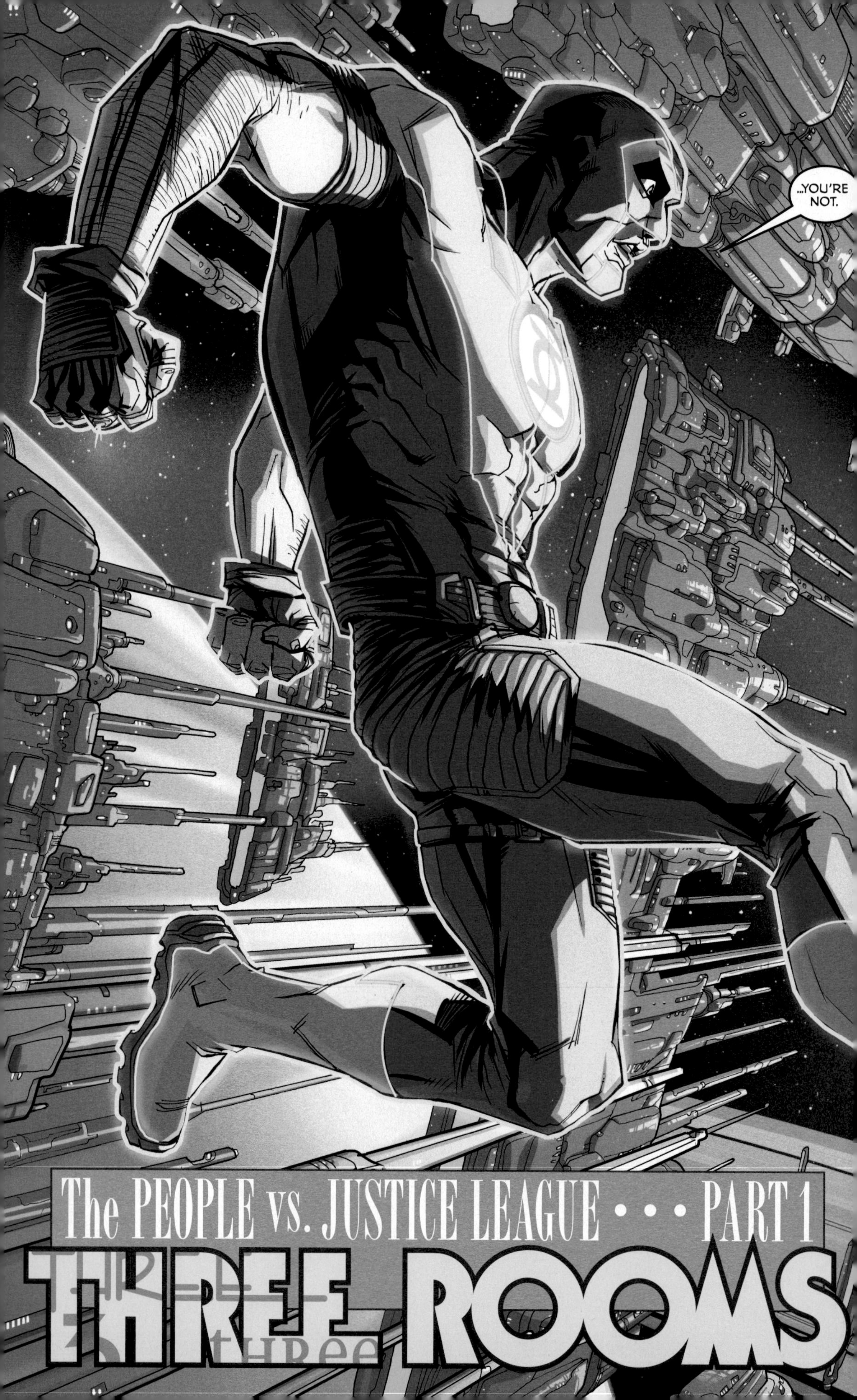
...YOU'RE NOT.
The PEOPLE vs. JUSTICE LEAGUE • • • PART 1
THREE ROOMS

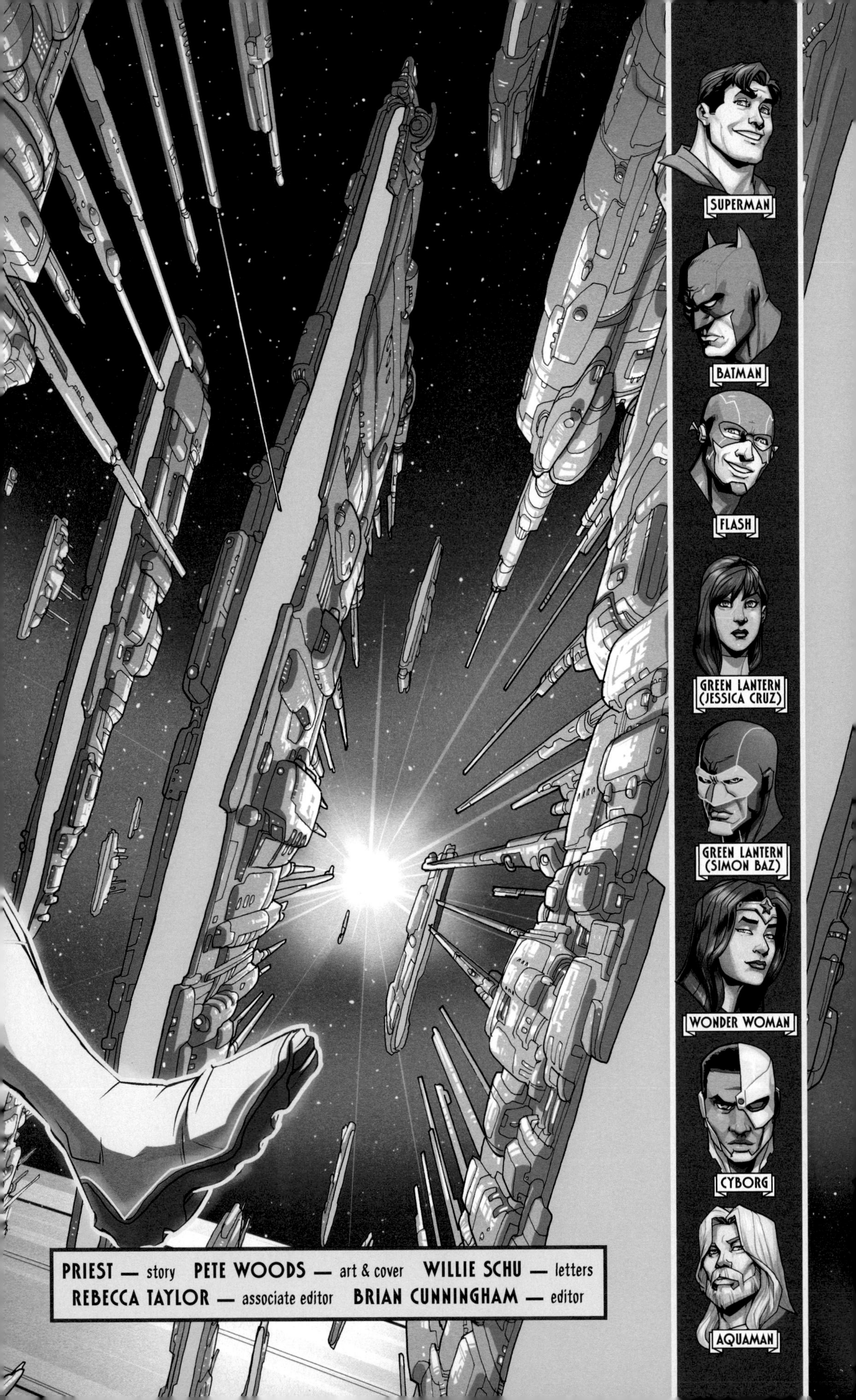
SUPERMAN
BATMAN
FLASH
GREEN LANTERN (JESSICA CRUZ)
GREEN LANTERN (SIMON BAZ)
WONDER WOMAN
CYBORG
AQUAMAN
PRIEST — story PETE WOODS — art & cover WILLIE SCHU — letters
REBECCA TAYLOR — associate editor BRIAN CUNNINGHAM — editor

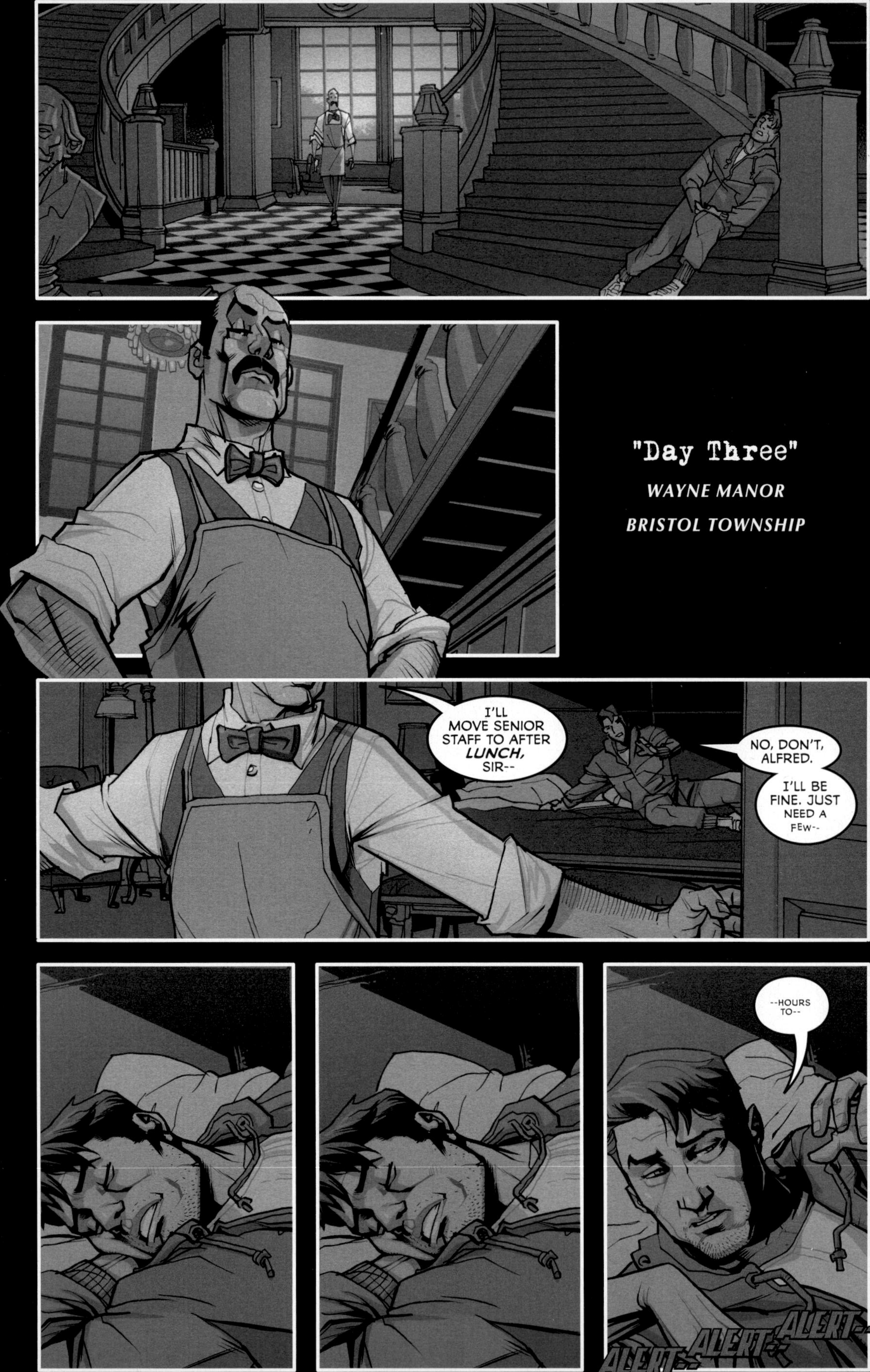
"Day Three"
WAYNE MANOR
BRISTOL TOWNSHIP
I'LL MOVE SENIOR STAFF TO AFTER *LUNCH,* SIR--
NO, DON'T, ALFRED.
I'LL BE FINE. JUST NEED A FEW--
--HOURS TO--
ALERT-- ALERT-- ALERT--

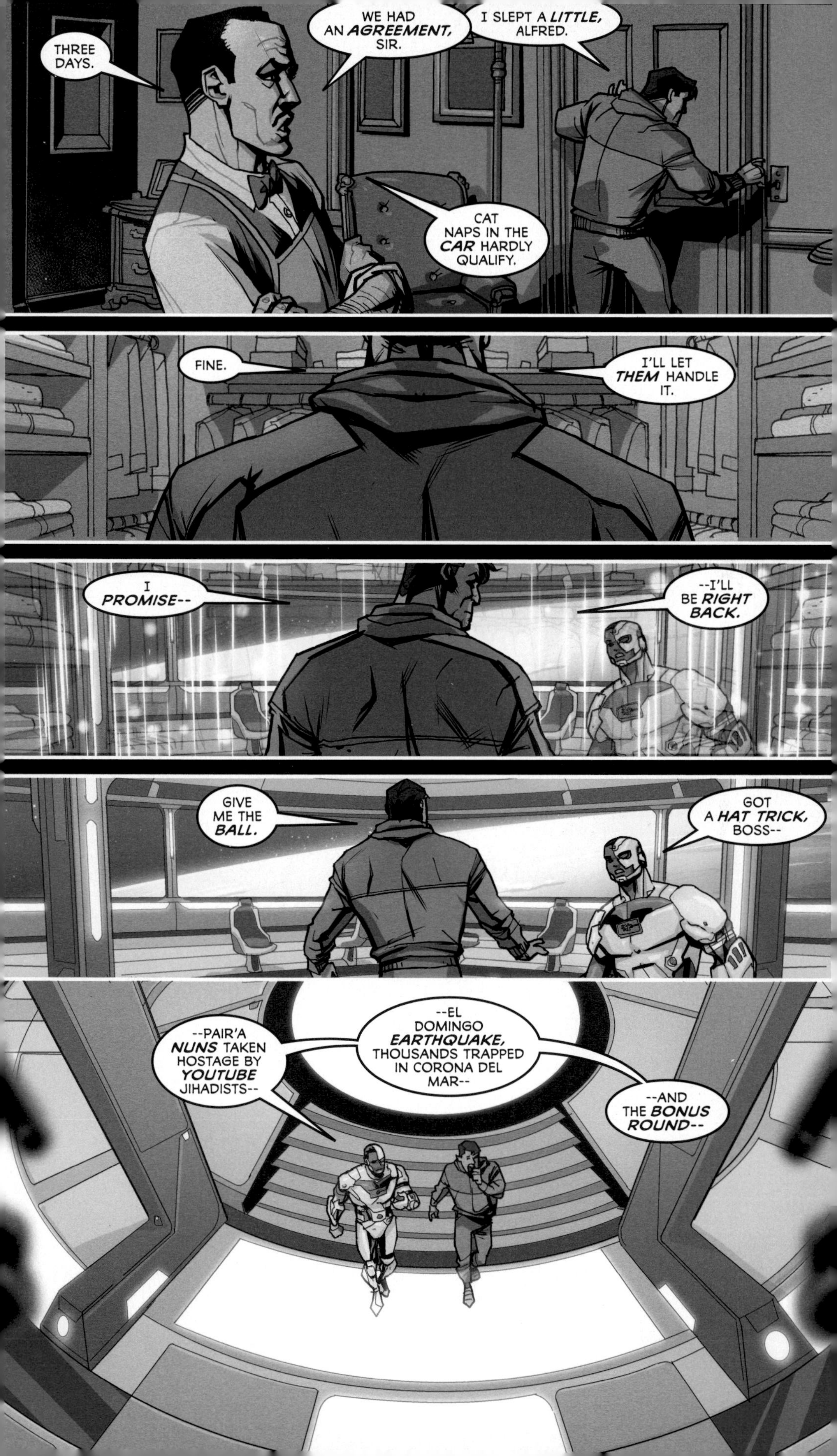
THREE DAYS.
WE HAD AN AGREEMENT, SIR.
I SLEPT A LITTLE, ALFRED.
CAT NAPS IN THE CAR HARDLY QUALIFY.
FINE.
I'LL LET THEM HANDLE IT.
I PROMISE--
--I'LL BE RIGHT BACK.
GIVE ME THE BALL.
GOT A HAT TRICK, BOSS--
--PAIR'A NUNS TAKEN HOSTAGE BY YOUTUBE JIHADISTS--
--EL DOMINGO EARTHQUAKE, THOUSANDS TRAPPED IN CORONA DEL MAR--
--AND THE BONUS ROUND--

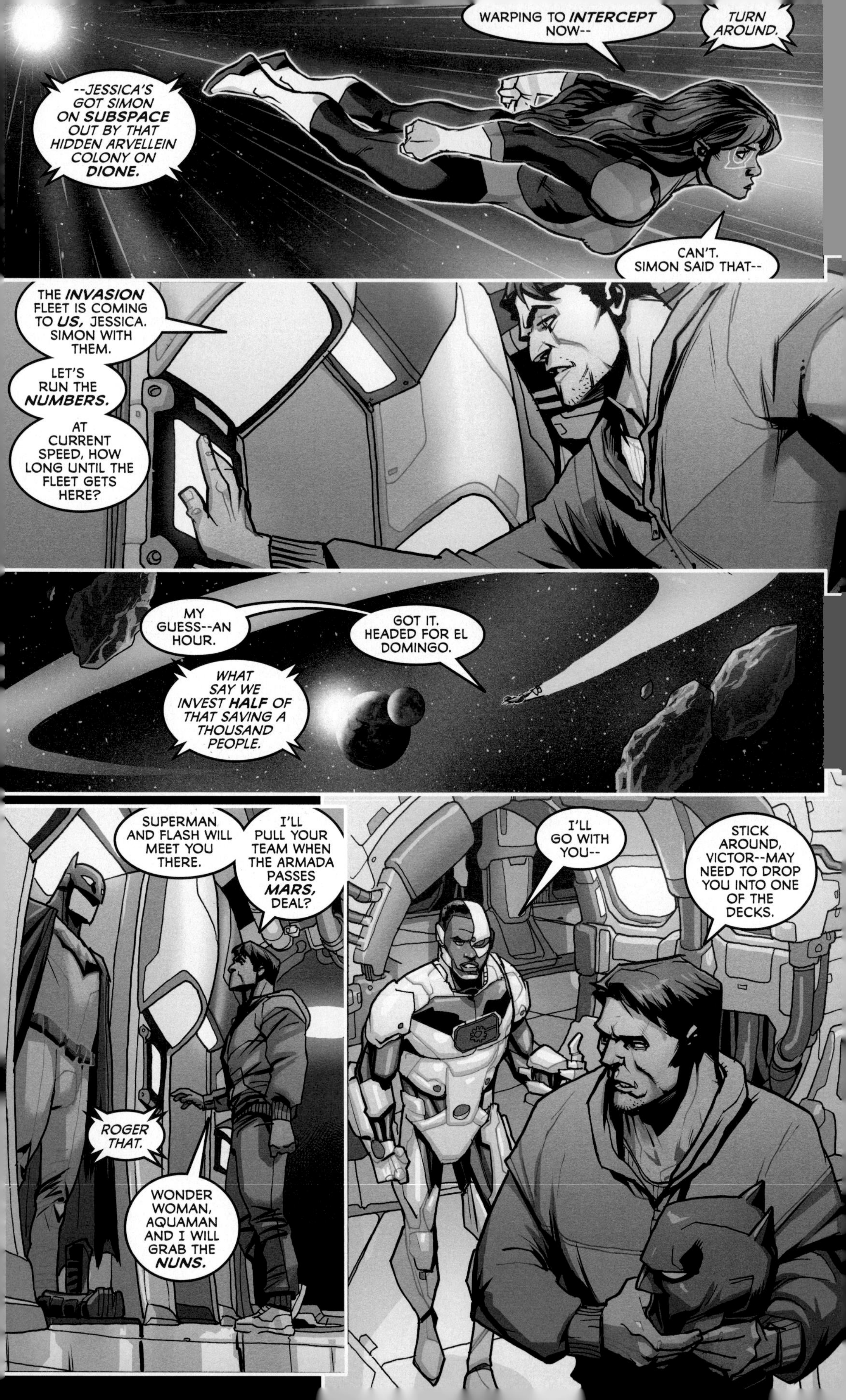
--JESSICA'S GOT SIMON ON SUBSPACE OUT BY THAT HIDDEN ARVELLEIN COLONY ON DIONE.
WARPING TO INTERCEPT NOW--
TURN AROUND.
CAN'T. SIMON SAID THAT--
THE INVASION FLEET IS COMING TO US, JESSICA. SIMON WITH THEM.
LET'S RUN THE NUMBERS.
AT CURRENT SPEED, HOW LONG UNTIL THE FLEET GETS HERE?
MY GUESS--AN HOUR.
GOT IT. HEADED FOR EL DOMINGO.
WHAT SAY WE INVEST HALF OF THAT SAVING A THOUSAND PEOPLE.
SUPERMAN AND FLASH WILL MEET YOU THERE.
I'LL PULL YOUR TEAM WHEN THE ARMADA PASSES MARS, DEAL?
ROGER THAT.
WONDER WOMAN, AQUAMAN AND I WILL GRAB THE NUNS.
I'LL GO WITH YOU--
STICK AROUND, VICTOR--MAY NEED TO DROP YOU INTO ONE OF THE DECKS.

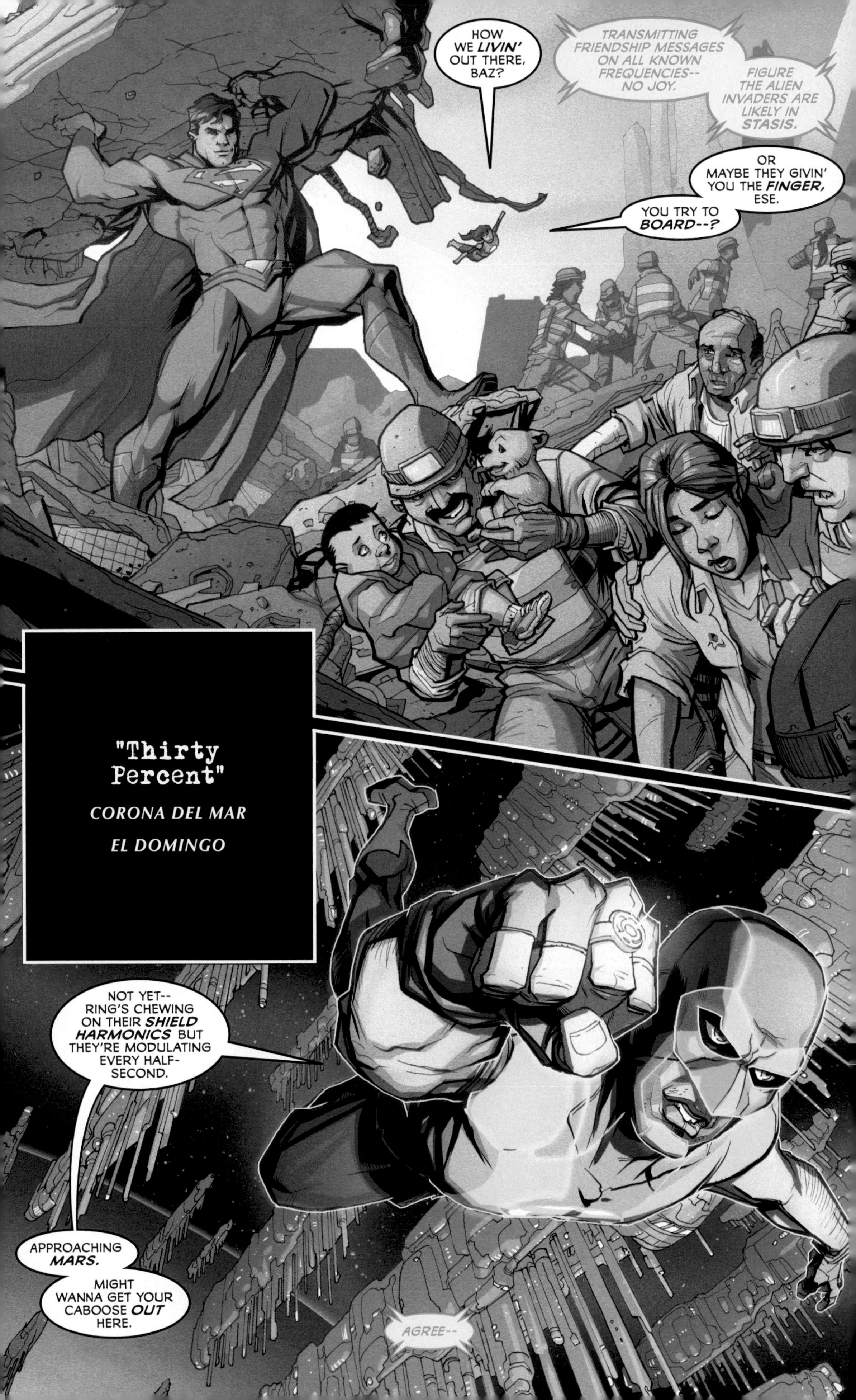
HOW WE LIVIN' OUT THERE, BAZ?
TRANSMITTING FRIENDSHIP MESSAGES ON ALL KNOWN FREQUENCIES-- NO JOY.
FIGURE THE ALIEN INVADERS ARE LIKELY IN STASIS.
OR MAYBE THEY GIVIN' YOU THE FINGER, ESE.
YOU TRY TO BOARD--?
"Thirty Percent"
CORONA DEL MAR
EL DOMINGO
NOT YET-- RING'S CHEWING ON THEIR SHIELD HARMONICS BUT THEY'RE MODULATING EVERY HALF-SECOND.
APPROACHING MARS.
MIGHT WANNA GET YOUR CABOOSE OUT HERE.
AGREE--

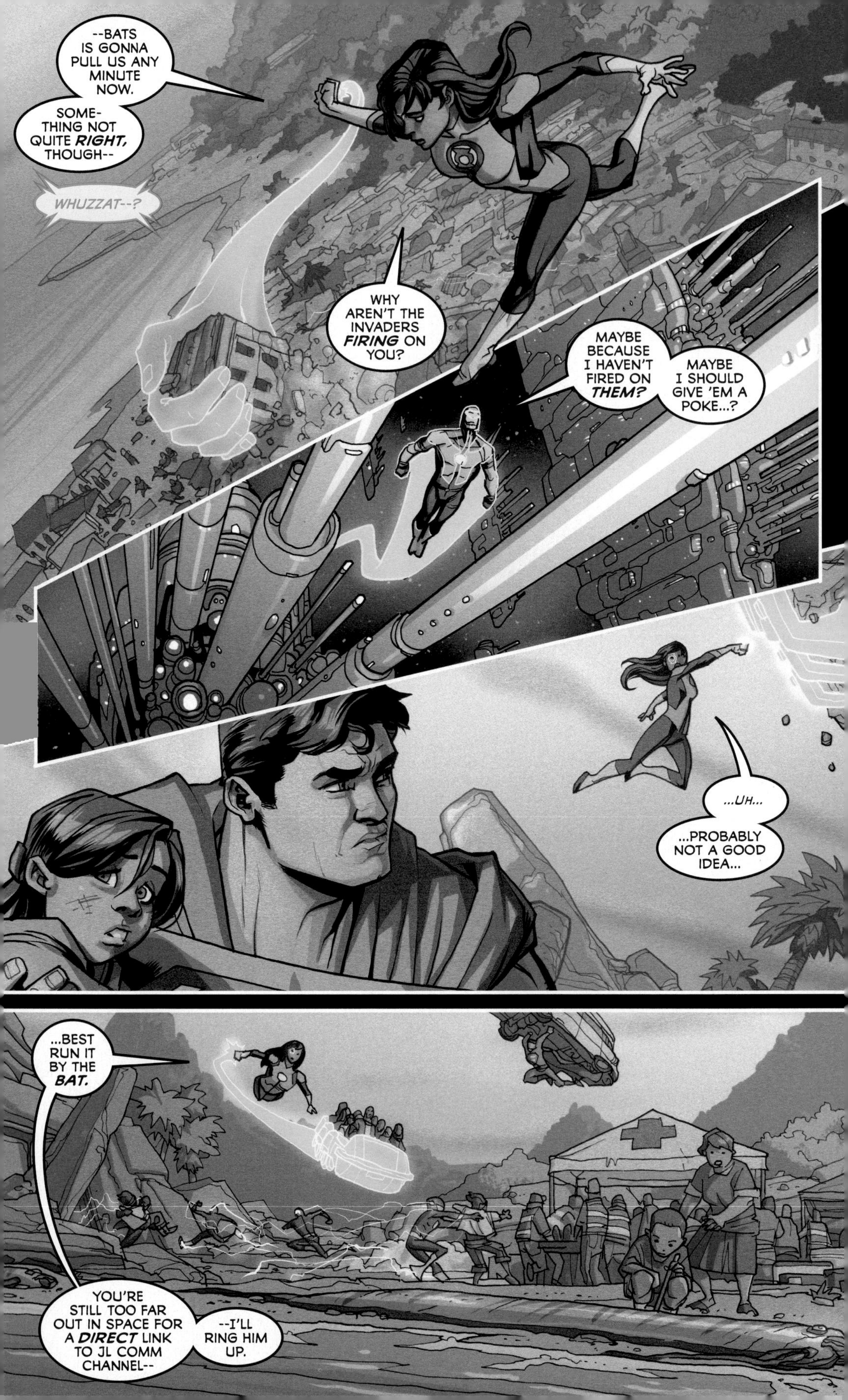
--BATS IS GONNA PULL US ANY MINUTE NOW.
SOME-THING NOT QUITE RIGHT, THOUGH--
WHUZZAT--?
WHY AREN'T THE INVADERS FIRING ON YOU?
MAYBE BECAUSE I HAVEN'T FIRED ON THEM?
MAYBE I SHOULD GIVE 'EM A POKE...?
...UH...
...PROBABLY NOT A GOOD IDEA...
...BEST RUN IT BY THE BAT.
YOU'RE STILL TOO FAR OUT IN SPACE FOR A DIRECT LINK TO JL COMM CHANNEL--
--I'LL RING HIM UP.

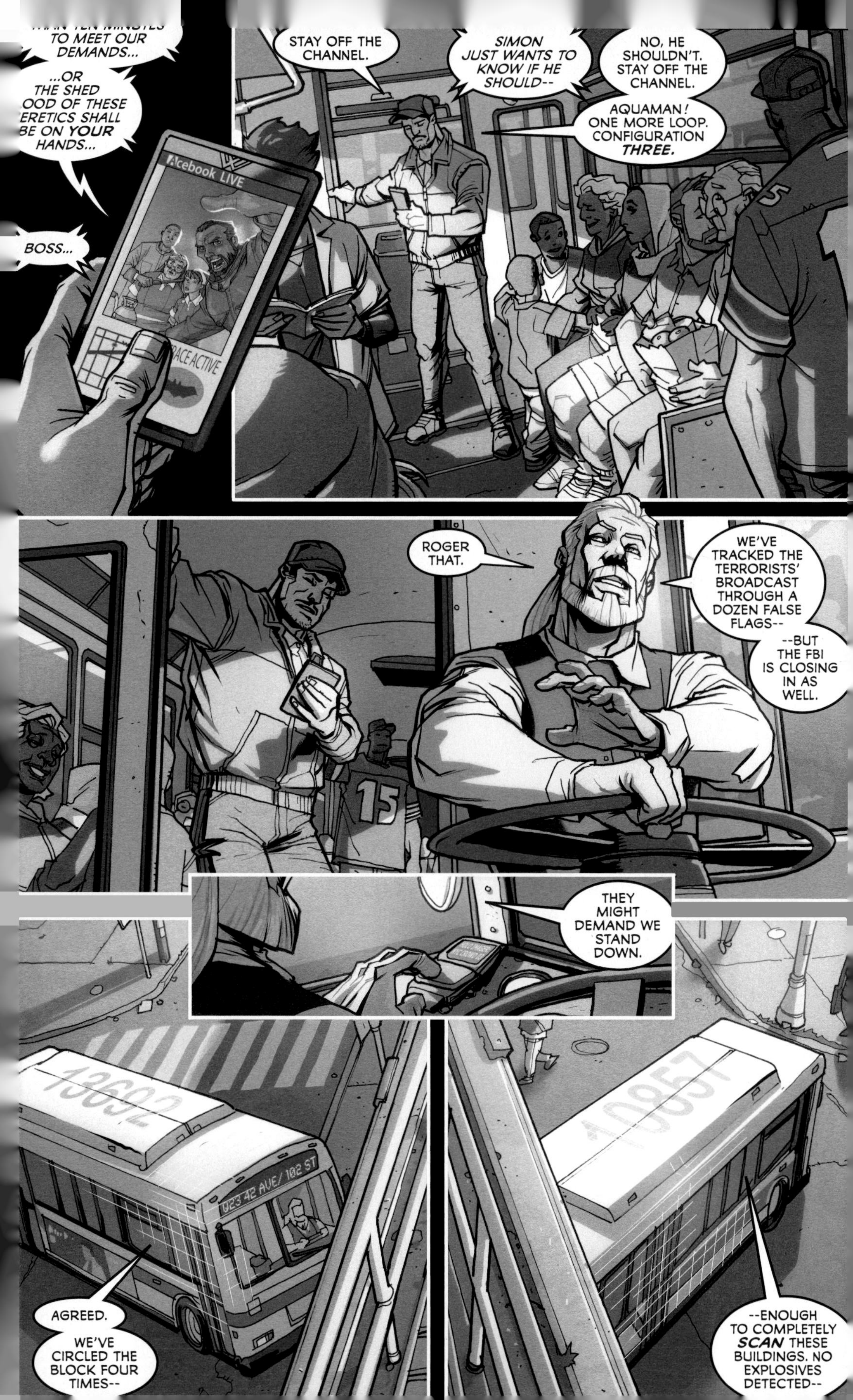
TO MEET OUR DEMANDS...
...OR THE SHED
OOD OF THESE
ERETICS SHALL BE ON YOUR HANDS...
Acebook LIVE
PACE ACTIVE
BOSS...
STAY OFF THE CHANNEL.
SIMON JUST WANTS TO KNOW IF HE SHOULD--
NO, HE SHOULDN'T. STAY OFF THE CHANNEL.
AQUAMAN! ONE MORE LOOP. CONFIGURATION THREE.
15
ROGER THAT.
WE'VE TRACKED THE TERRORISTS' BROADCAST THROUGH A DOZEN FALSE FLAGS--
--BUT THE FBI IS CLOSING IN AS WELL.
15
THEY MIGHT DEMAND WE STAND DOWN.
13692
023 42 AVE/ 102 ST
AGREED.
WE'VE CIRCLED THE BLOCK FOUR TIMES--
10857
--ENOUGH TO COMPLETELY SCAN THESE BUILDINGS. NO EXPLOSIVES DETECTED--

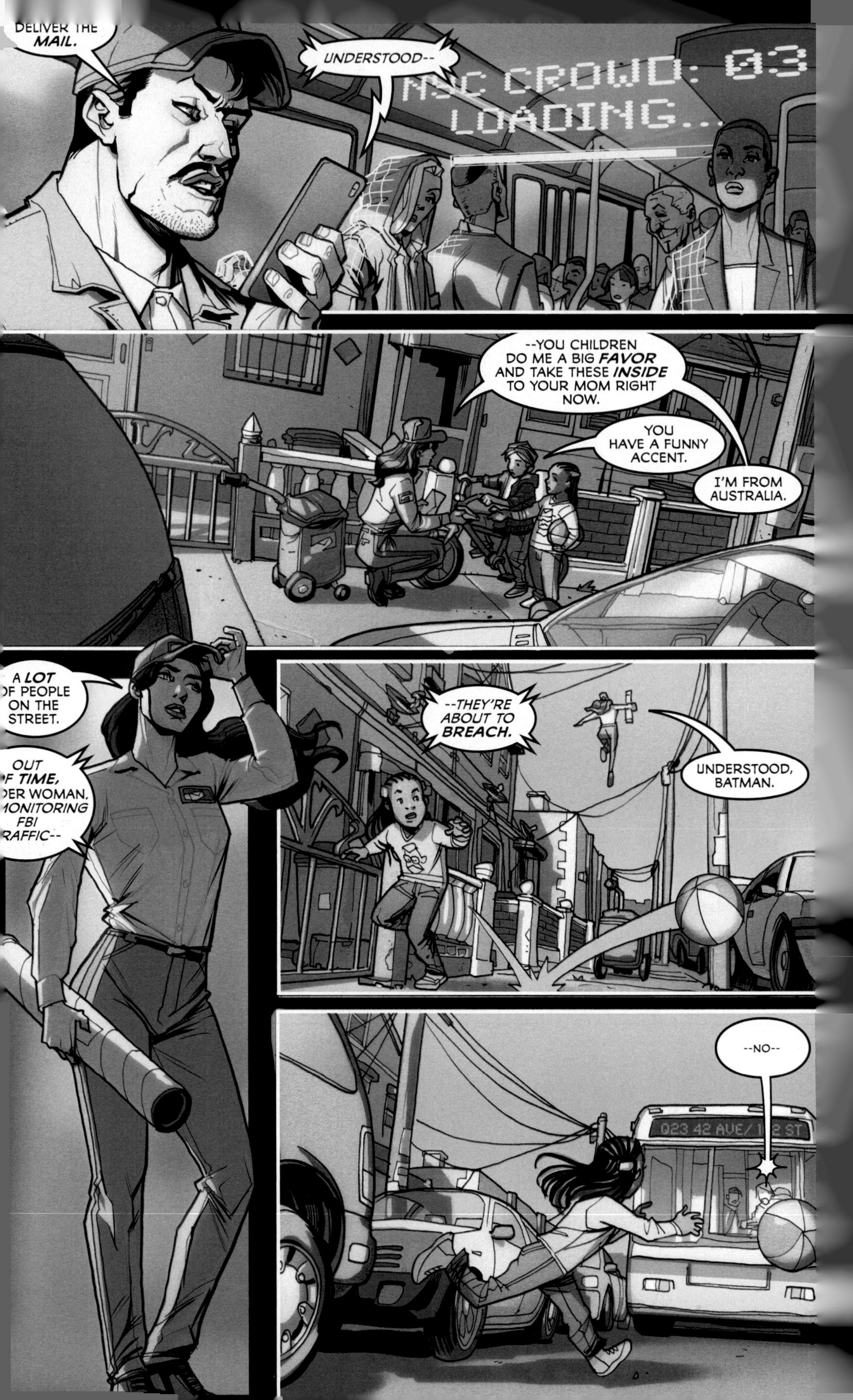
DELIVER THE MAIL.
UNDERSTOOD--
NSC CROWD: 03
LOADING...
--YOU CHILDREN DO ME A BIG FAVOR AND TAKE THESE INSIDE TO YOUR MOM RIGHT NOW.
YOU HAVE A FUNNY ACCENT.
I'M FROM AUSTRALIA.
A LOT OF PEOPLE ON THE STREET.
OUT OF TIME, DER WOMAN. MONITORING FBI RAFFIC--
--THEY'RE ABOUT TO BREACH.
UNDERSTOOD, BATMAN.
--NO--

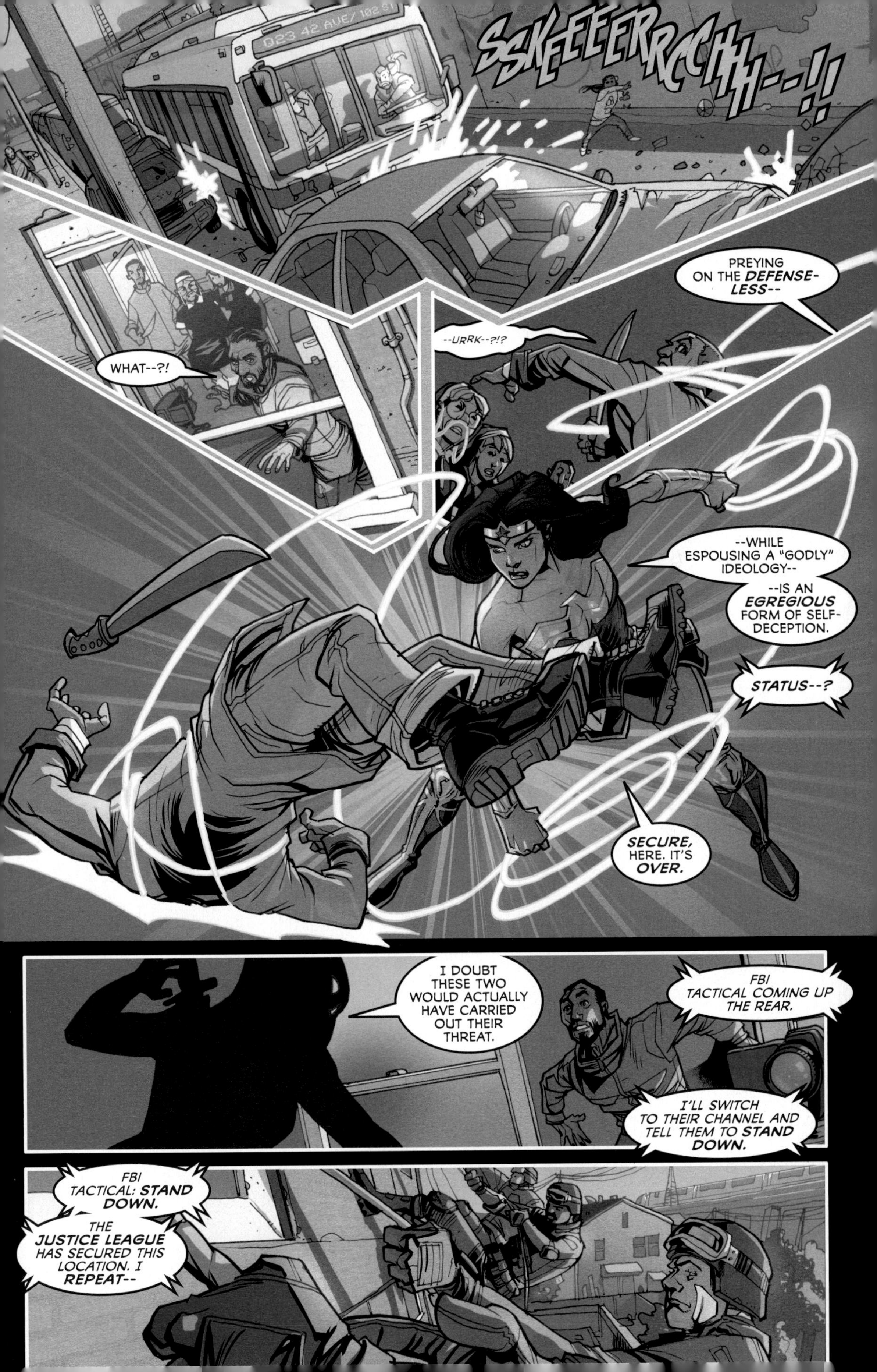
SSKEEEERRCCHHH--!!
Q23 42 AVE/ 102 ST
WHAT--?!
PREYING ON THE DEFENSE-LESS--
--URRK--?!?
--WHILE ESPOUSING A "GODLY" IDEOLOGY--
--IS AN EGREGIOUS FORM OF SELF-DECEPTION.
STATUS--?
SECURE, HERE. IT'S OVER.
I DOUBT THESE TWO WOULD ACTUALLY HAVE CARRIED OUT THEIR THREAT.
FBI TACTICAL COMING UP THE REAR.
I'LL SWITCH TO THEIR CHANNEL AND TELL THEM TO STAND DOWN.
FBI TACTICAL: STAND DOWN.
THE JUSTICE LEAGUE HAS SECURED THIS LOCATION. I REPEAT--

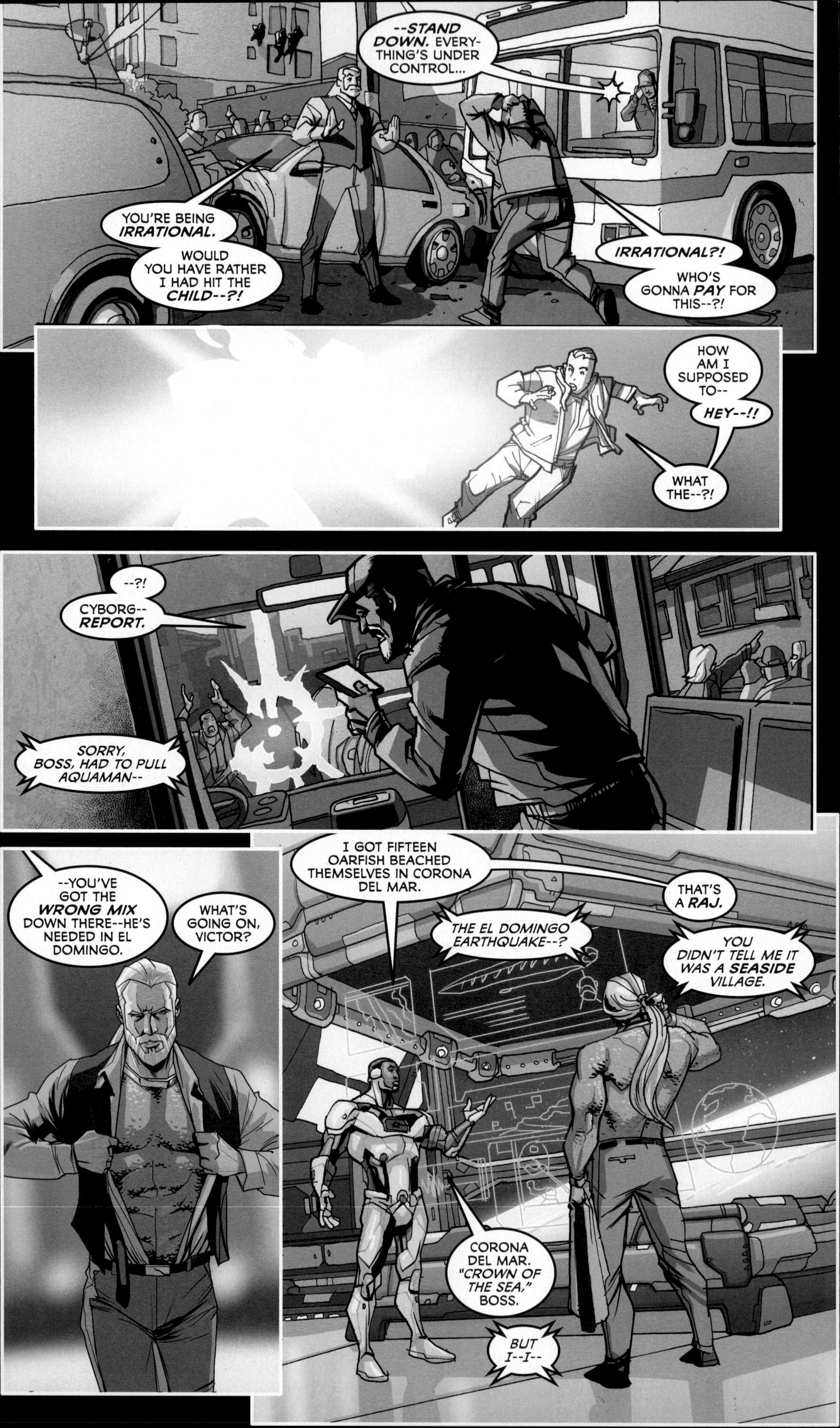

--STAND DOWN. EVERYTHING'S UNDER CONTROL...
YOU'RE BEING IRRATIONAL.
WOULD YOU HAVE RATHER I HAD HIT THE CHILD--?!
IRRATIONAL?!
WHO'S GONNA PAY FOR THIS--?!
HOW AM I SUPPOSED TO--
HEY--!!
WHAT THE--?!
--?!
CYBORG-- REPORT.
SORRY, BOSS, HAD TO PULL AQUAMAN--
--YOU'VE GOT THE WRONG MIX DOWN THERE--HE'S NEEDED IN EL DOMINGO.
WHAT'S GOING ON, VICTOR?
I GOT FIFTEEN OARFISH BEACHED THEMSELVES IN CORONA DEL MAR.
THAT'S A RAJ.
THE EL DOMINGO EARTHQUAKE--?
YOU DIDN'T TELL ME IT WAS A SEASIDE VILLAGE.
CORONA DEL MAR. "CROWN OF THE SEA," BOSS.
BUT I--I--

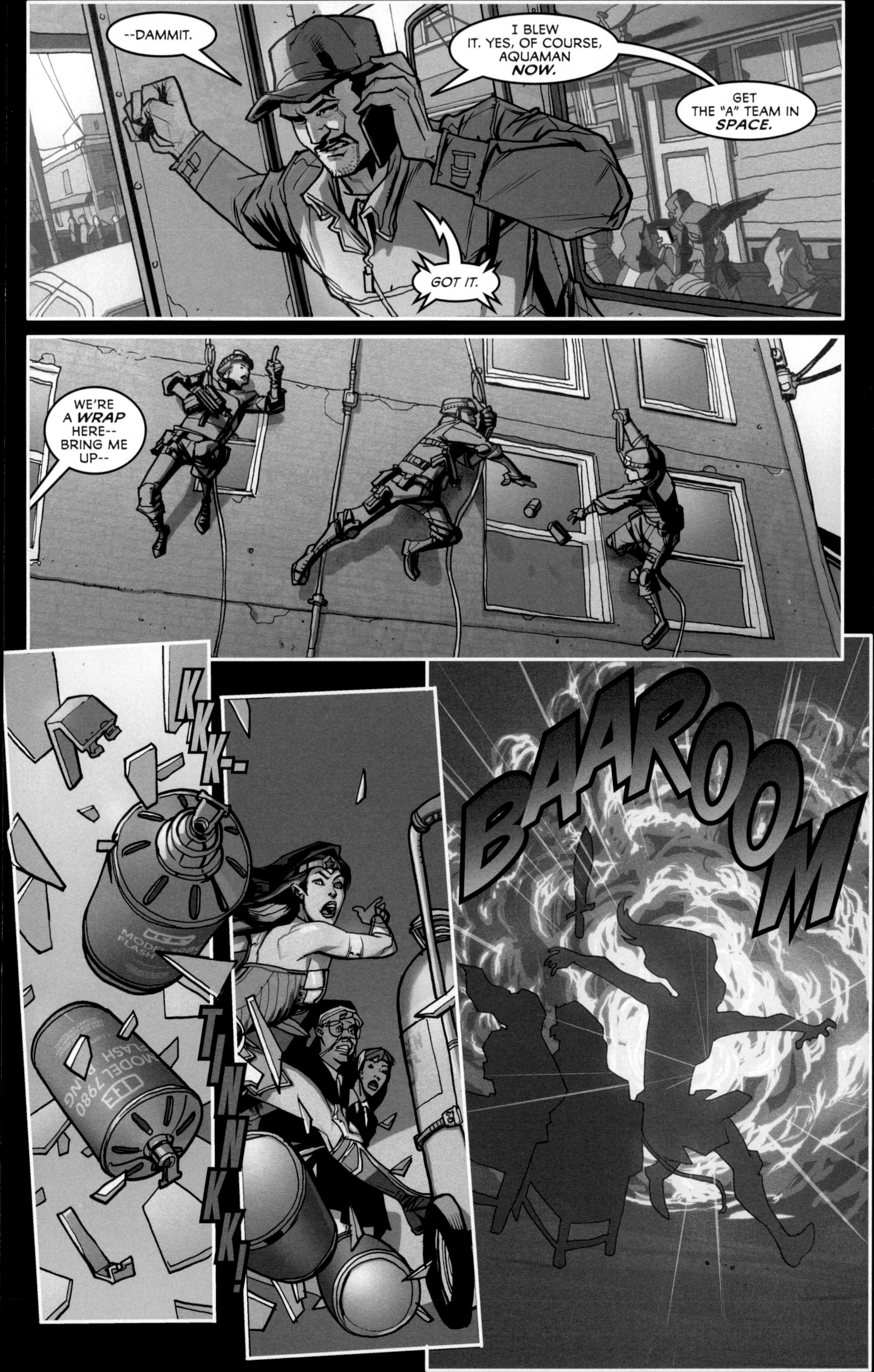
--DAMMIT.
I BLEW IT. YES, OF COURSE, AQUAMAN **NOW.**
GET THE "A" TEAM IN ***SPACE.***
GOT IT.
WE'RE A ***WRAP*** HERE-- BRING ME UP--
KKK--
TINNNKKK!
BAAROOOM

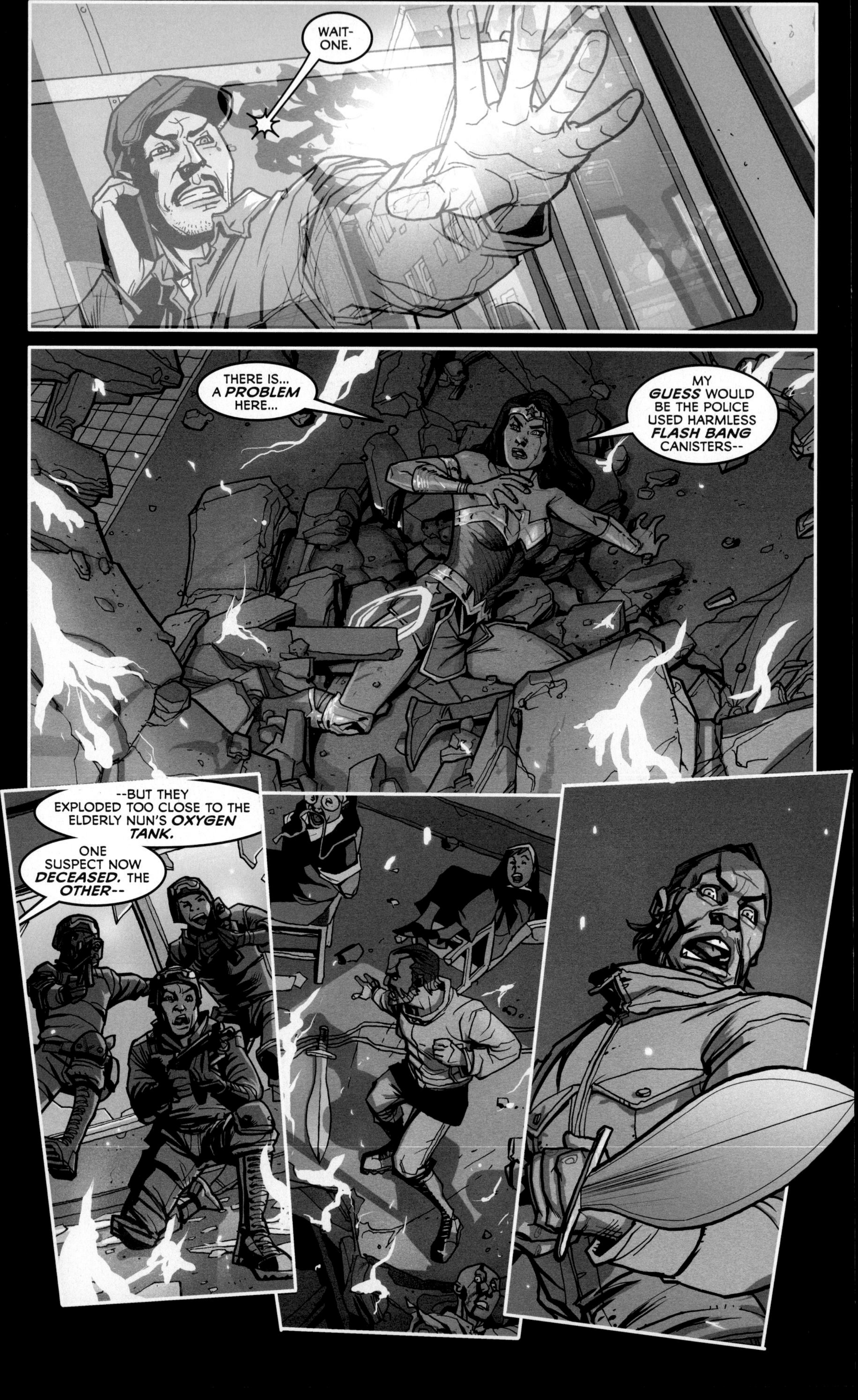
WAIT-ONE.
THERE IS... A PROBLEM HERE...
MY GUESS WOULD BE THE POLICE USED HARMLESS FLASH BANG CANISTERS--
--BUT THEY EXPLODED TOO CLOSE TO THE ELDERLY NUN'S OXYGEN TANK.
ONE SUSPECT NOW DECEASED. THE OTHER--

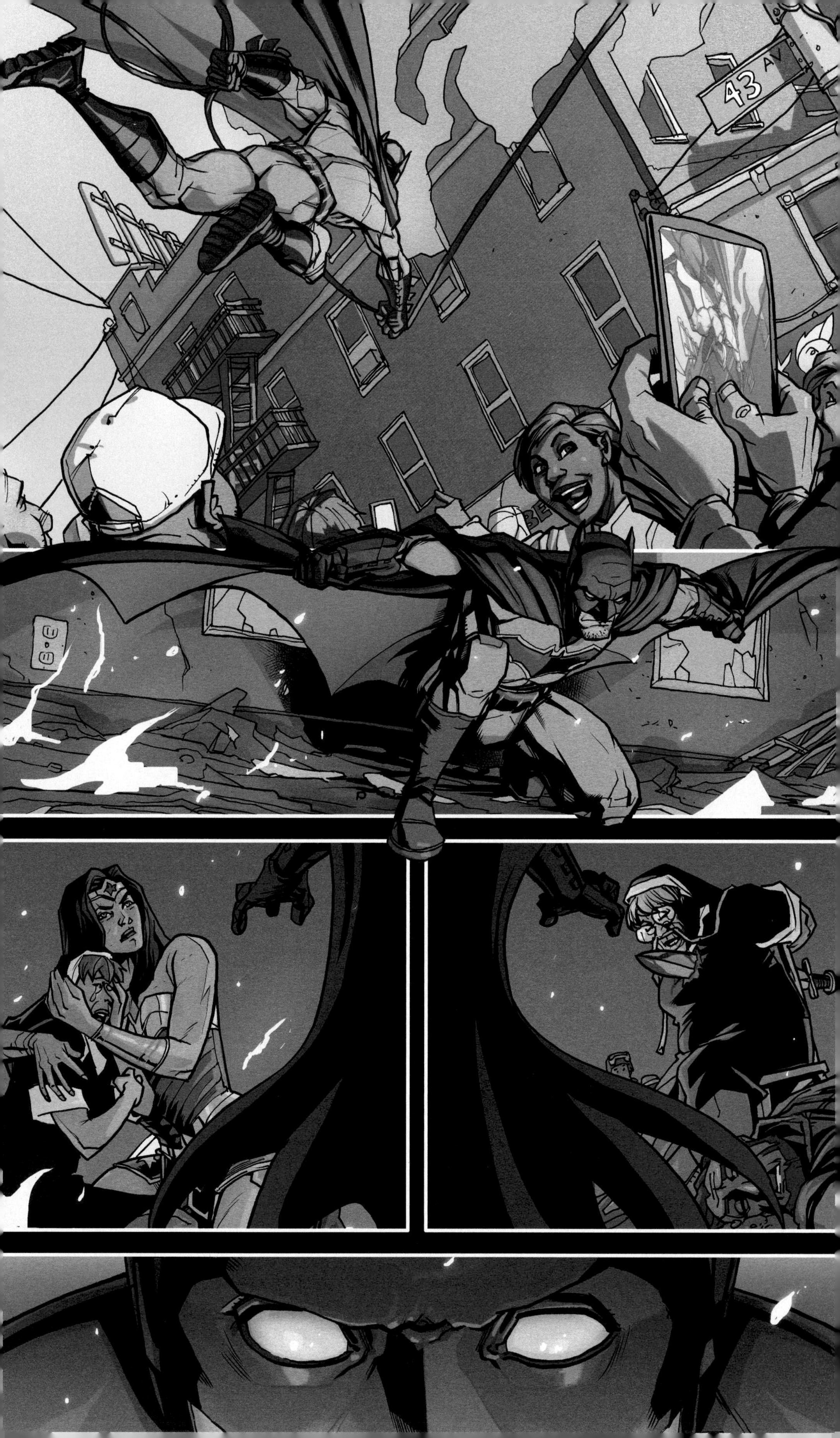
43 AV

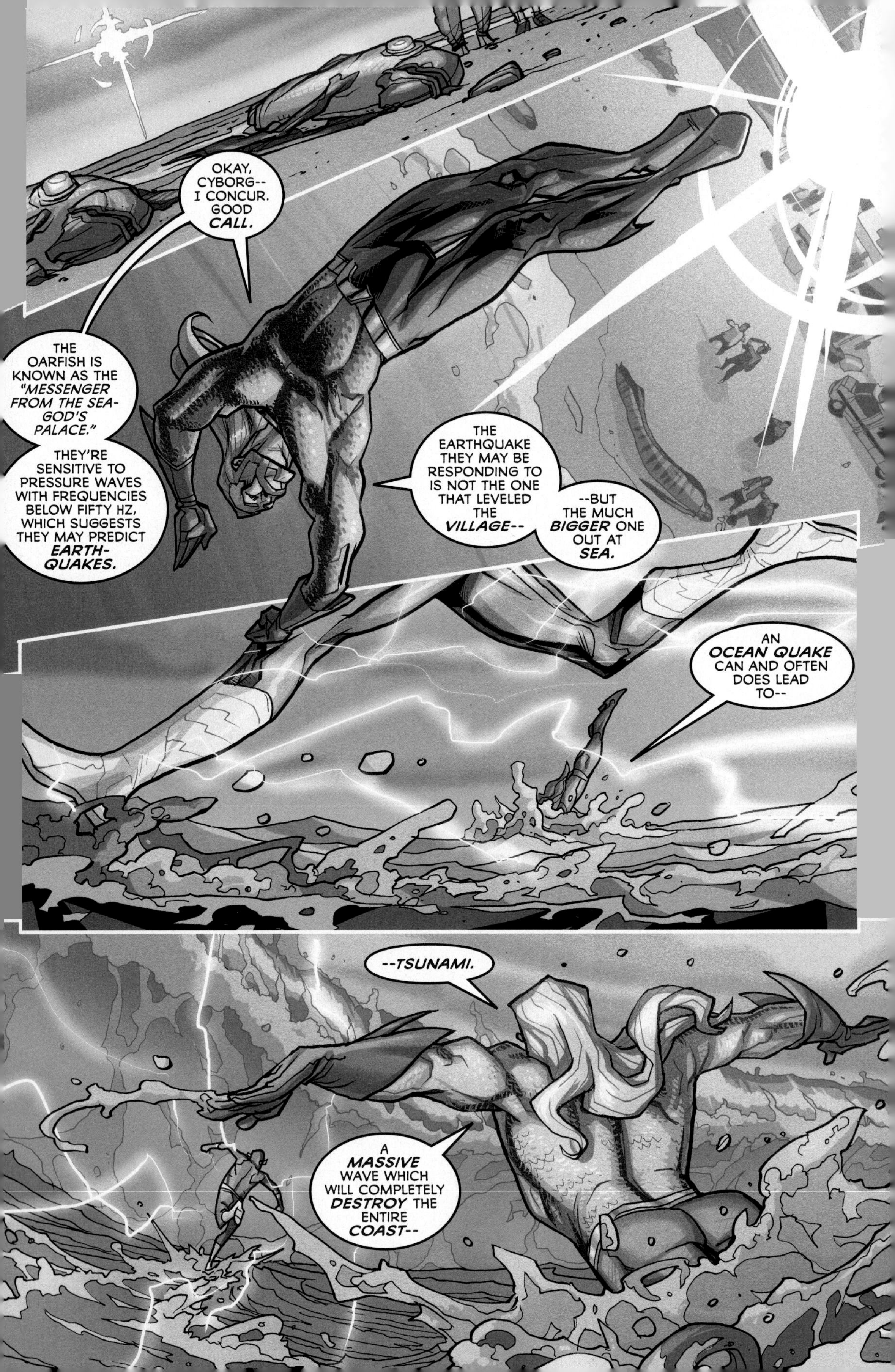
OKAY, CYBORG-- I CONCUR. GOOD CALL.
THE OARFISH IS KNOWN AS THE "MESSENGER FROM THE SEA-GOD'S PALACE."
THEY'RE SENSITIVE TO PRESSURE WAVES WITH FREQUENCIES BELOW FIFTY HZ, WHICH SUGGESTS THEY MAY PREDICT EARTH-QUAKES.
THE EARTHQUAKE THEY MAY BE RESPONDING TO IS NOT THE ONE THAT LEVELED THE VILLAGE--
--BUT THE MUCH BIGGER ONE OUT AT SEA.
AN OCEAN QUAKE CAN AND OFTEN DOES LEAD TO--
--TSUNAMI.
A MASSIVE WAVE WHICH WILL COMPLETELY DESTROY THE ENTIRE COAST--

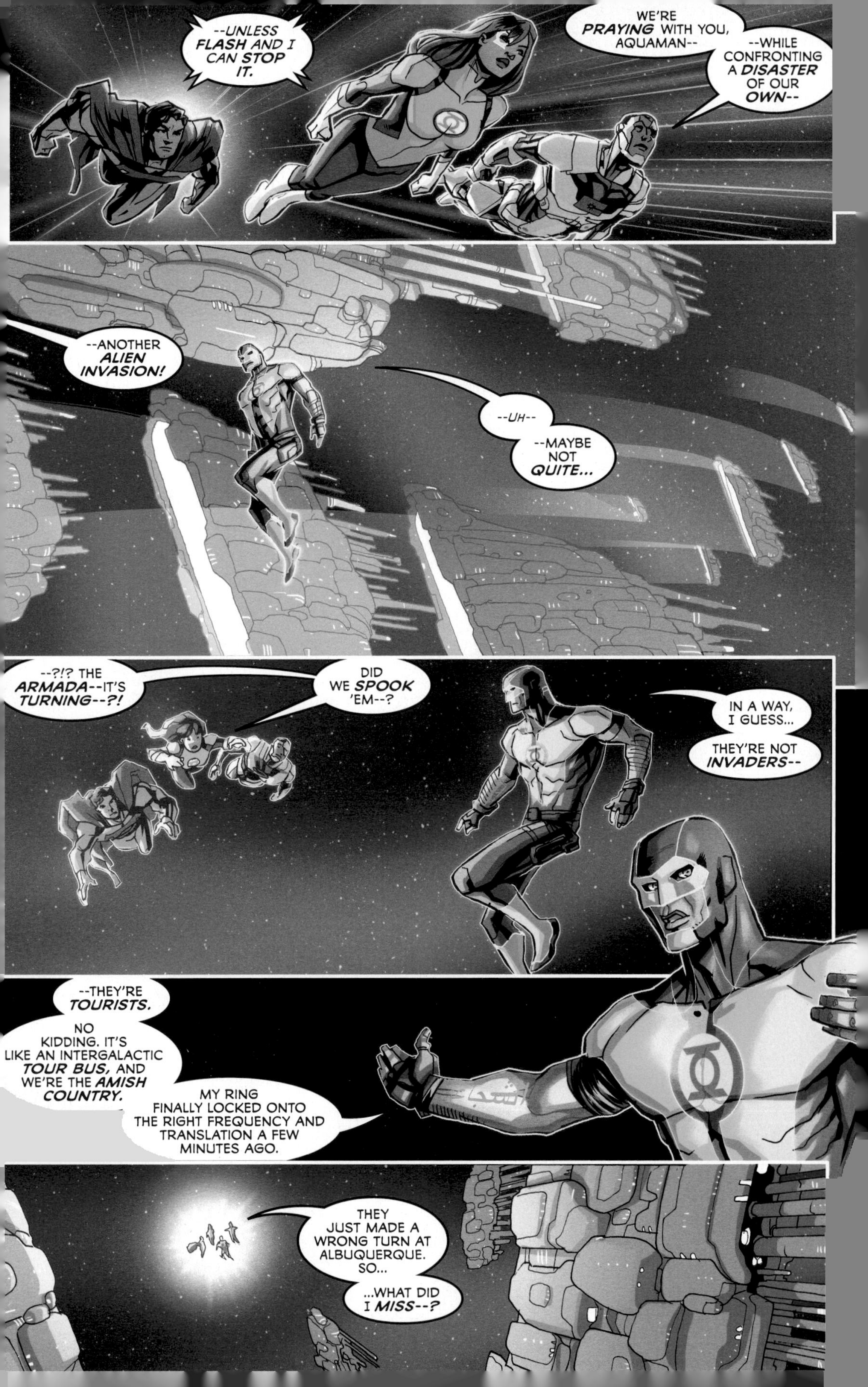
--UNLESS FLASH AND I CAN STOP IT.
WE'RE PRAYING WITH YOU, AQUAMAN--
--WHILE CONFRONTING A DISASTER OF OUR OWN--
--ANOTHER ALIEN INVASION!
--UH--
--MAYBE NOT QUITE...
--?!? THE ARMADA--IT'S TURNING--?!
DID WE SPOOK 'EM--?
IN A WAY, I GUESS...
THEY'RE NOT INVADERS--
--THEY'RE TOURISTS.
NO KIDDING. IT'S LIKE AN INTERGALACTIC TOUR BUS, AND WE'RE THE AMISH COUNTRY.
MY RING FINALLY LOCKED ONTO THE RIGHT FREQUENCY AND TRANSLATION A FEW MINUTES AGO.
THEY JUST MADE A WRONG TURN AT ALBUQUERQUE. SO...
...WHAT DID I MISS--?

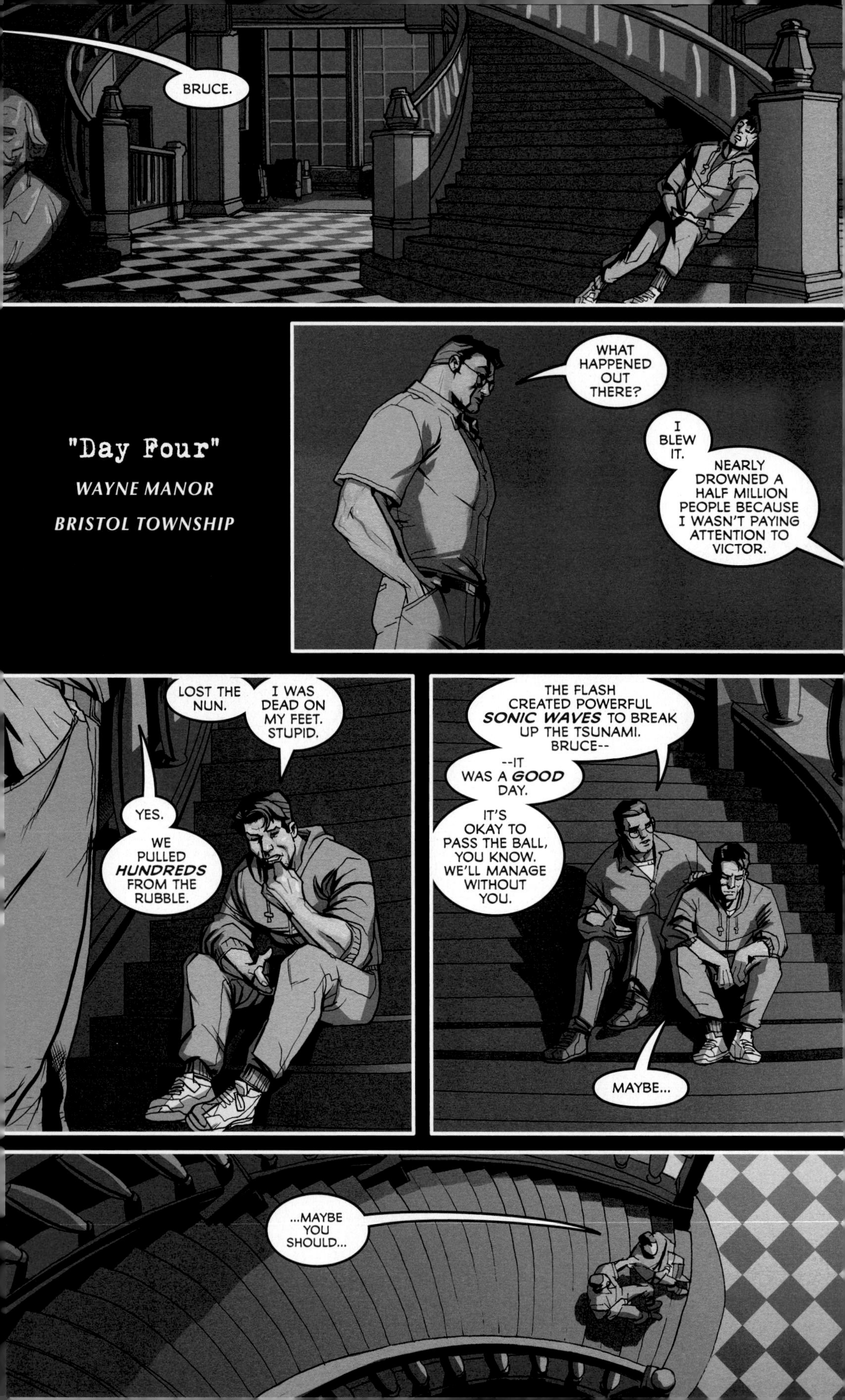
BRUCE.
"Day Four"
WAYNE MANOR
BRISTOL TOWNSHIP
WHAT HAPPENED OUT THERE?
I BLEW IT.
NEARLY DROWNED A HALF MILLION PEOPLE BECAUSE I WASN'T PAYING ATTENTION TO VICTOR.
LOST THE NUN.
I WAS DEAD ON MY FEET. STUPID.
YES.
WE PULLED HUNDREDS FROM THE RUBBLE.
THE FLASH CREATED POWERFUL SONIC WAVES TO BREAK UP THE TSUNAMI. BRUCE--
--IT WAS A GOOD DAY.
IT'S OKAY TO PASS THE BALL, YOU KNOW. WE'LL MANAGE WITHOUT YOU.
MAYBE...
...MAYBE YOU SHOULD...

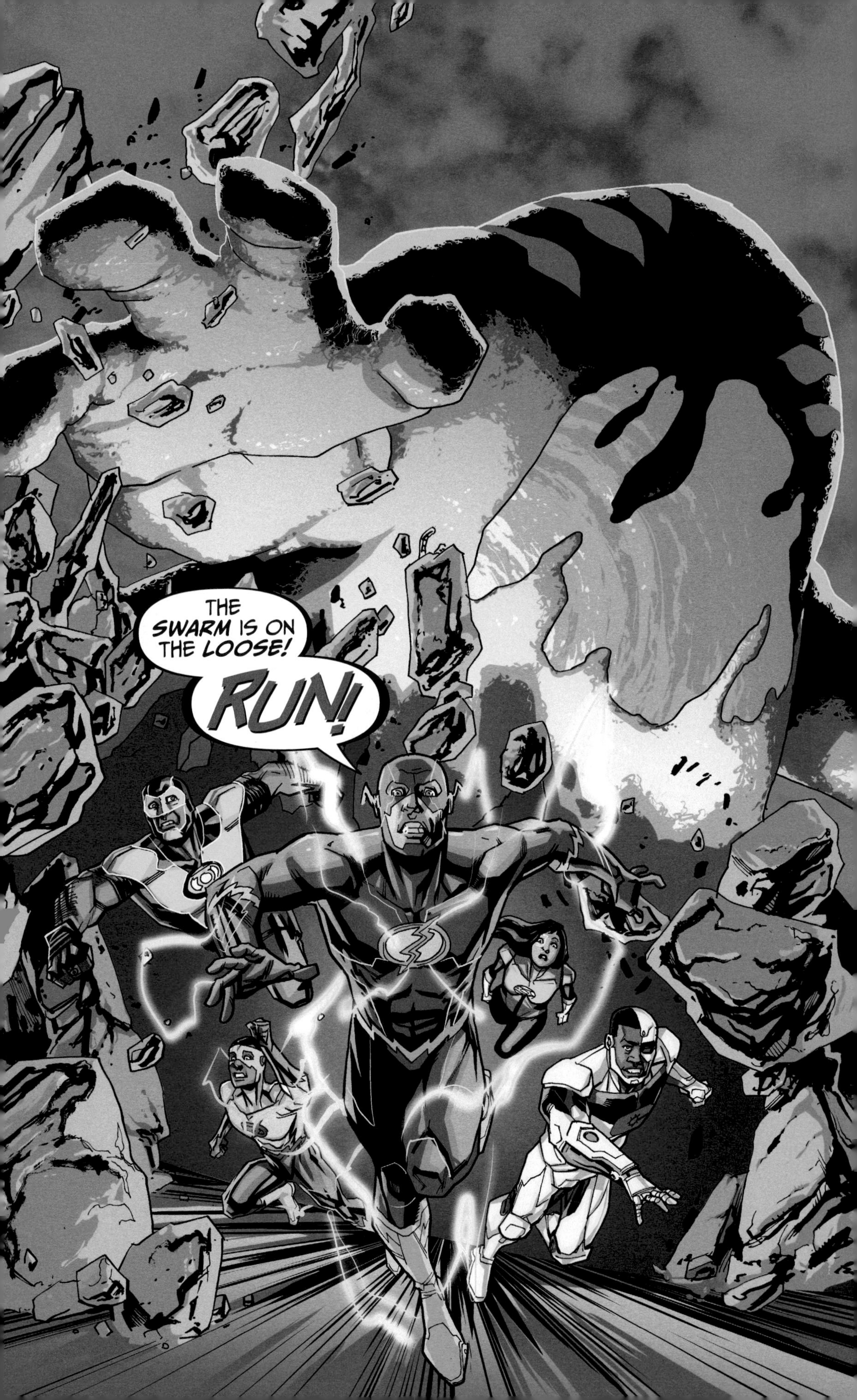
THE SWARM IS ON THE LOOSE!
RUN!

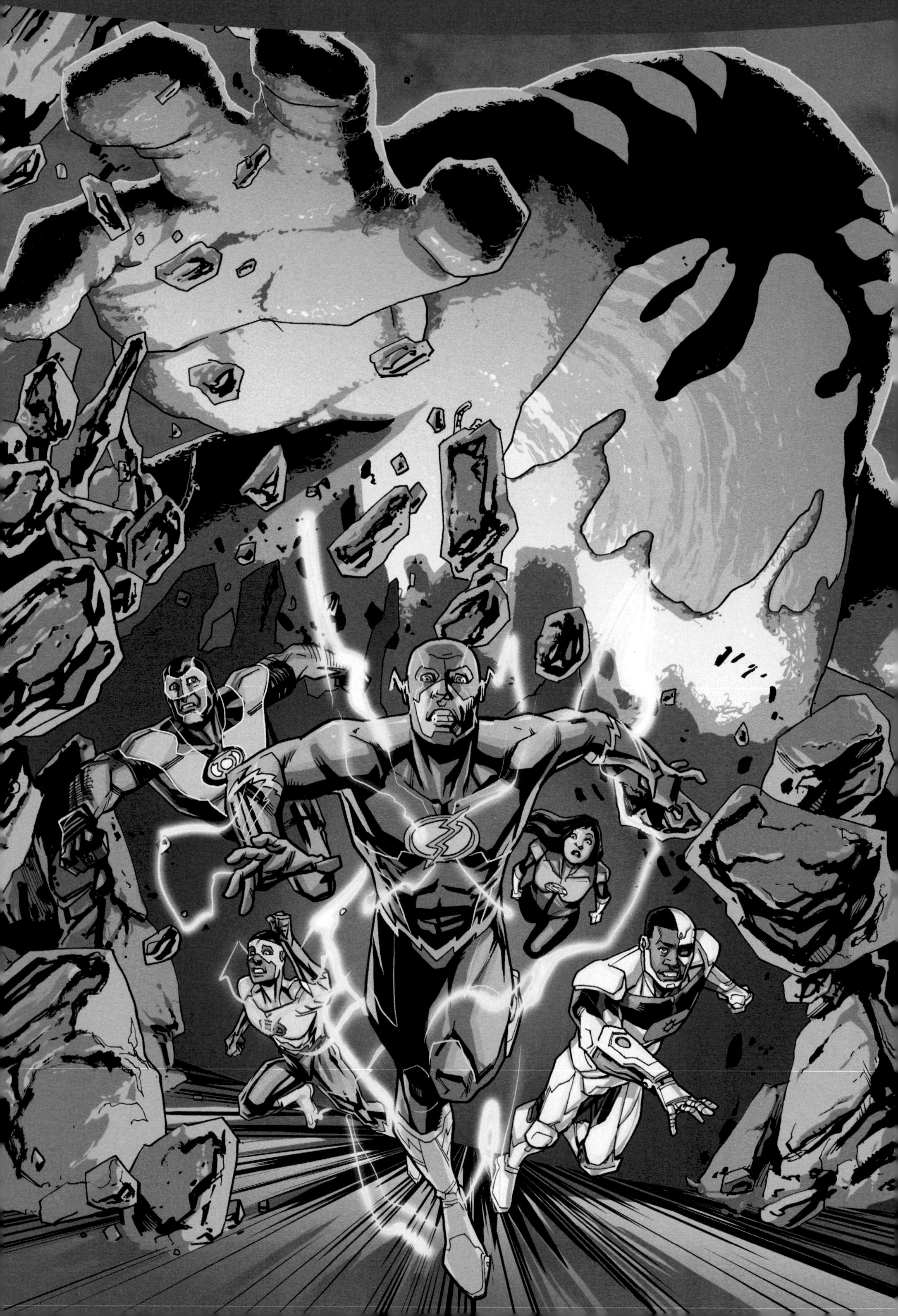

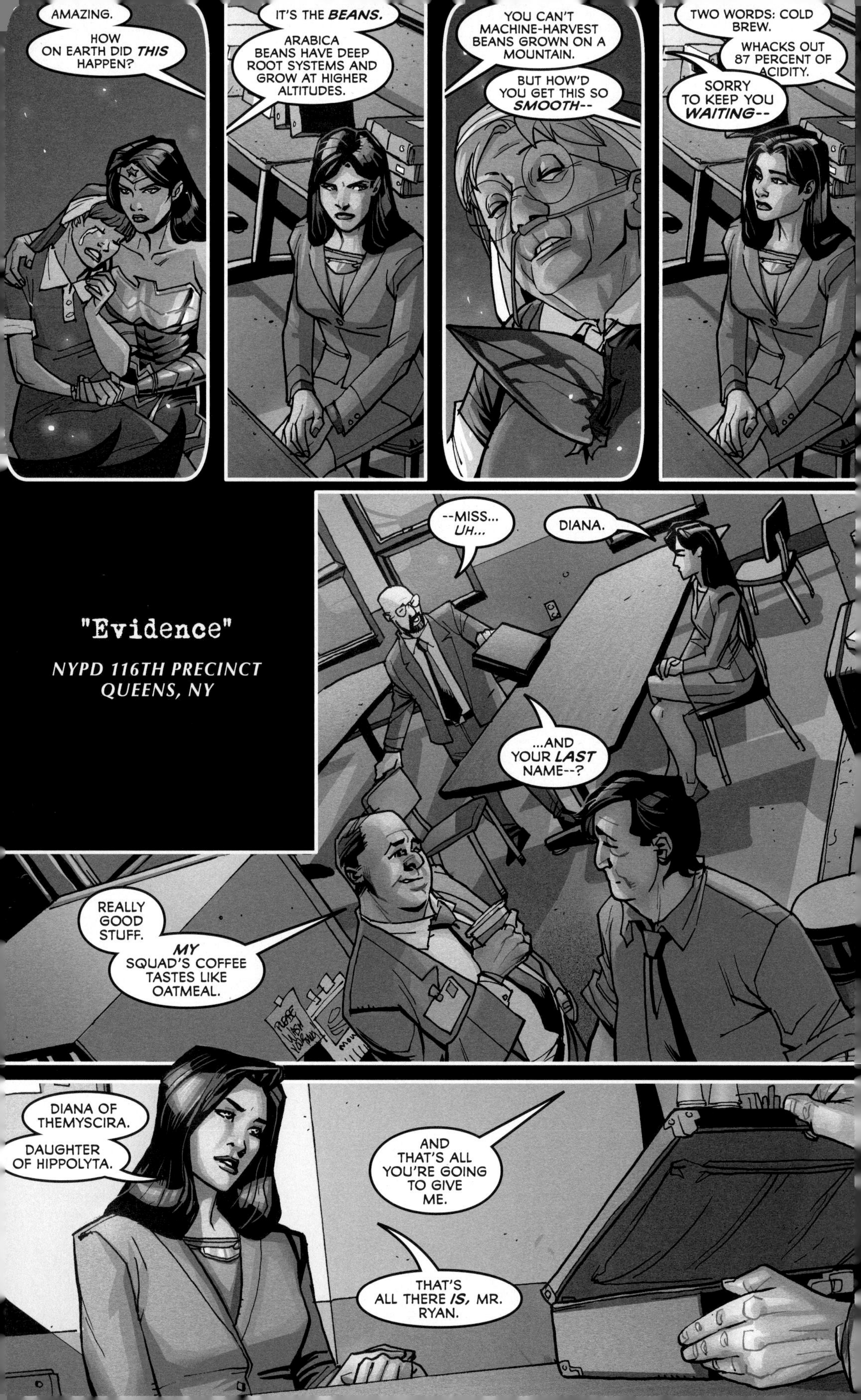
AMAZING.
HOW ON EARTH DID THIS HAPPEN?
IT'S THE BEANS.
ARABICA BEANS HAVE DEEP ROOT SYSTEMS AND GROW AT HIGHER ALTITUDES.
YOU CAN'T MACHINE-HARVEST BEANS GROWN ON A MOUNTAIN.
BUT HOW'D YOU GET THIS SO SMOOTH--
TWO WORDS: COLD BREW.
WHACKS OUT 87 PERCENT OF ACIDITY.
SORRY TO KEEP YOU WAITING--
"Evidence"
NYPD 116TH PRECINCT
QUEENS, NY
--MISS... UH...
DIANA.
...AND YOUR LAST NAME--?
REALLY GOOD STUFF.
MY SQUAD'S COFFEE TASTES LIKE OATMEAL.
DIANA OF THEMYSCIRA.
DAUGHTER OF HIPPOLYTA.
AND THAT'S ALL YOU'RE GOING TO GIVE ME.
THAT'S ALL THERE IS, MR. RYAN.

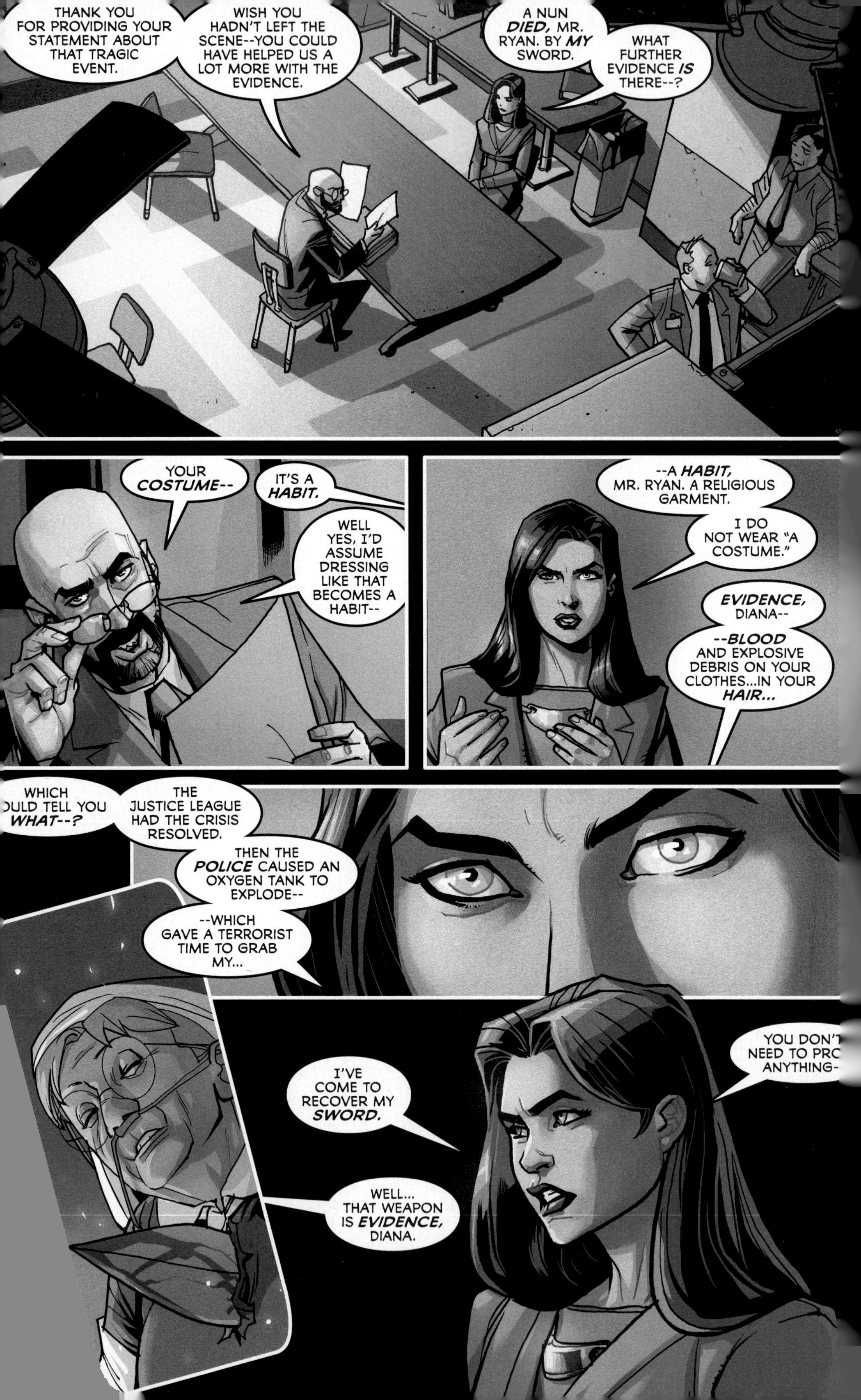
THANK YOU FOR PROVIDING YOUR STATEMENT ABOUT THAT TRAGIC EVENT.
WISH YOU HADN'T LEFT THE SCENE--YOU COULD HAVE HELPED US A LOT MORE WITH THE EVIDENCE.
A NUN *DIED,* MR. RYAN. BY *MY* SWORD.
WHAT FURTHER EVIDENCE *IS* THERE--?
YOUR *COSTUME--*
IT'S A *HABIT.*
WELL YES, I'D ASSUME DRESSING LIKE THAT BECOMES A HABIT--
--A *HABIT,* MR. RYAN. A RELIGIOUS GARMENT.
I DO NOT WEAR "A COSTUME."
EVIDENCE, DIANA--
--BLOOD AND EXPLOSIVE DEBRIS ON YOUR CLOTHES...IN YOUR *HAIR...*
WHICH OULD TELL YOU *WHAT--?*
THE JUSTICE LEAGUE HAD THE CRISIS RESOLVED.
THEN THE *POLICE* CAUSED AN OXYGEN TANK TO EXPLODE--
--WHICH GAVE A TERRORIST TIME TO GRAB MY...
I'VE COME TO RECOVER MY *SWORD.*
YOU DON'T NEED TO PRO ANYTHING-
WELL... THAT WEAPON IS *EVIDENCE,* DIANA.

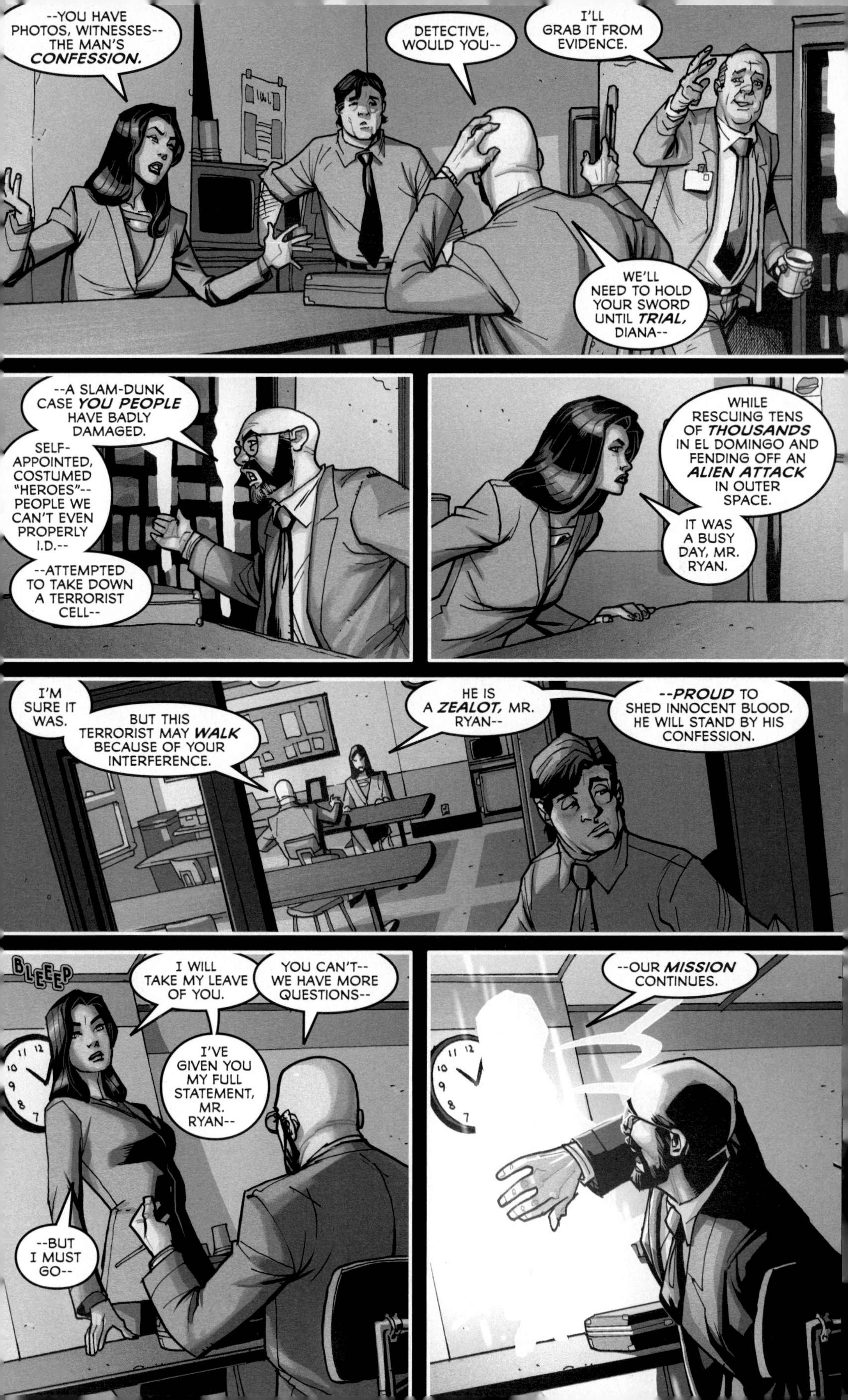
--YOU HAVE PHOTOS, WITNESSES-- THE MAN'S CONFESSION.
DETECTIVE, WOULD YOU--
I'LL GRAB IT FROM EVIDENCE.
WE'LL NEED TO HOLD YOUR SWORD UNTIL TRIAL, DIANA--
--A SLAM-DUNK CASE YOU PEOPLE HAVE BADLY DAMAGED.
SELF-APPOINTED, COSTUMED "HEROES"--PEOPLE WE CAN'T EVEN PROPERLY I.D.--
--ATTEMPTED TO TAKE DOWN A TERRORIST CELL--
WHILE RESCUING TENS OF THOUSANDS IN EL DOMINGO AND FENDING OFF AN ALIEN ATTACK IN OUTER SPACE.
IT WAS A BUSY DAY, MR. RYAN.
I'M SURE IT WAS.
BUT THIS TERRORIST MAY WALK BECAUSE OF YOUR INTERFERENCE.
HE IS A ZEALOT, MR. RYAN--
--PROUD TO SHED INNOCENT BLOOD. HE WILL STAND BY HIS CONFESSION.
BLEEEP
I WILL TAKE MY LEAVE OF YOU.
YOU CAN'T-- WE HAVE MORE QUESTIONS--
I'VE GIVEN YOU MY FULL STATEMENT, MR. RYAN--
--BUT I MUST GO--
--OUR MISSION CONTINUES.

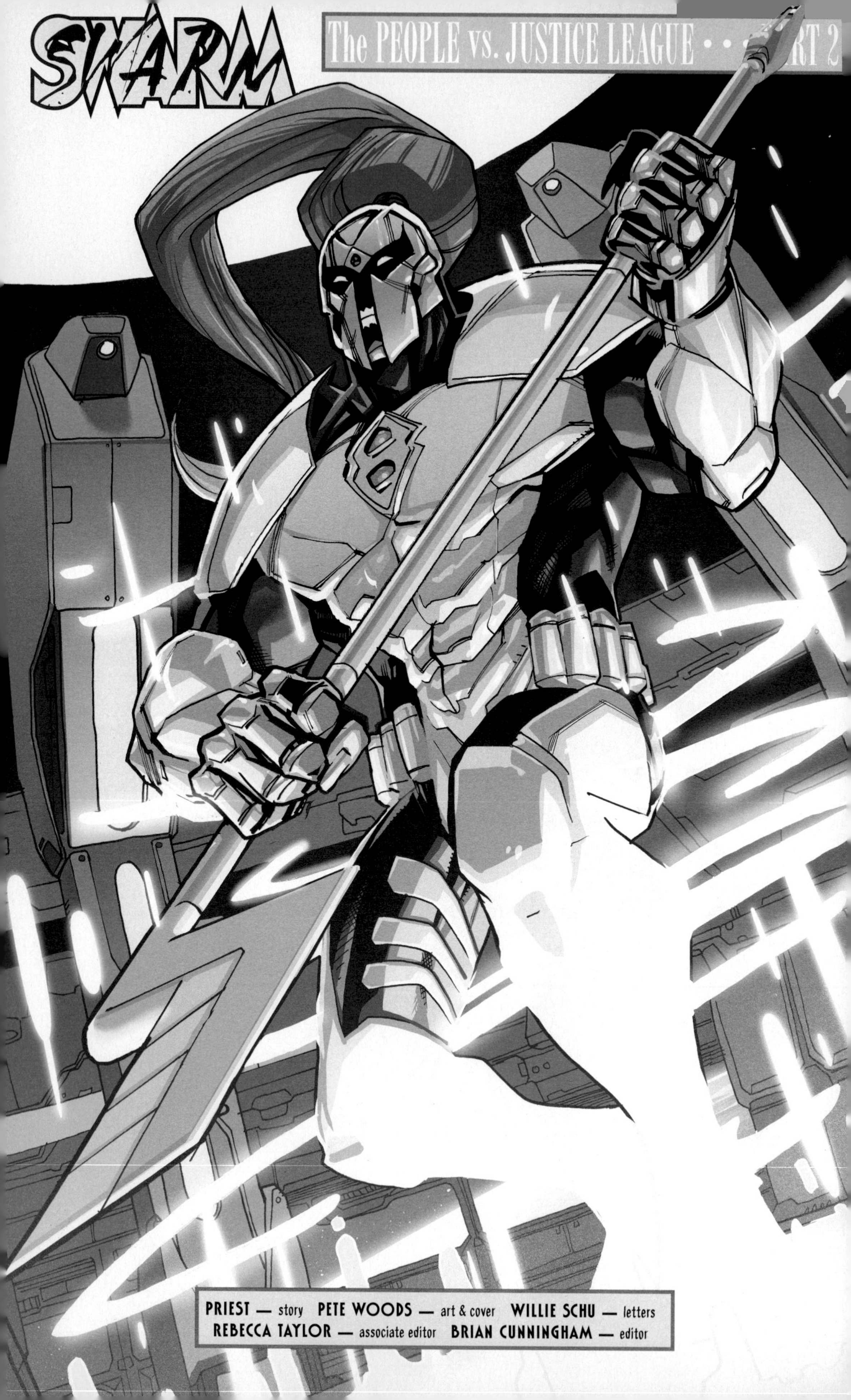
SWARM
The PEOPLE vs. JUSTICE LEAGUE • • • RT 2
PRIEST — story PETE WOODS — art & cover WILLIE SCHU — letters
REBECCA TAYLOR — associate editor BRIAN CUNNINGHAM — editor

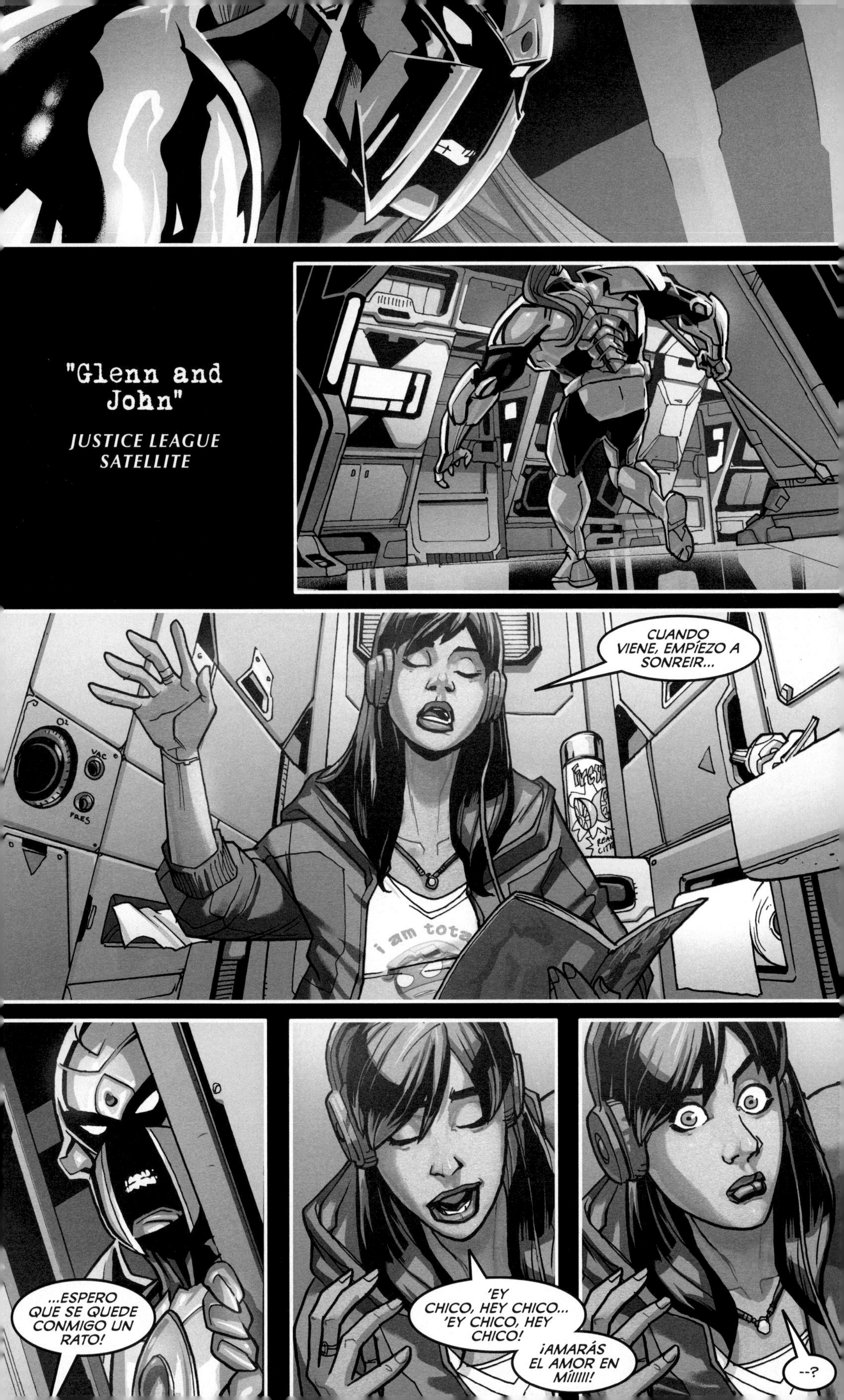
"Glenn and John"
JUSTICE LEAGUE SATELLITE
CUANDO VIENE, EMPÍEZO A SONREIR...
...ESPERO QUE SE QUEDE CONMIGO UN RATO!
'EY CHICO, HEY CHICO... 'EY CHICO, HEY CHICO!
¡AMARÁS EL AMOR EN MÍÍÍÍÍÍ!
--?

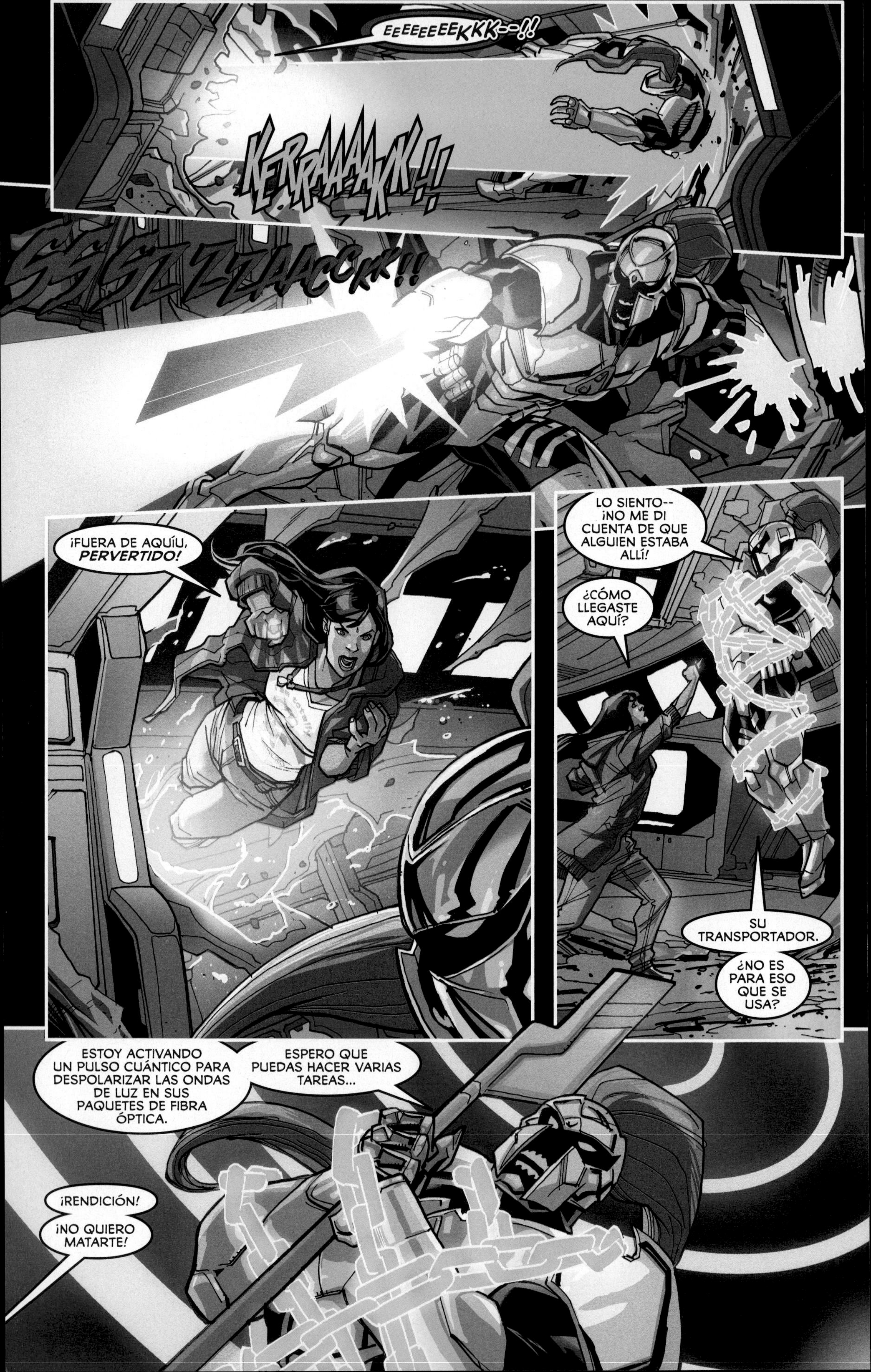
EEEEEEEEKKK--!!
KERRAAAAKK!!
SSSSZ ZZAACCKK!!
¡FUERA DE AQUÍU, *PERVERTIDO!*
LO SIENTO-- ¡NO ME DI CUENTA DE QUE ALGUIEN ESTABA ALLÍ!
¿CÓMO LLEGASTE AQUÍ?
SU TRANSPORTADOR.
¿NO ES PARA ESO QUE SE USA?
ESTOY ACTIVANDO UN PULSO CUÁNTICO PARA DESPOLARIZAR LAS ONDAS DE LUZ EN SUS PAQUETES DE FIBRA ÓPTICA.
ESPERO QUE PUEDAS HACER VARIAS TAREAS...
¡RENDICIÓN!
¡NO QUIERO MATARTE!

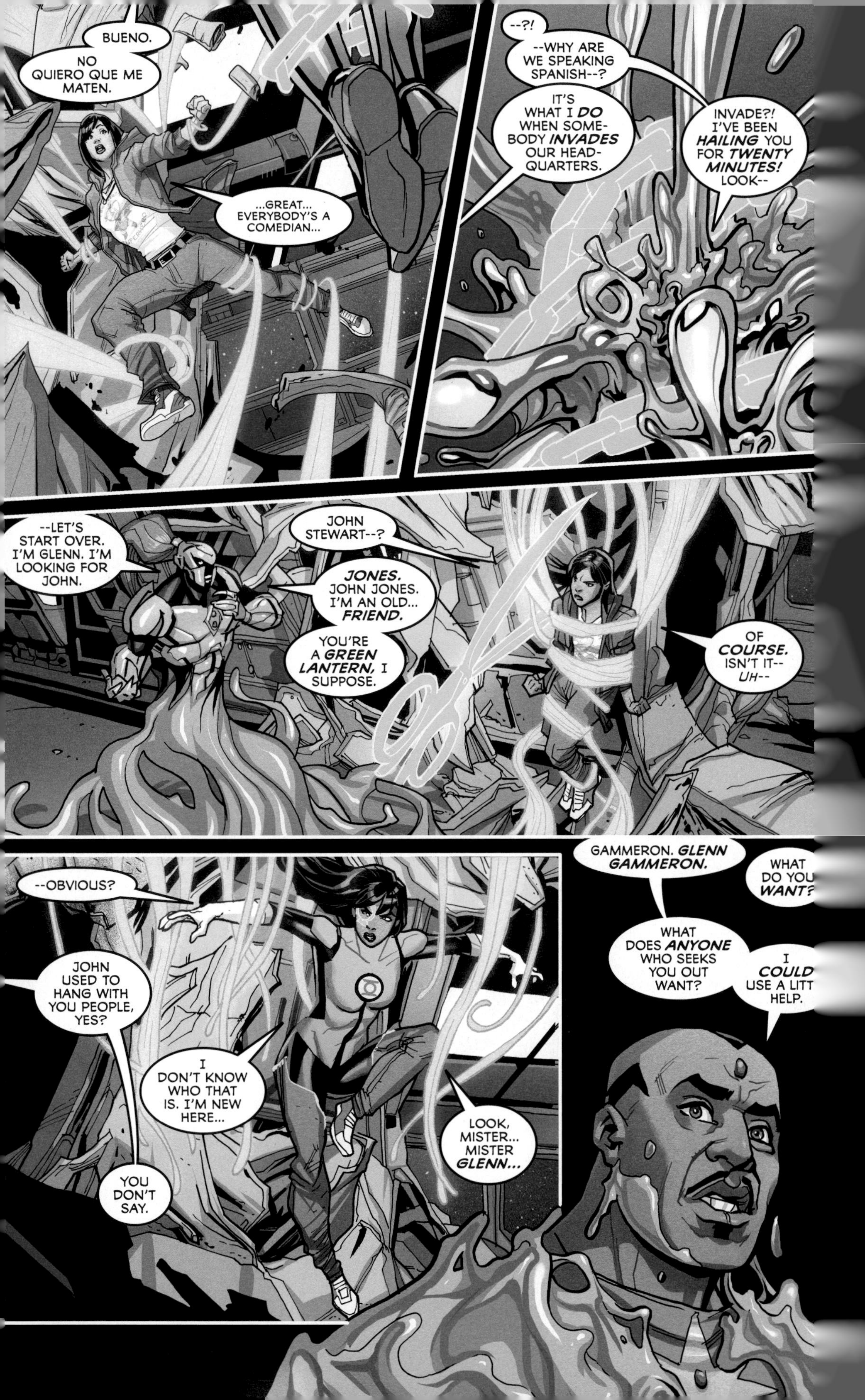
BUENO.
NO QUIERO QUE ME MATEN.
...GREAT... EVERYBODY'S A COMEDIAN...
--?!
--WHY ARE WE SPEAKING SPANISH--?
IT'S WHAT I *DO* WHEN SOMEBODY *INVADES* OUR HEADQUARTERS.
INVADE?! I'VE BEEN *HAILING* YOU FOR *TWENTY MINUTES!* LOOK--
--LET'S START OVER. I'M GLENN. I'M LOOKING FOR JOHN.
JOHN STEWART--?
JONES. JOHN JONES. I'M AN OLD... *FRIEND.*
YOU'RE A *GREEN LANTERN,* I SUPPOSE.
OF *COURSE.* ISN'T IT-- *UH--*
--OBVIOUS?
JOHN USED TO HANG WITH YOU PEOPLE, YES?
I DON'T KNOW WHO THAT IS. I'M NEW HERE...
YOU DON'T SAY.
LOOK, MISTER... MISTER *GLENN...*
GAMMERON. *GLENN GAMMERON.*
WHAT DO YOU *WANT?*
WHAT DOES *ANYONE* WHO SEEKS YOU OUT WANT?
I *COULD* USE A LITT HELP.

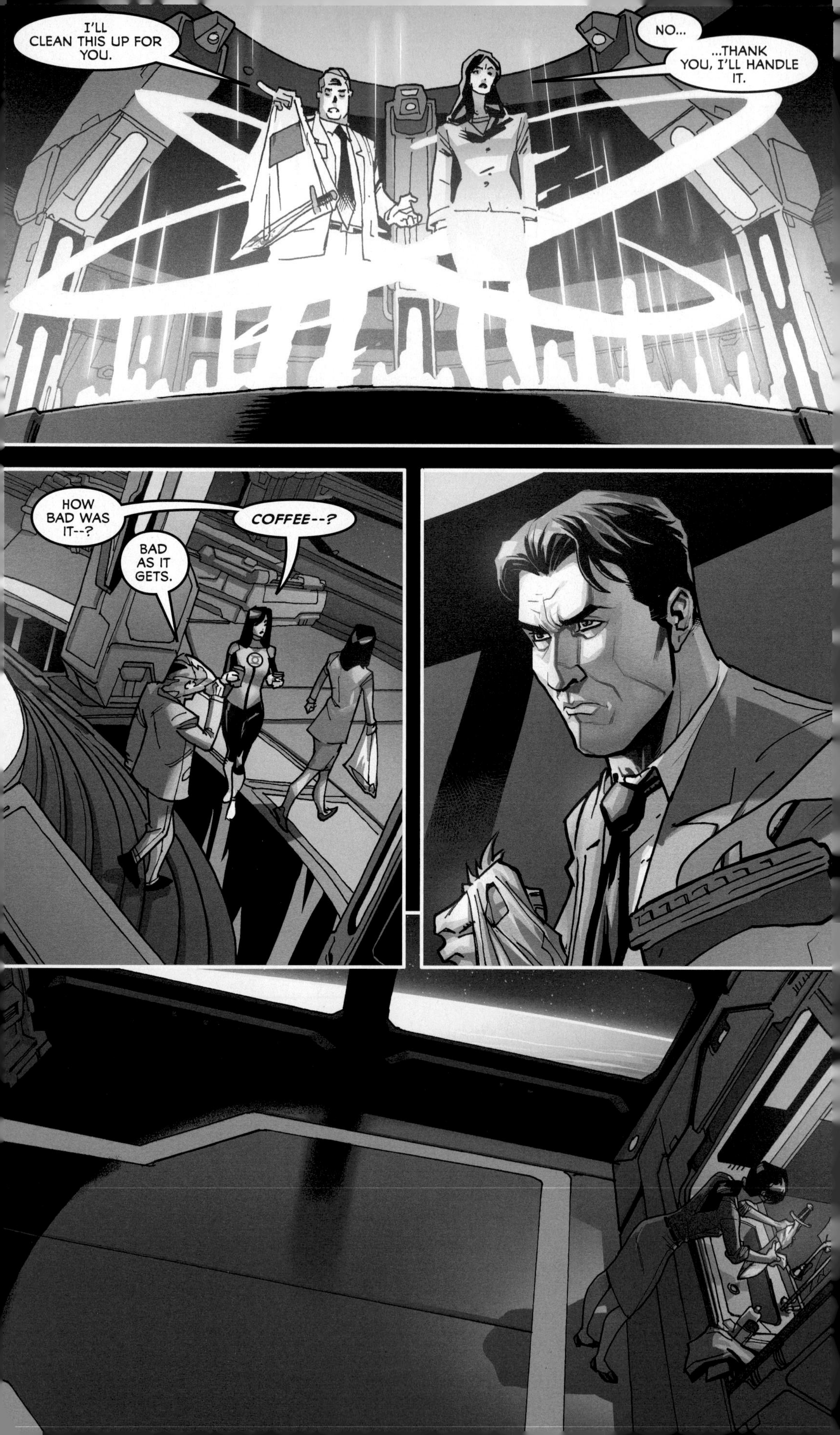
I'LL CLEAN THIS UP FOR YOU.
NO...
...THANK YOU, I'LL HANDLE IT.
HOW BAD WAS IT--?
COFFEE--?
BAD AS IT GETS.

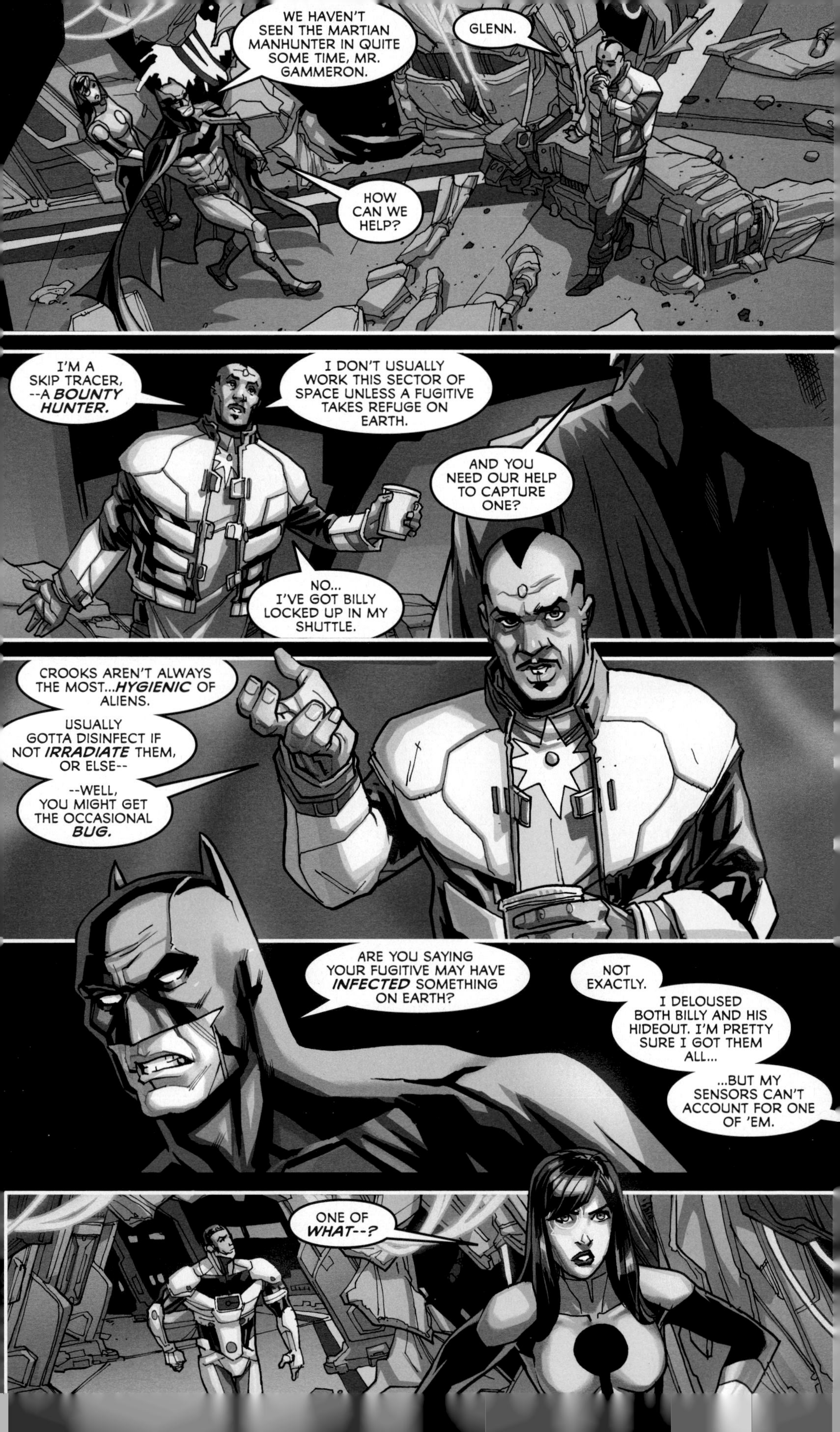
WE HAVEN'T SEEN THE MARTIAN MANHUNTER IN QUITE SOME TIME, MR. GAMMERON.
GLENN.
HOW CAN WE HELP?
I'M A SKIP TRACER, --A *BOUNTY HUNTER.*
I DON'T USUALLY WORK THIS SECTOR OF SPACE UNLESS A FUGITIVE TAKES REFUGE ON EARTH.
AND YOU NEED OUR HELP TO CAPTURE ONE?
NO... I'VE GOT BILLY LOCKED UP IN MY SHUTTLE.
CROOKS AREN'T ALWAYS THE MOST...*HYGIENIC* OF ALIENS.
USUALLY GOTTA DISINFECT IF NOT *IRRADIATE* THEM, OR ELSE--
--WELL, YOU MIGHT GET THE OCCASIONAL *BUG.*
ARE YOU SAYING YOUR FUGITIVE MAY HAVE *INFECTED* SOMETHING ON EARTH?
NOT EXACTLY.
I DELOUSED BOTH BILLY AND HIS HIDEOUT. I'M PRETTY SURE I GOT THEM ALL...
...BUT MY SENSORS CAN'T ACCOUNT FOR ONE OF 'EM.
ONE OF *WHAT--?*

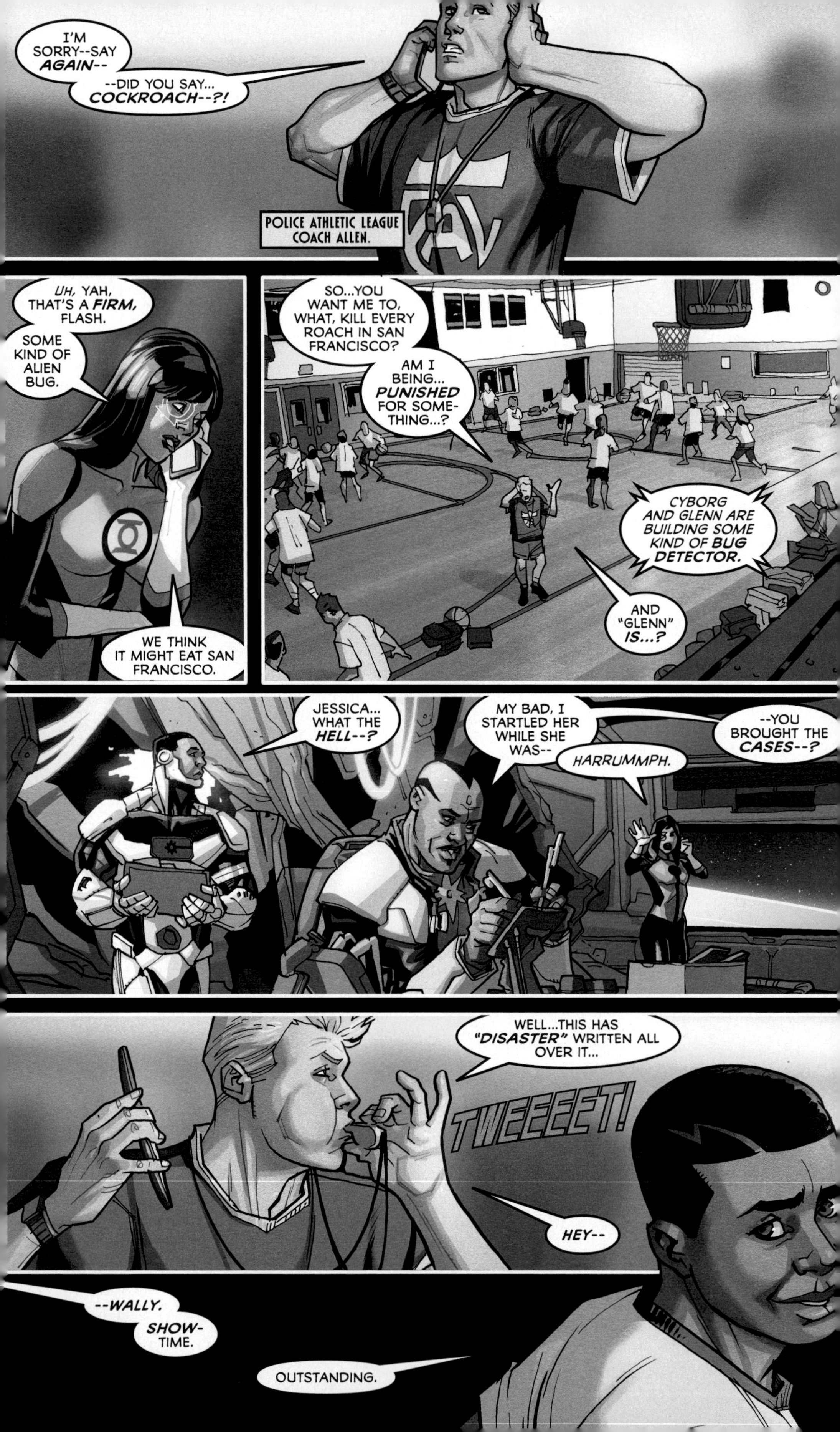

I'M SORRY--SAY AGAIN--
--DID YOU SAY... COCKROACH--?!
POLICE ATHLETIC LEAGUE COACH ALLEN.
UH, YAH, THAT'S A FIRM, FLASH.
SOME KIND OF ALIEN BUG.
WE THINK IT MIGHT EAT SAN FRANCISCO.
SO...YOU WANT ME TO, WHAT, KILL EVERY ROACH IN SAN FRANCISCO?
AM I BEING... PUNISHED FOR SOME-THING...?
CYBORG AND GLENN ARE BUILDING SOME KIND OF BUG DETECTOR.
AND "GLENN" IS...?
JESSICA... WHAT THE HELL--?
MY BAD, I STARTLED HER WHILE SHE WAS--
HARRUMMPH.
--YOU BROUGHT THE CASES--?
WELL...THIS HAS "DISASTER" WRITTEN ALL OVER IT...
TWEEEEET!
HEY--
--WALLY.
SHOW-TIME.
OUTSTANDING.

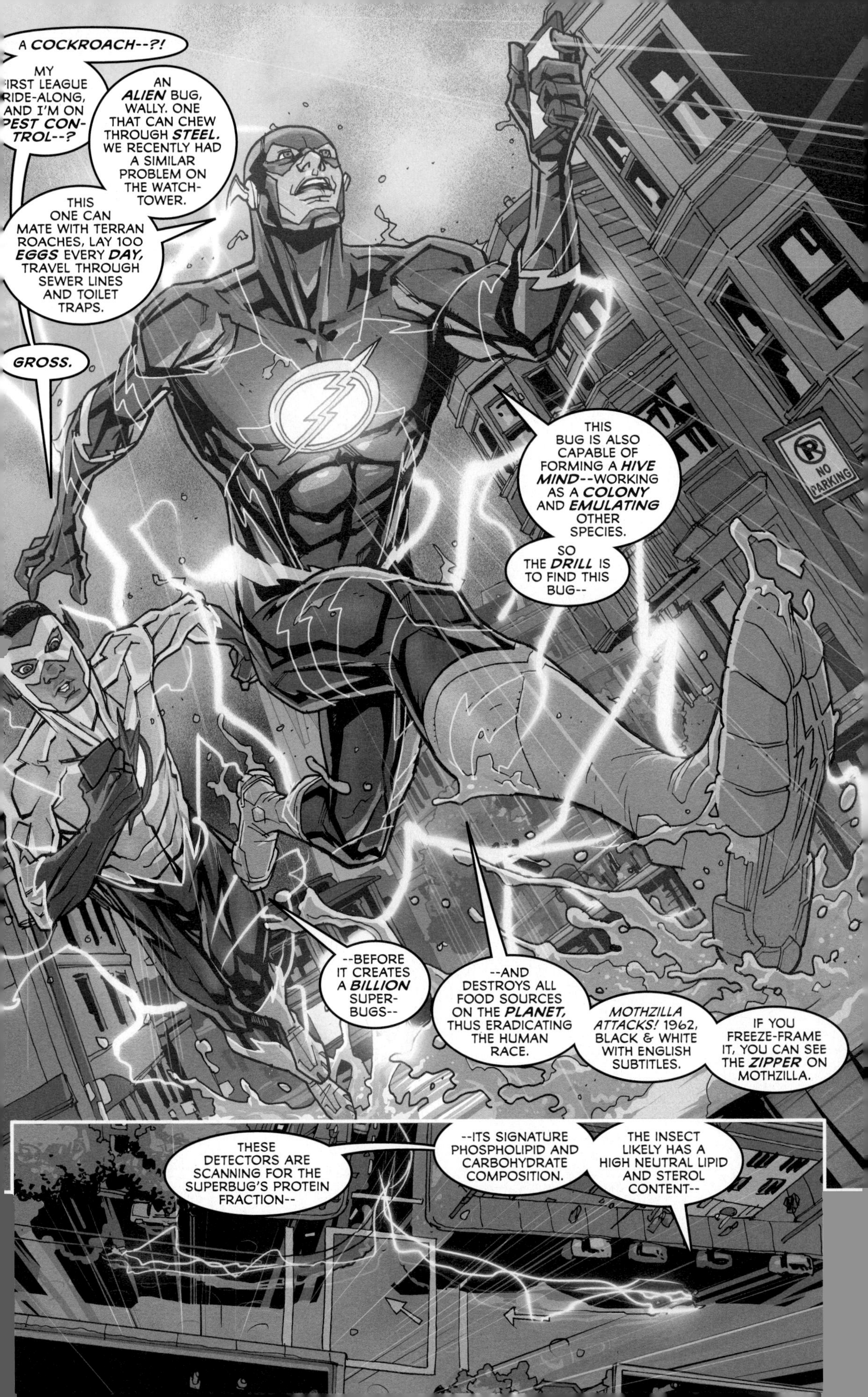
A COCKROACH--?!
MY FIRST LEAGUE RIDE-ALONG, AND I'M ON PEST CON-TROL--?
AN ALIEN BUG, WALLY. ONE THAT CAN CHEW THROUGH STEEL. WE RECENTLY HAD A SIMILAR PROBLEM ON THE WATCH-TOWER.
THIS ONE CAN MATE WITH TERRAN ROACHES, LAY 100 EGGS EVERY DAY, TRAVEL THROUGH SEWER LINES AND TOILET TRAPS.
GROSS.
THIS BUG IS ALSO CAPABLE OF FORMING A HIVE MIND--WORKING AS A COLONY AND EMULATING OTHER SPECIES.
NO PARKING
SO THE DRILL IS TO FIND THIS BUG--
--BEFORE IT CREATES A BILLION SUPER-BUGS--
--AND DESTROYS ALL FOOD SOURCES ON THE PLANET, THUS ERADICATING THE HUMAN RACE.
MOTHZILLA ATTACKS! 1962, BLACK & WHITE WITH ENGLISH SUBTITLES.
IF YOU FREEZE-FRAME IT, YOU CAN SEE THE ZIPPER ON MOTHZILLA.
THESE DETECTORS ARE SCANNING FOR THE SUPERBUG'S PROTEIN FRACTION--
--ITS SIGNATURE PHOSPHOLIPID AND CARBOHYDRATE COMPOSITION.
THE INSECT LIKELY HAS A HIGH NEUTRAL LIPID AND STEROL CONTENT--

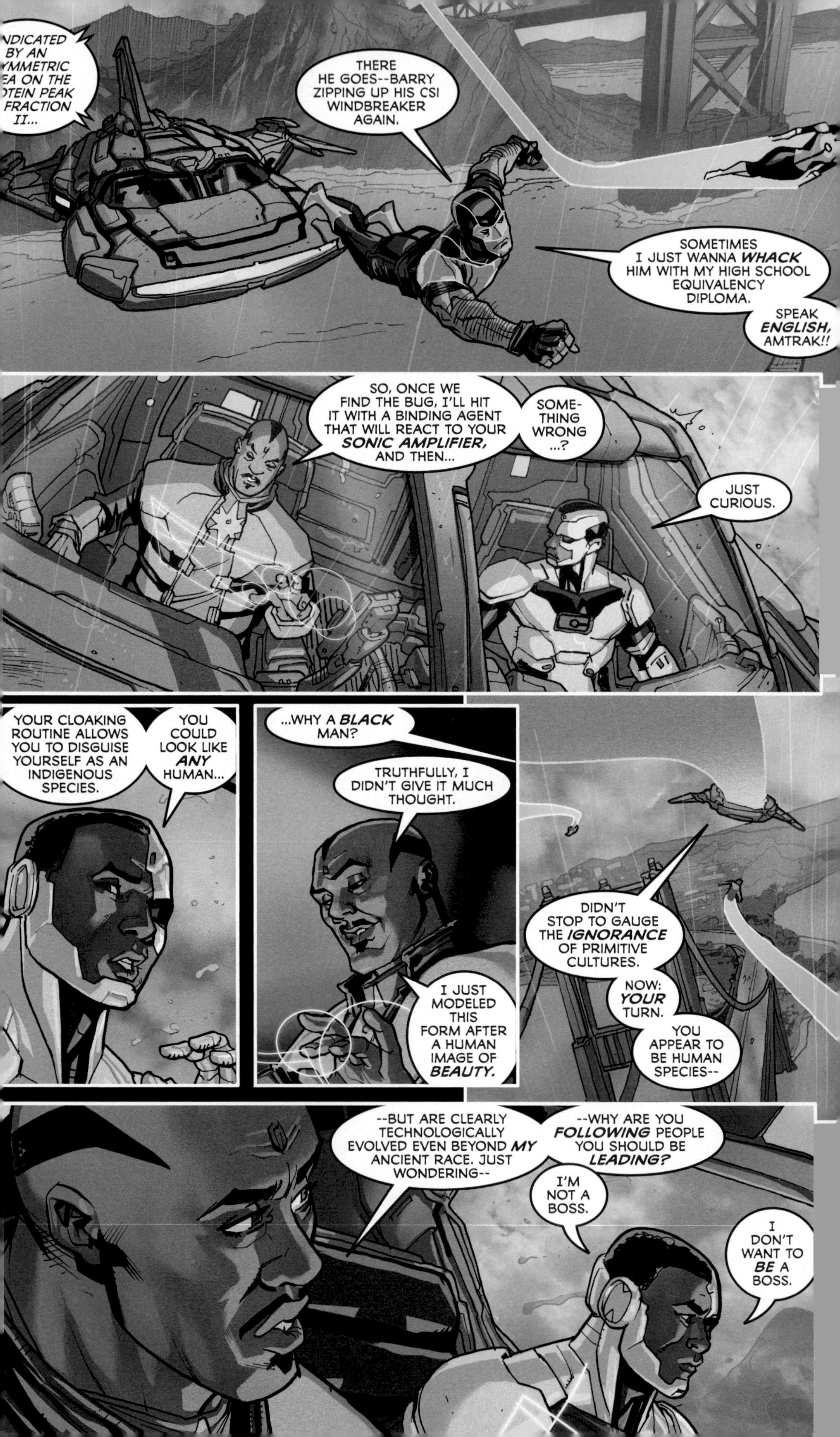

NDICATED BY AN YMMETRIC EA ON THE OTEIN PEAK FRACTION II...
THERE HE GOES--BARRY ZIPPING UP HIS CSI WINDBREAKER AGAIN.
SOMETIMES I JUST WANNA WHACK HIM WITH MY HIGH SCHOOL EQUIVALENCY DIPLOMA.
SPEAK ENGLISH, AMTRAK!!
SO, ONCE WE FIND THE BUG, I'LL HIT IT WITH A BINDING AGENT THAT WILL REACT TO YOUR SONIC AMPLIFIER, AND THEN...
SOME-THING WRONG ...?
JUST CURIOUS.
YOUR CLOAKING ROUTINE ALLOWS YOU TO DISGUISE YOURSELF AS AN INDIGENOUS SPECIES.
YOU COULD LOOK LIKE ANY HUMAN...
...WHY A BLACK MAN?
TRUTHFULLY, I DIDN'T GIVE IT MUCH THOUGHT.
I JUST MODELED THIS FORM AFTER A HUMAN IMAGE OF BEAUTY.
DIDN'T STOP TO GAUGE THE IGNORANCE OF PRIMITIVE CULTURES.
NOW: YOUR TURN.
YOU APPEAR TO BE HUMAN SPECIES--
--BUT ARE CLEARLY TECHNOLOGICALLY EVOLVED EVEN BEYOND MY ANCIENT RACE. JUST WONDERING--
--WHY ARE YOU FOLLOWING PEOPLE YOU SHOULD BE LEADING?
I'M NOT A BOSS.
I DON'T WANT TO BE A BOSS.

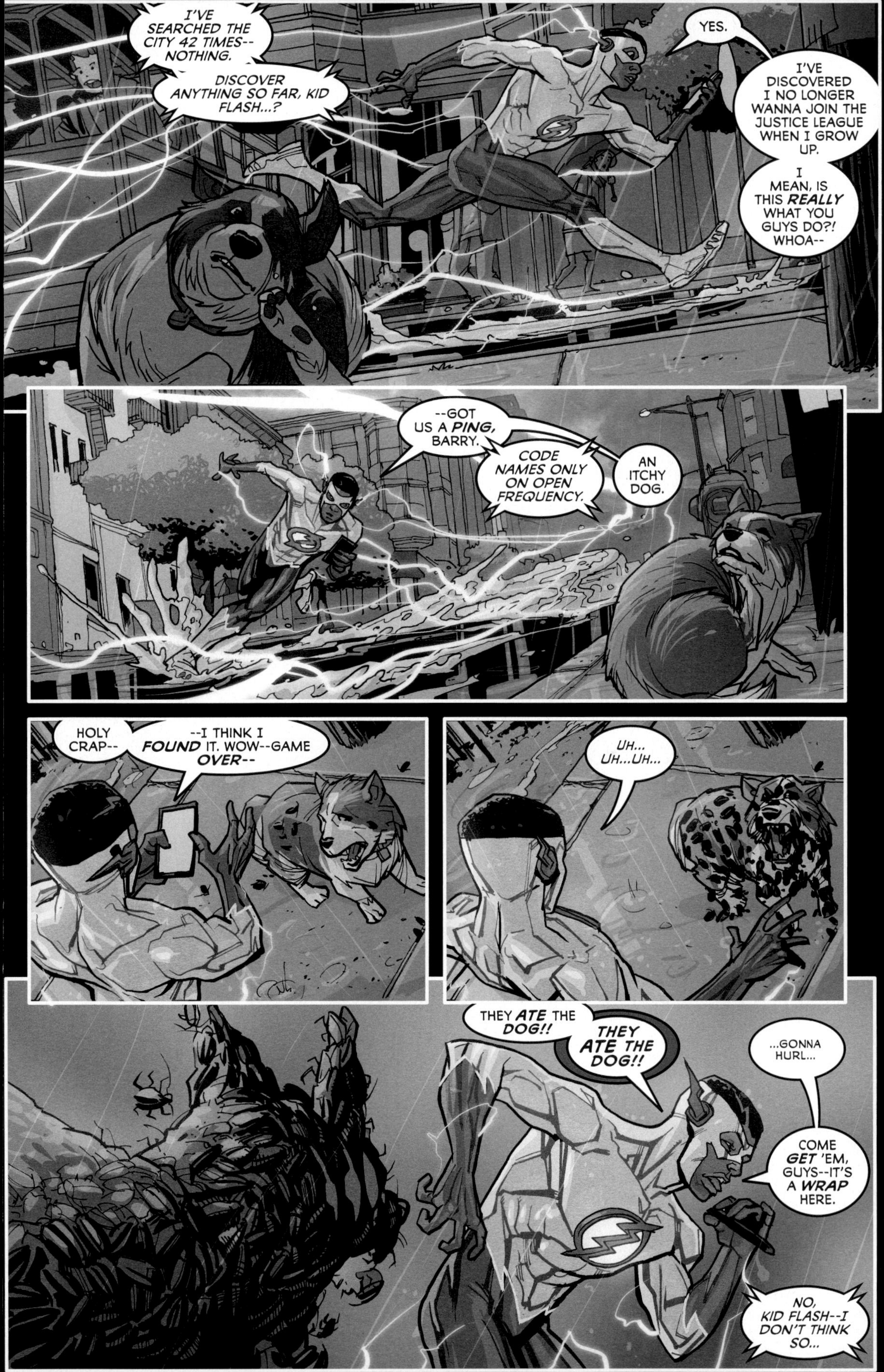
I'VE SEARCHED THE CITY 42 TIMES--NOTHING.
DISCOVER ANYTHING SO FAR, KID FLASH...?
YES.
I'VE DISCOVERED I NO LONGER WANNA JOIN THE JUSTICE LEAGUE WHEN I GROW UP.
I MEAN, IS THIS REALLY WHAT YOU GUYS DO?! WHOA--
--GOT US A PING, BARRY.
CODE NAMES ONLY ON OPEN FREQUENCY.
AN ITCHY DOG.
HOLY CRAP--
--I THINK I FOUND IT. WOW--GAME OVER--
UH... UH...UH...
THEY ATE THE DOG!!
THEY ATE THE DOG!!
...GONNA HURL...
COME GET 'EM, GUYS--IT'S A WRAP HERE.
NO, KID FLASH--I DON'T THINK SO...

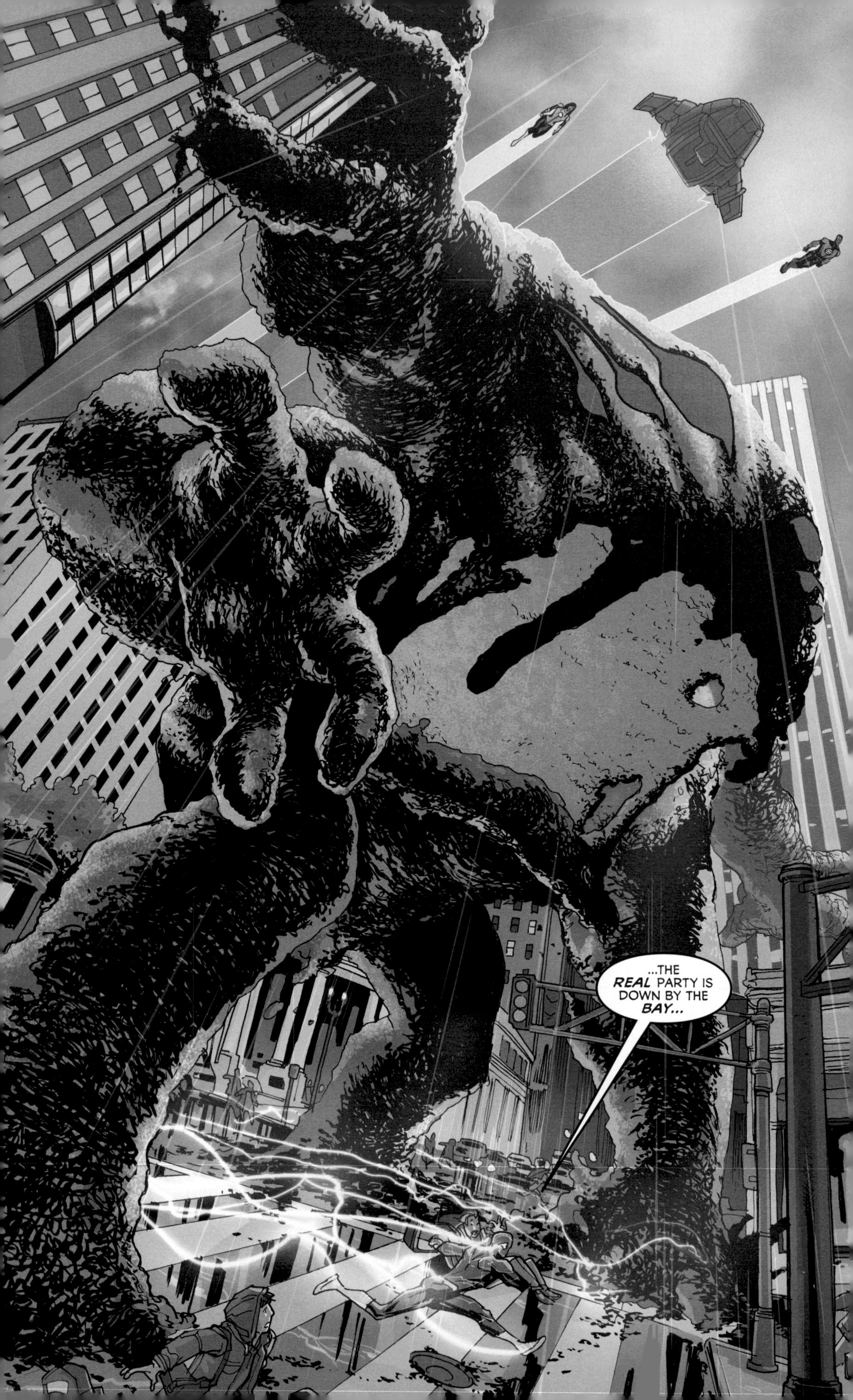
...THE
REAL PARTY IS
DOWN BY THE
BAY...

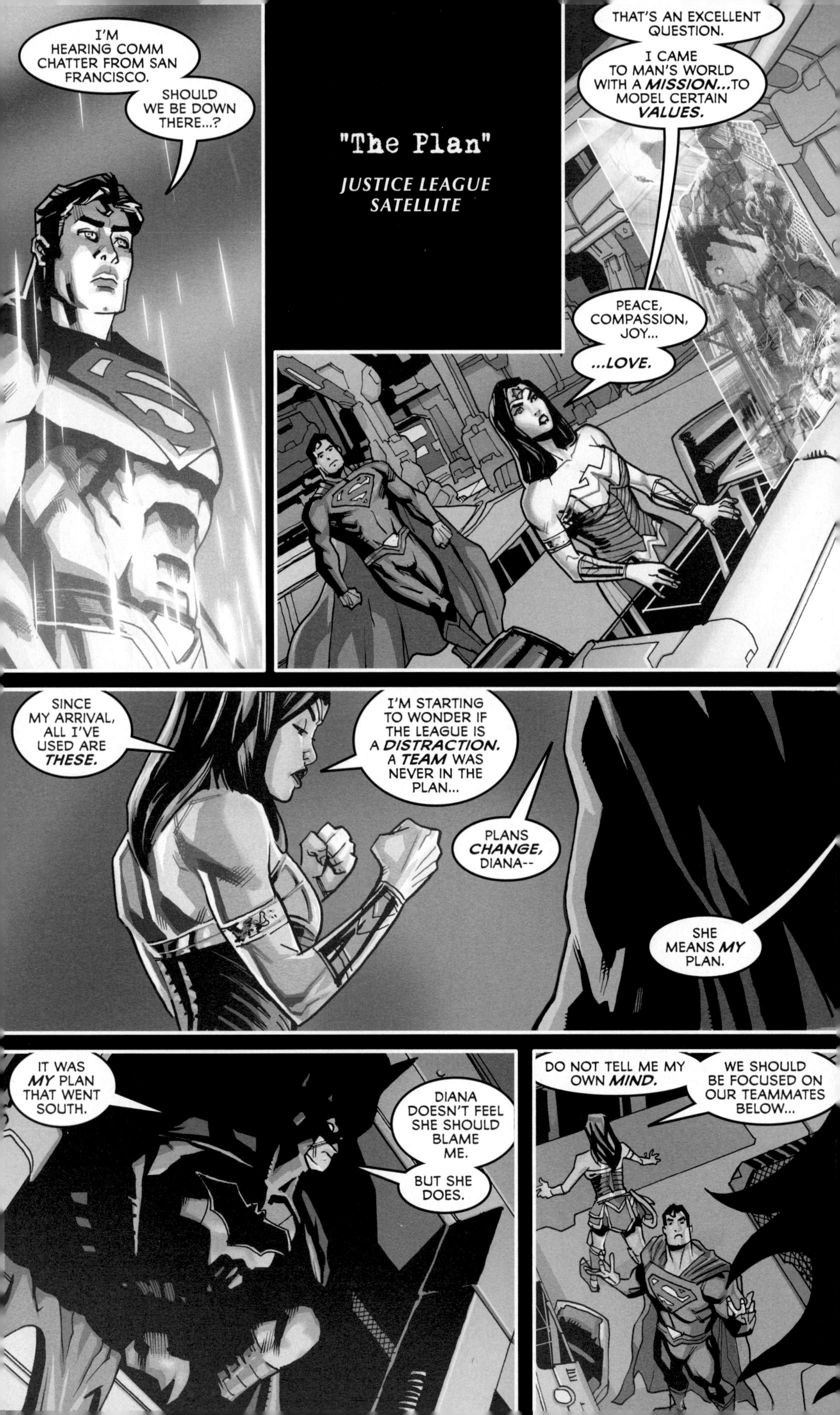
I'M HEARING COMM CHATTER FROM SAN FRANCISCO.
SHOULD WE BE DOWN THERE...?
"The Plan"
JUSTICE LEAGUE SATELLITE
THAT'S AN EXCELLENT QUESTION.
I CAME TO MAN'S WORLD WITH A MISSION...TO MODEL CERTAIN VALUES.
PEACE, COMPASSION, JOY...
...LOVE.
SINCE MY ARRIVAL, ALL I'VE USED ARE THESE.
I'M STARTING TO WONDER IF THE LEAGUE IS A DISTRACTION. A TEAM WAS NEVER IN THE PLAN...
PLANS CHANGE, DIANA--
SHE MEANS MY PLAN.
IT WAS MY PLAN THAT WENT SOUTH.
DIANA DOESN'T FEEL SHE SHOULD BLAME ME.
BUT SHE DOES.
DO NOT TELL ME MY OWN MIND.
WE SHOULD BE FOCUSED ON OUR TEAMMATES BELOW...

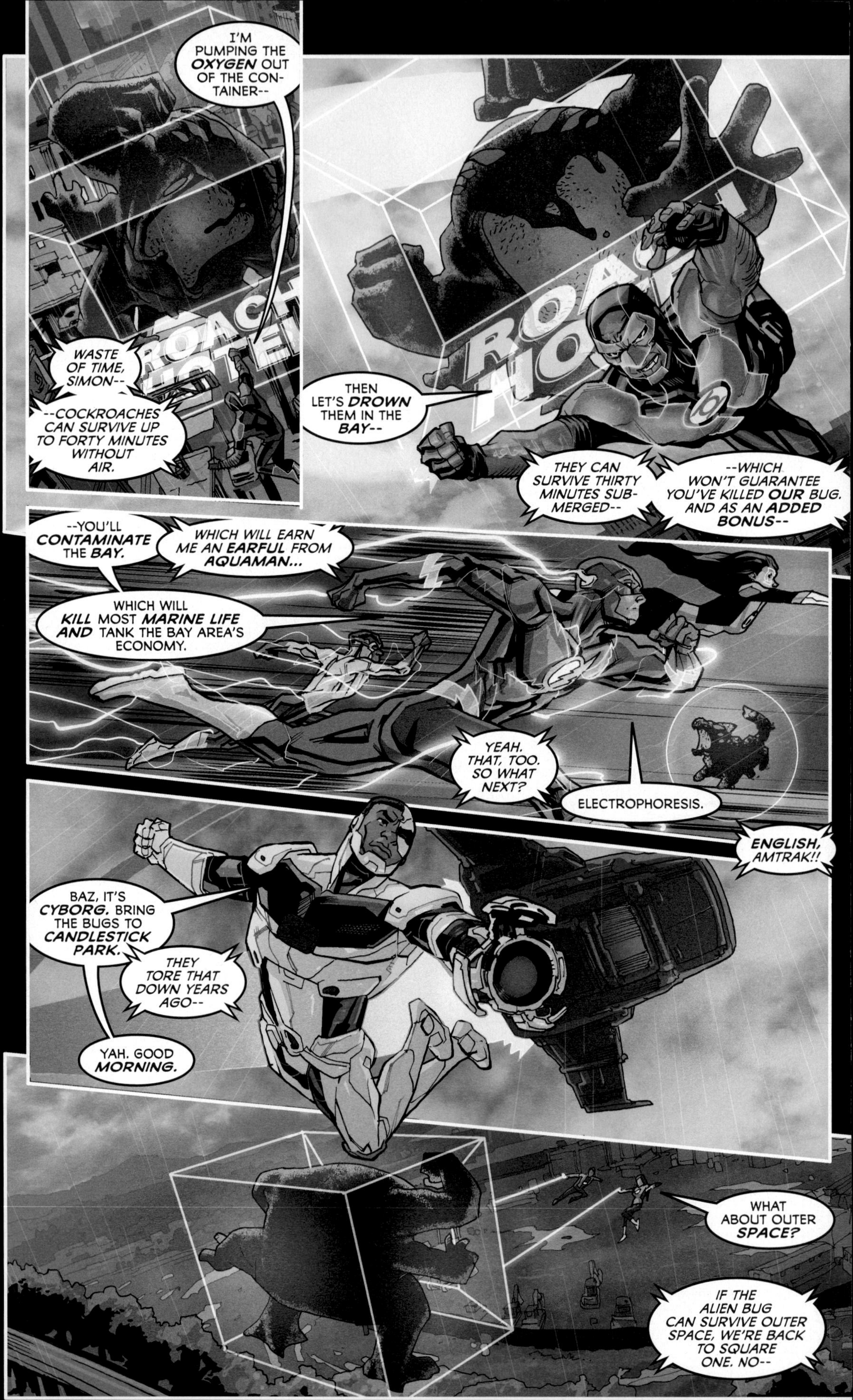
I'M PUMPING THE OXYGEN OUT OF THE CONTAINER--
ROACH HOTEL
WASTE OF TIME, SIMON--
--COCKROACHES CAN SURVIVE UP TO FORTY MINUTES WITHOUT AIR.
THEN LET'S DROWN THEM IN THE BAY--
THEY CAN SURVIVE THIRTY MINUTES SUBMERGED--
--WHICH WON'T GUARANTEE YOU'VE KILLED OUR BUG. AND AS AN ADDED BONUS--
--YOU'LL CONTAMINATE THE BAY.
WHICH WILL EARN ME AN EARFUL FROM AQUAMAN...
WHICH WILL KILL MOST MARINE LIFE AND TANK THE BAY AREA'S ECONOMY.
YEAH. THAT, TOO. SO WHAT NEXT?
ELECTROPHORESIS.
ENGLISH, AMTRAK!!
BAZ, IT'S CYBORG. BRING THE BUGS TO CANDLESTICK PARK.
THEY TORE THAT DOWN YEARS AGO--
YAH. GOOD MORNING.
WHAT ABOUT OUTER SPACE?
IF THE ALIEN BUG CAN SURVIVE OUTER SPACE, WE'RE BACK TO SQUARE ONE. NO--

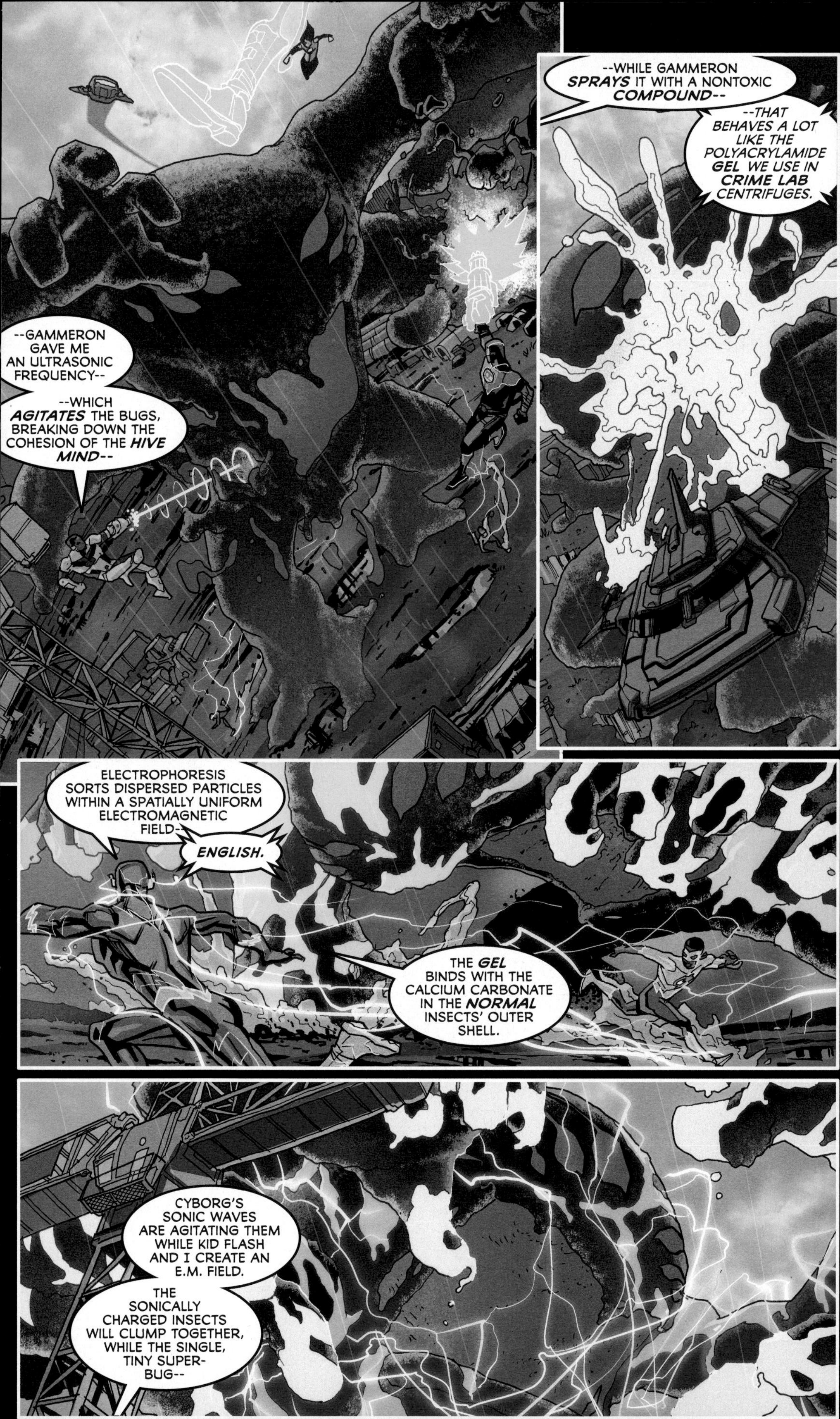
--GAMMERON GAVE ME AN ULTRASONIC FREQUENCY--
--WHICH *AGITATES* THE BUGS, BREAKING DOWN THE COHESION OF THE *HIVE MIND*--
--WHILE GAMMERON *SPRAYS* IT WITH A NONTOXIC *COMPOUND*--
--THAT BEHAVES A LOT LIKE THE POLYACRYLAMIDE *GEL* WE USE IN *CRIME LAB* CENTRIFUGES.
ELECTROPHORESIS SORTS DISPERSED PARTICLES WITHIN A SPATIALLY UNIFORM ELECTROMAGNETIC FIELD--
ENGLISH.
THE *GEL* BINDS WITH THE CALCIUM CARBONATE IN THE *NORMAL* INSECTS' OUTER SHELL.
CYBORG'S SONIC WAVES ARE AGITATING THEM WHILE KID FLASH AND I CREATE AN E.M. FIELD.
THE SONICALLY CHARGED INSECTS WILL CLUMP TOGETHER, WHILE THE SINGLE, TINY SUPER-BUG--

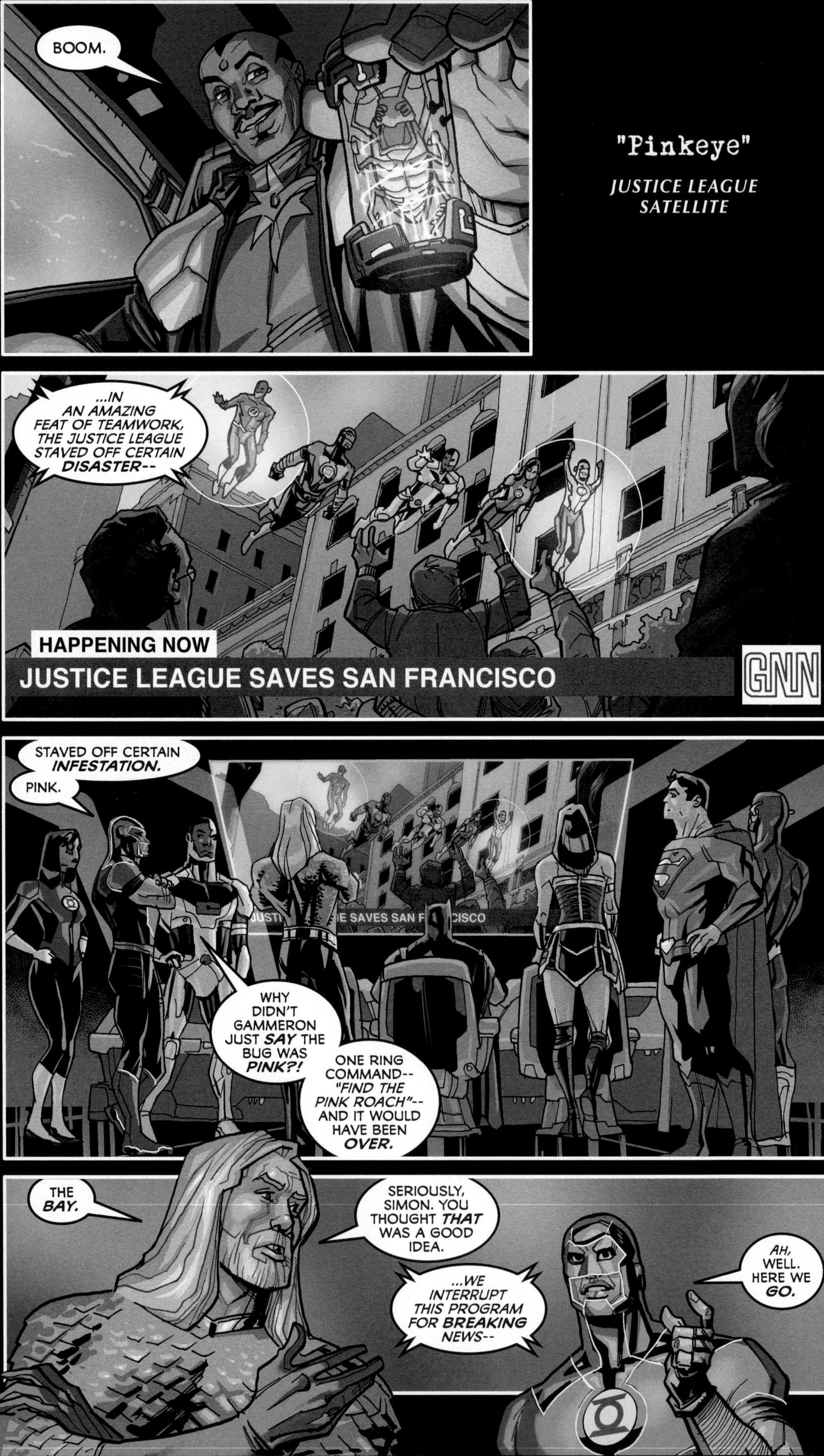
BOOM.
"Pinkeye"
JUSTICE LEAGUE SATELLITE
...IN AN AMAZING FEAT OF TEAMWORK, THE JUSTICE LEAGUE STAVED OFF CERTAIN DISASTER--
HAPPENING NOW
JUSTICE LEAGUE SAVES SAN FRANCISCO
GNN
STAVED OFF CERTAIN INFESTATION.
PINK.
WHY DIDN'T GAMMERON JUST SAY THE BUG WAS PINK?!
ONE RING COMMAND-- "FIND THE PINK ROACH"-- AND IT WOULD HAVE BEEN OVER.
THE BAY.
SERIOUSLY, SIMON. YOU THOUGHT THAT WAS A GOOD IDEA.
...WE INTERRUPT THIS PROGRAM FOR BREAKING NEWS--
AH, WELL. HERE WE GO.

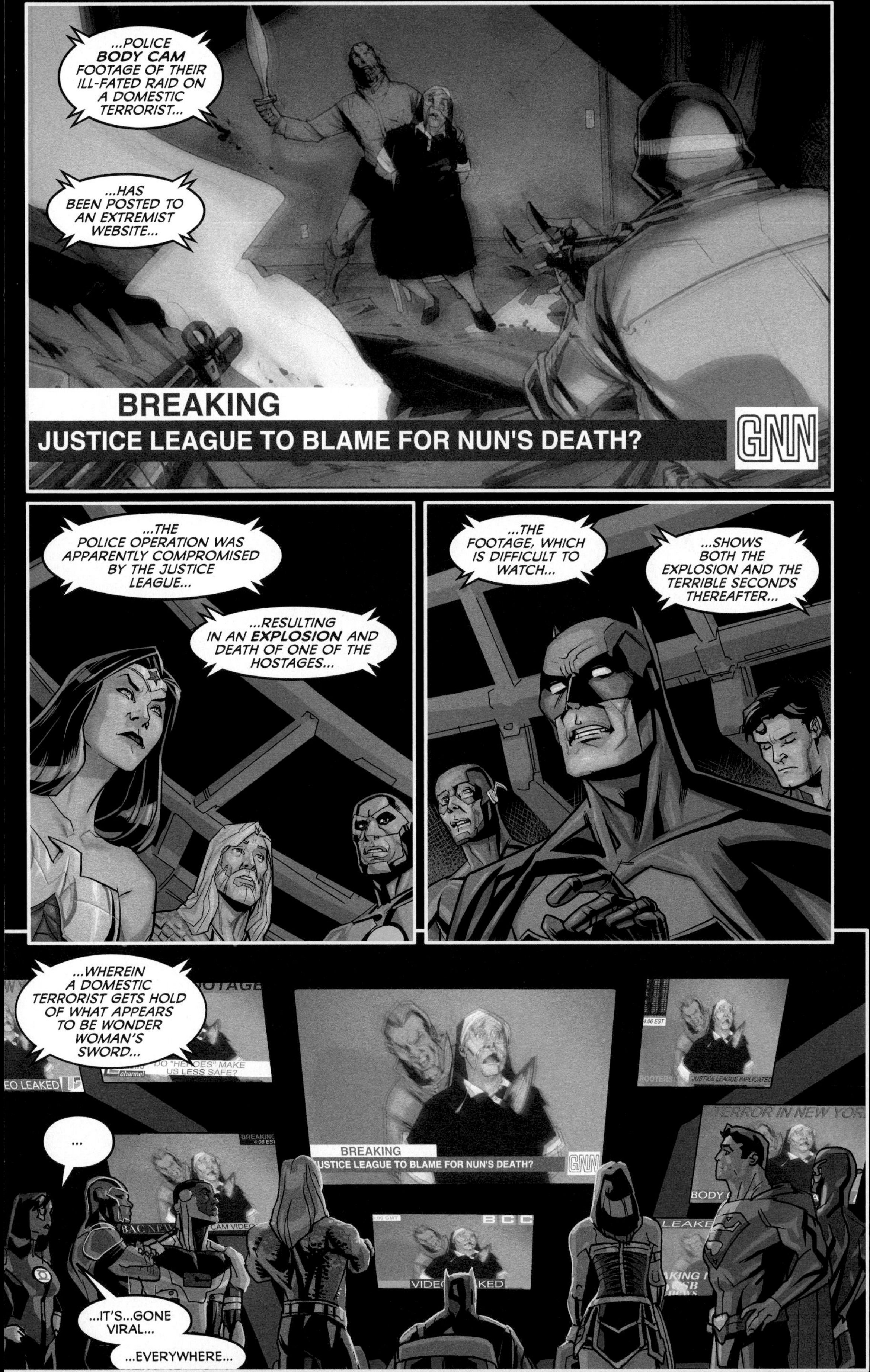

...POLICE BODY CAM FOOTAGE OF THEIR ILL-FATED RAID ON A DOMESTIC TERRORIST...
...HAS BEEN POSTED TO AN EXTREMIST WEBSITE...
BREAKING
JUSTICE LEAGUE TO BLAME FOR NUN'S DEATH?
GNN
...THE POLICE OPERATION WAS APPARENTLY COMPROMISED BY THE JUSTICE LEAGUE...
...RESULTING IN AN EXPLOSION AND DEATH OF ONE OF THE HOSTAGES...
...THE FOOTAGE, WHICH IS DIFFICULT TO WATCH...
...SHOWS BOTH THE EXPLOSION AND THE TERRIBLE SECONDS THEREAFTER...
...WHEREIN A DOMESTIC TERRORIST GETS HOLD OF WHAT APPEARS TO BE WONDER WOMAN'S SWORD...
DO "HEROES" MAKE US LESS SAFE?
JUSTICE LEAGUE IMPLICATED
BREAKING
JUSTICE LEAGUE TO BLAME FOR NUN'S DEATH?
...
...IT'S...GONE VIRAL...
...EVERYWHERE...

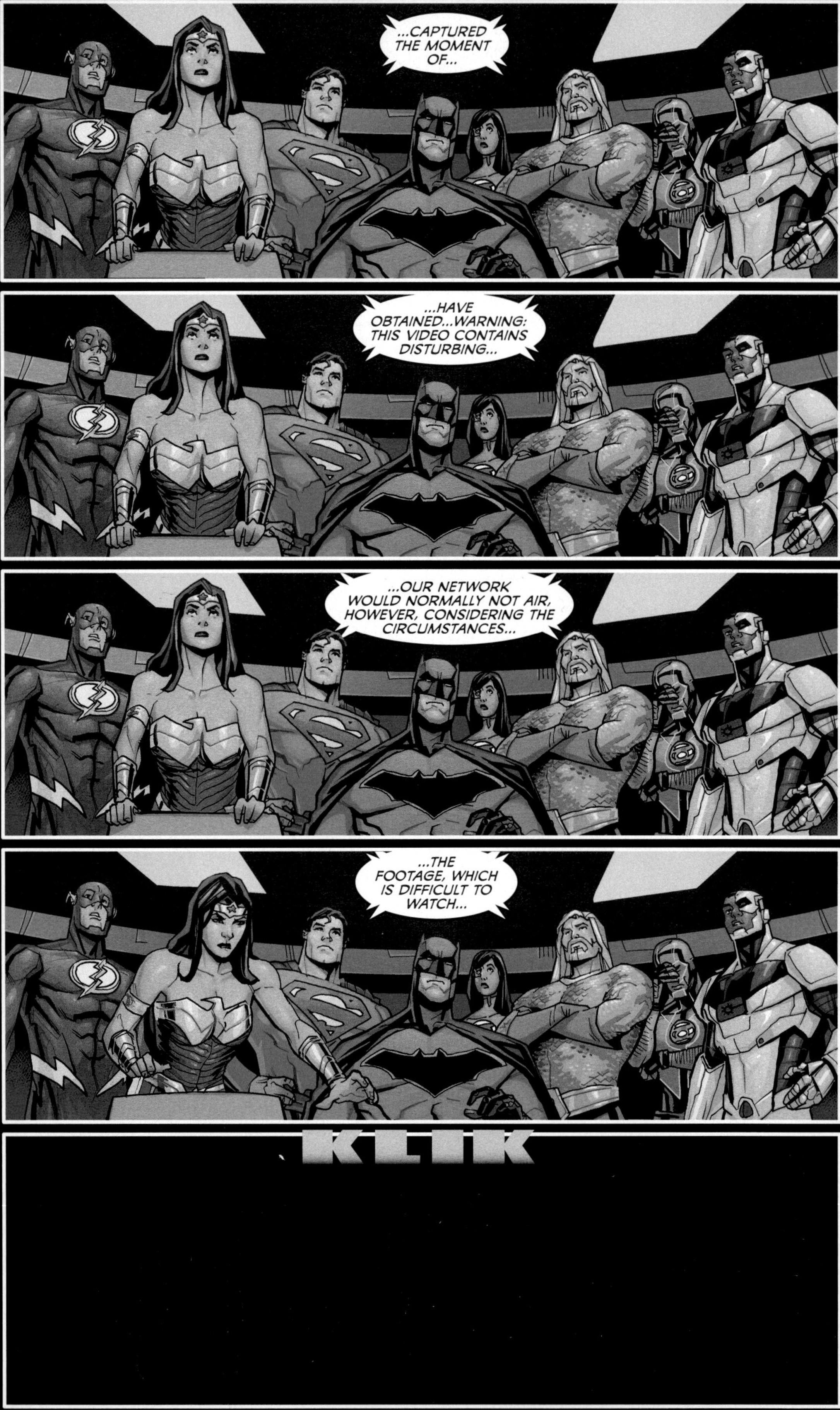
...CAPTURED THE MOMENT OF...
...HAVE OBTAINED...WARNING: THIS VIDEO CONTAINS DISTURBING...
...OUR NETWORK WOULD NORMALLY NOT AIR, HOWEVER, CONSIDERING THE CIRCUMSTANCES...
...THE FOOTAGE, WHICH IS DIFFICULT TO WATCH...
KLIK

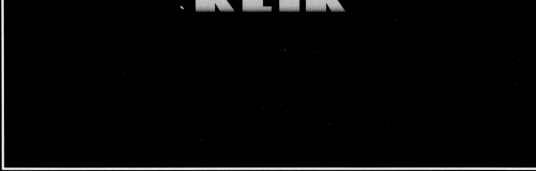

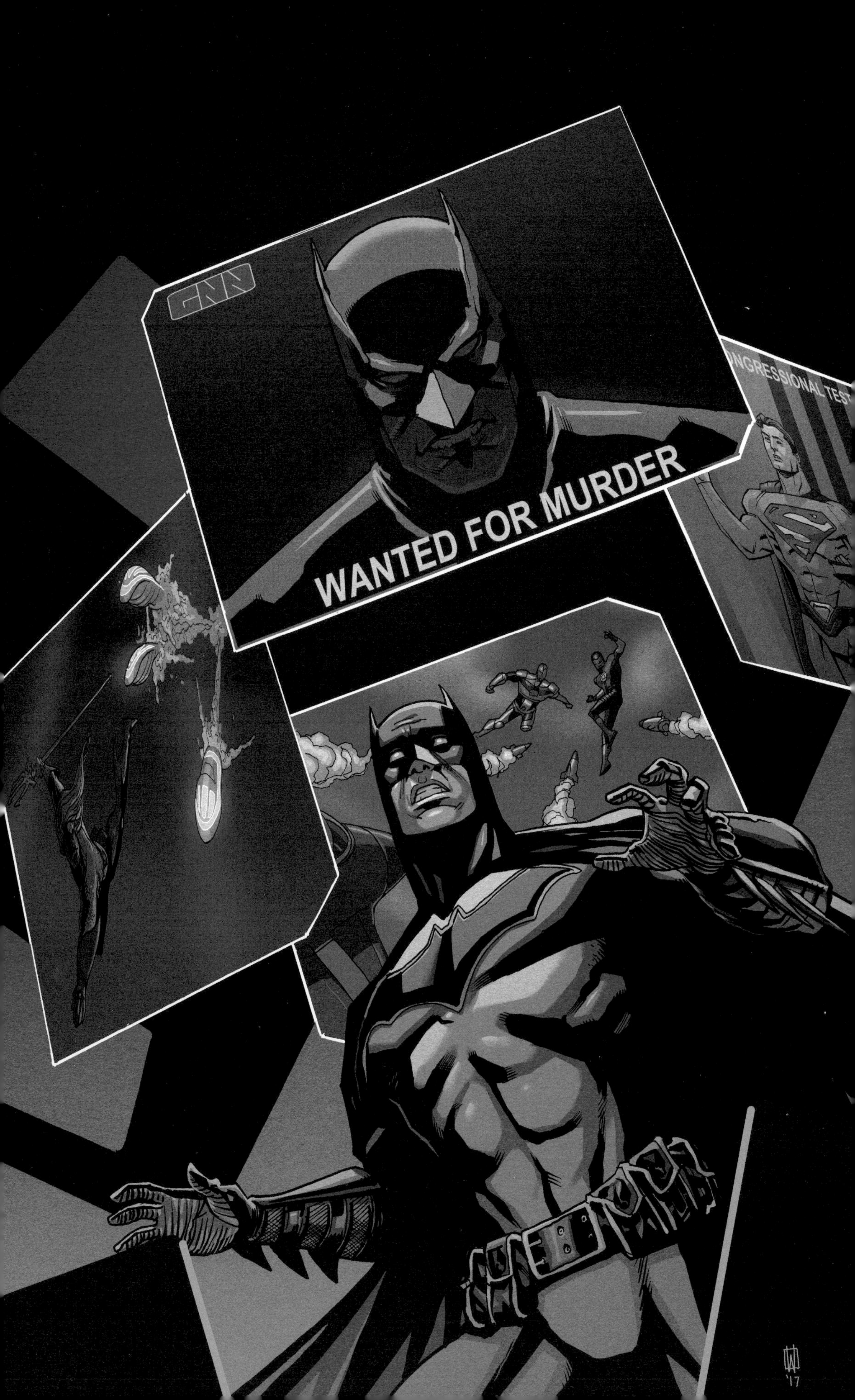
GNN
WANTED FOR MURDER

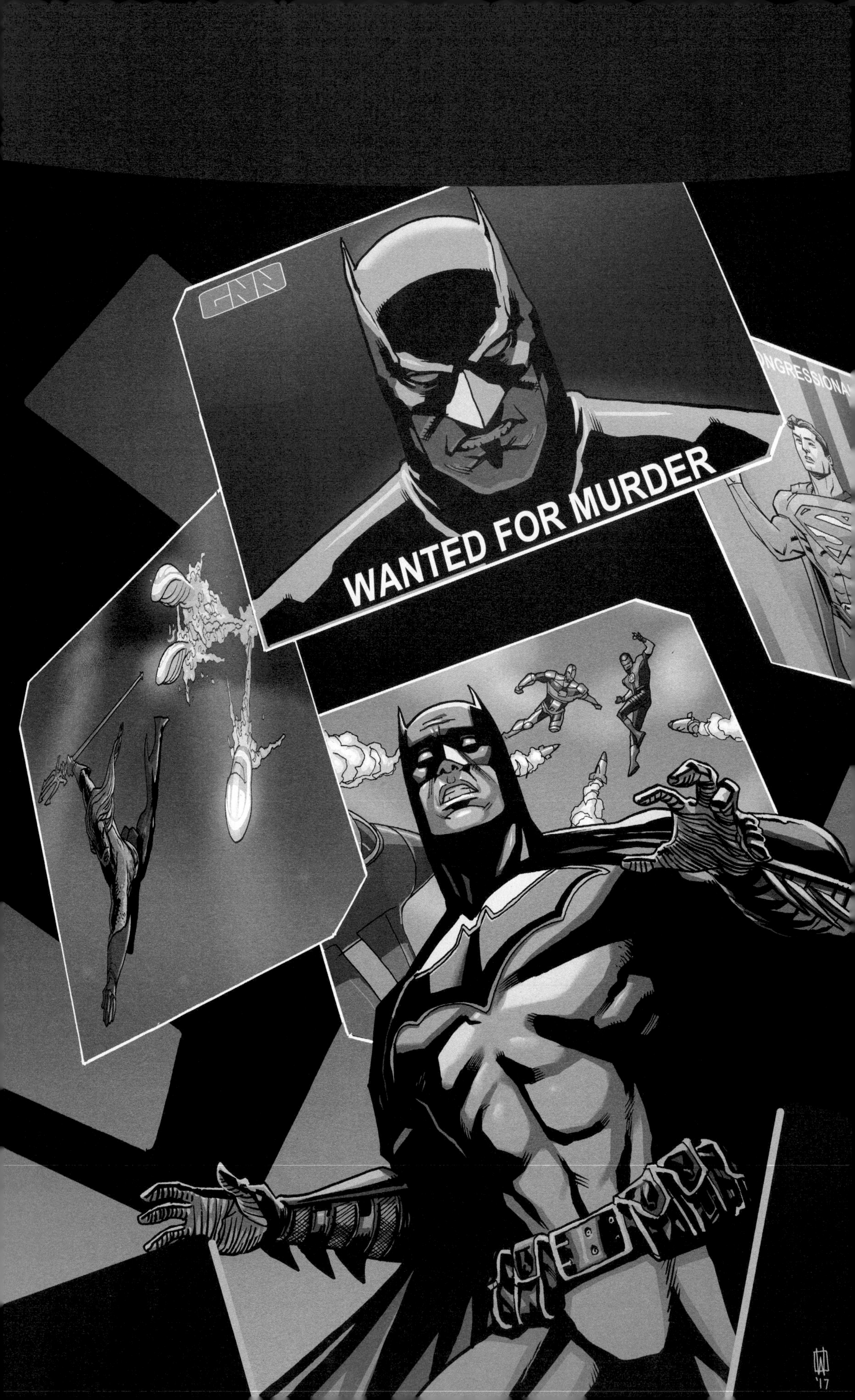
WANTED FOR MURDER

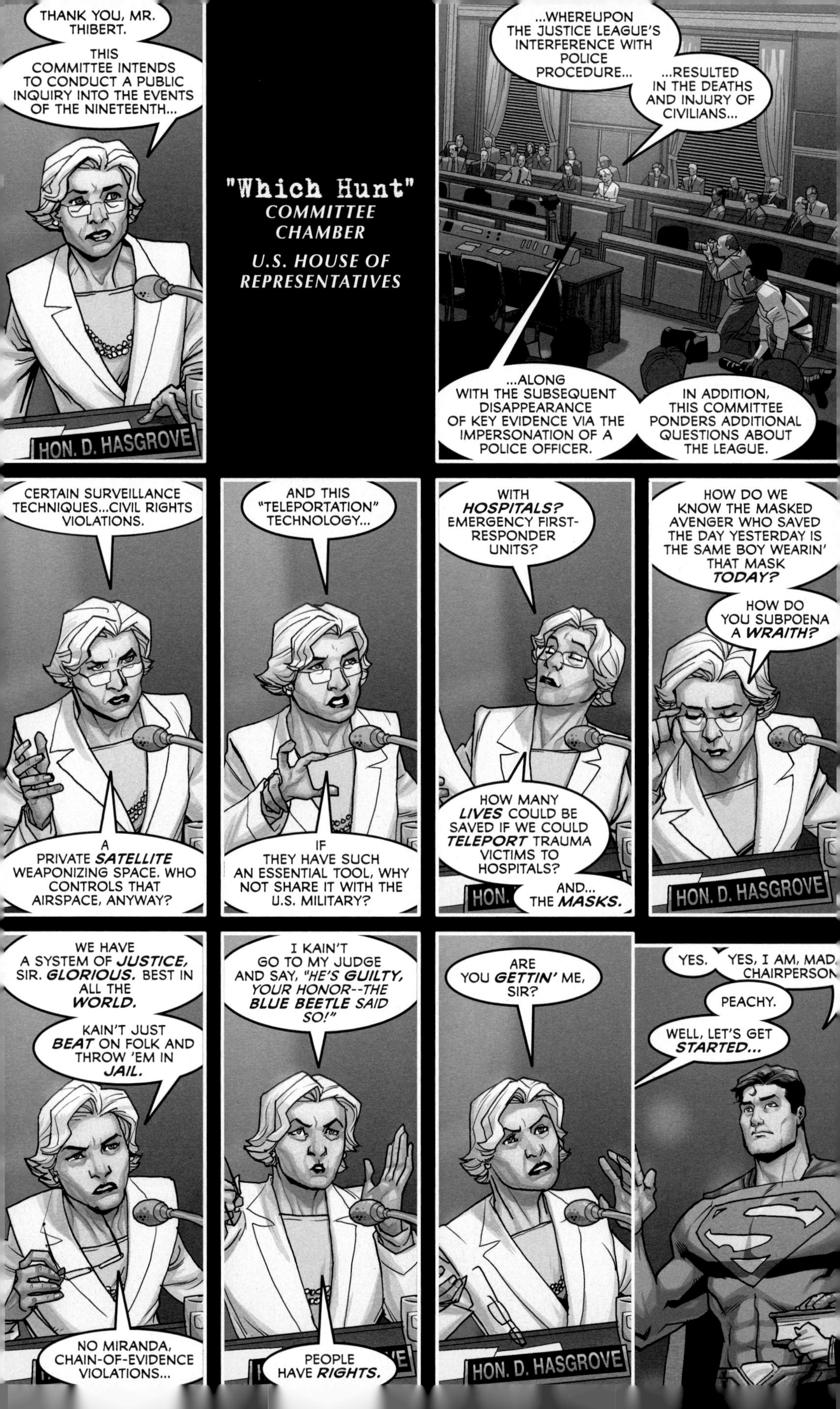
THANK YOU, MR. THIBERT.
THIS COMMITTEE INTENDS TO CONDUCT A PUBLIC INQUIRY INTO THE EVENTS OF THE NINETEENTH...
HON. D. HASGROVE
"Which Hunt"
COMMITTEE CHAMBER
U.S. HOUSE OF REPRESENTATIVES
...WHEREUPON THE JUSTICE LEAGUE'S INTERFERENCE WITH POLICE PROCEDURE...
...RESULTED IN THE DEATHS AND INJURY OF CIVILIANS...
...ALONG WITH THE SUBSEQUENT DISAPPEARANCE OF KEY EVIDENCE VIA THE IMPERSONATION OF A POLICE OFFICER.
IN ADDITION, THIS COMMITTEE PONDERS ADDITIONAL QUESTIONS ABOUT THE LEAGUE.
CERTAIN SURVEILLANCE TECHNIQUES...CIVIL RIGHTS VIOLATIONS.
A PRIVATE SATELLITE WEAPONIZING SPACE. WHO CONTROLS THAT AIRSPACE, ANYWAY?
AND THIS "TELEPORTATION" TECHNOLOGY...
IF THEY HAVE SUCH AN ESSENTIAL TOOL, WHY NOT SHARE IT WITH THE U.S. MILITARY?
WITH HOSPITALS? EMERGENCY FIRST-RESPONDER UNITS?
HOW MANY LIVES COULD BE SAVED IF WE COULD TELEPORT TRAUMA VICTIMS TO HOSPITALS?
AND... THE MASKS.
HOW DO WE KNOW THE MASKED AVENGER WHO SAVED THE DAY YESTERDAY IS THE SAME BOY WEARIN' THAT MASK TODAY?
HOW DO YOU SUBPOENA A WRAITH?
HON. D. HASGROVE
WE HAVE A SYSTEM OF JUSTICE, SIR. GLORIOUS. BEST IN ALL THE WORLD.
KAIN'T JUST BEAT ON FOLK AND THROW 'EM IN JAIL.
NO MIRANDA, CHAIN-OF-EVIDENCE VIOLATIONS...
I KAIN'T GO TO MY JUDGE AND SAY, "HE'S GUILTY, YOUR HONOR--THE BLUE BEETLE SAID SO!"
PEOPLE HAVE RIGHTS.
ARE YOU GETTIN' ME, SIR?
HON. D. HASGROVE
YES.
YES, I AM, MAD
CHAIRPERSON
PEACHY.
WELL, LET'S GET STARTED...

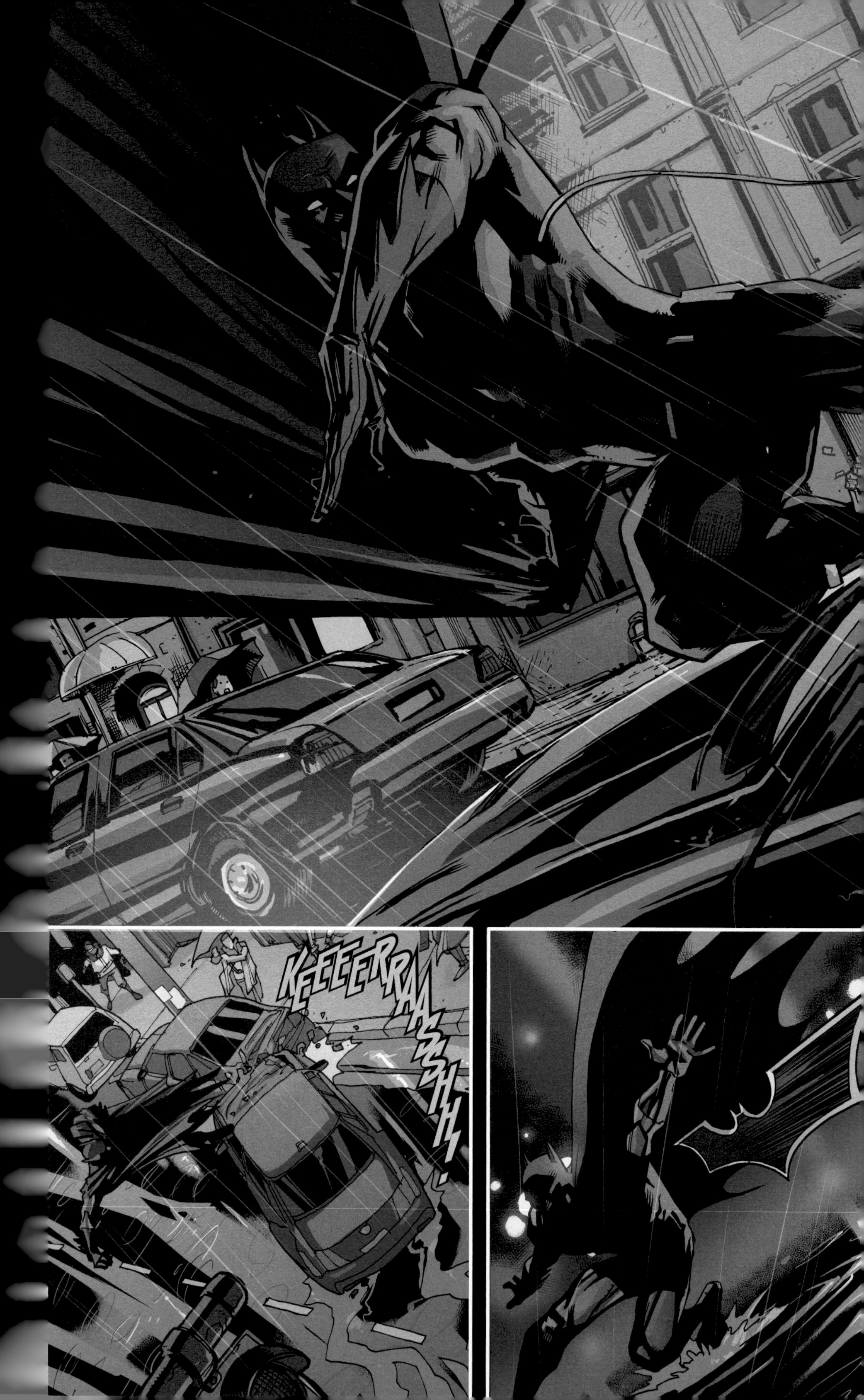
KEEEERRAASSHH!

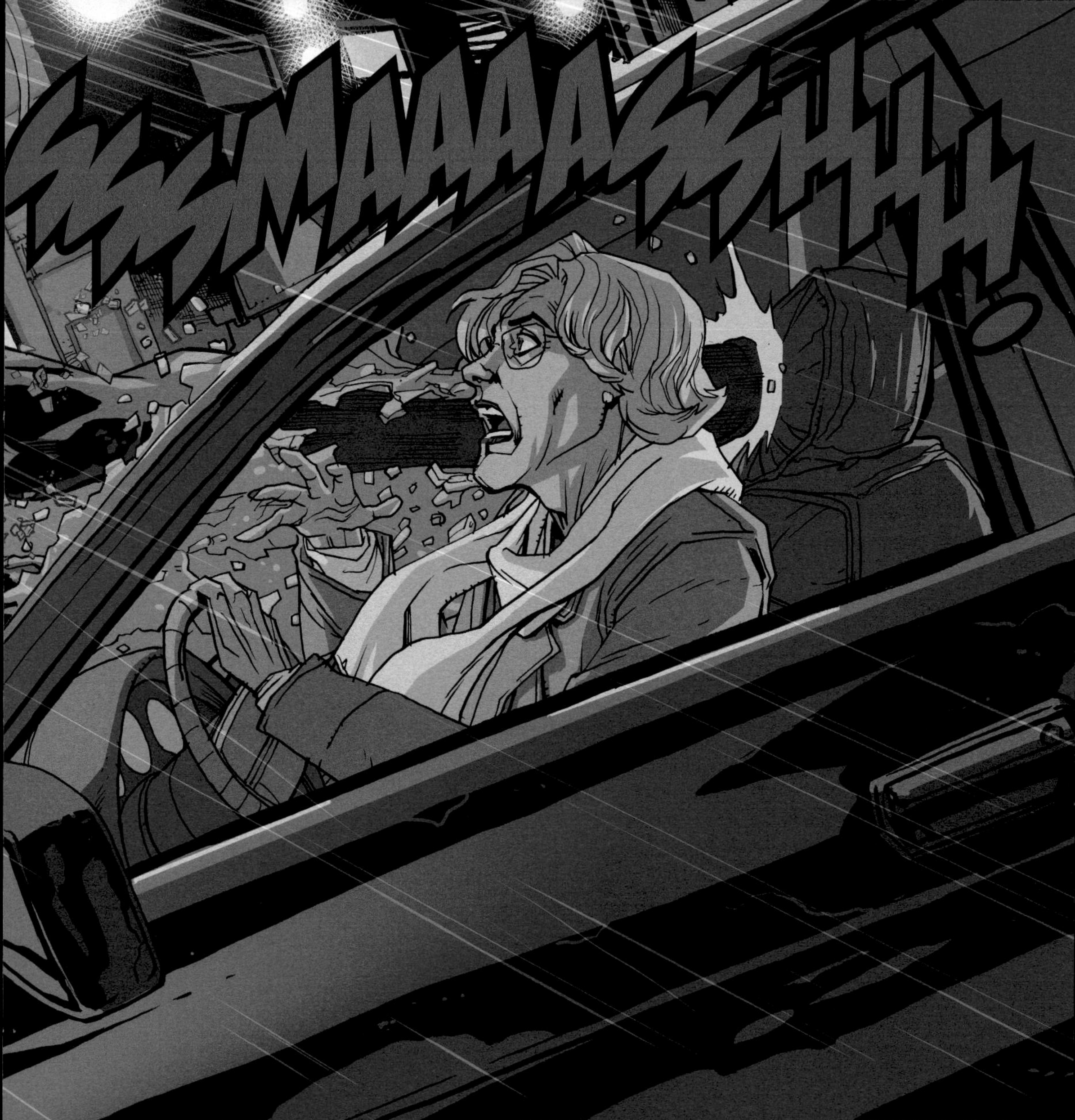
SSMAAAASHHH!
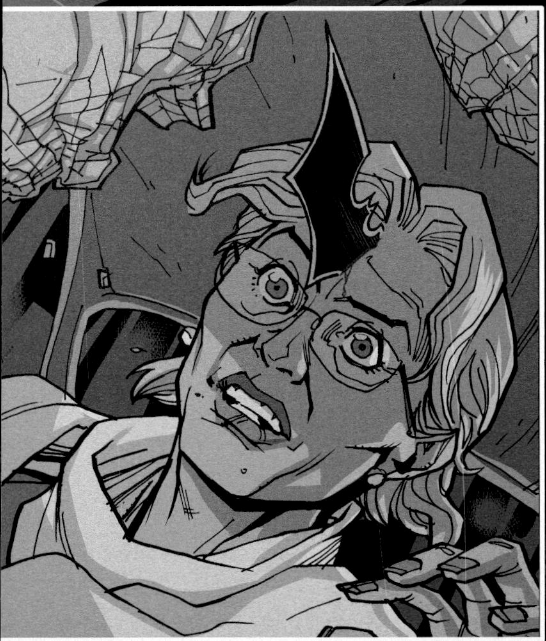
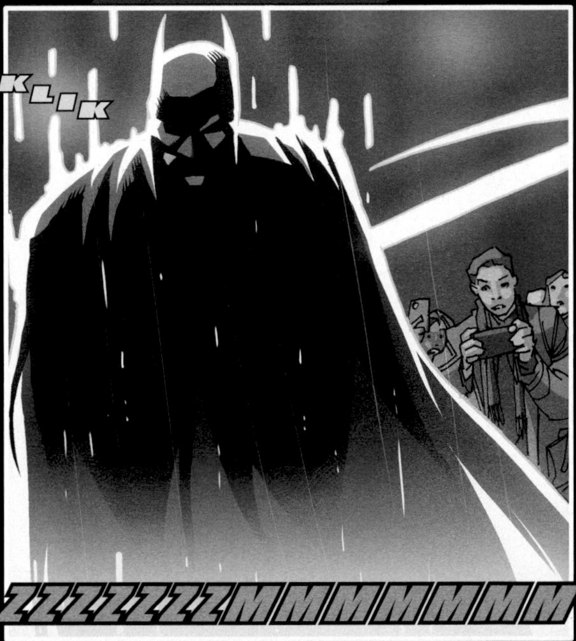
KLIK
ZZZZZZZMMMMMMM

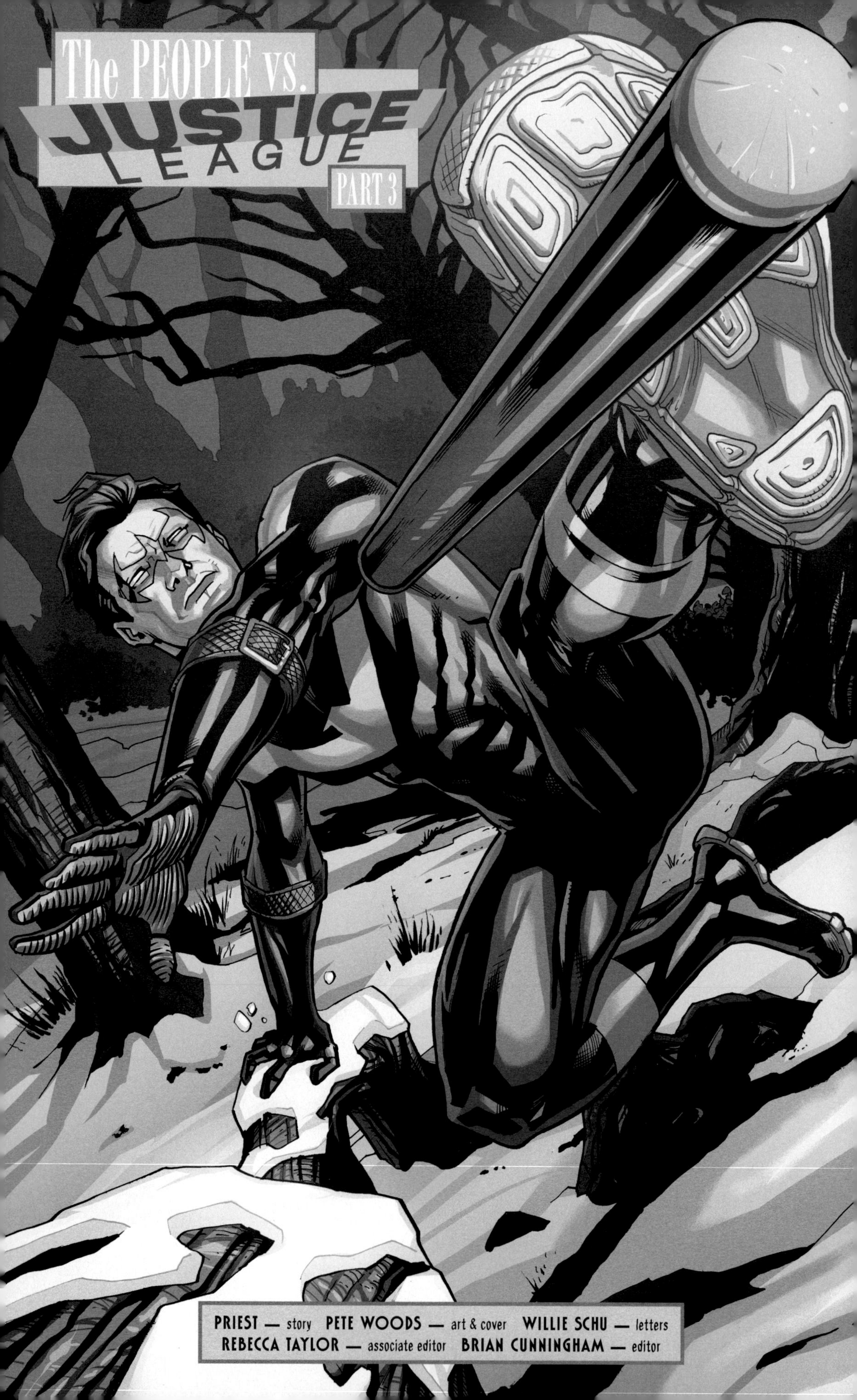
The PEOPLE vs.
JUSTICE LEAGUE
PART 3
PRIEST — story PETE WOODS — art & cover WILLIE SCHU — letters
REBECCA TAYLOR — associate editor BRIAN CUNNINGHAM — editor

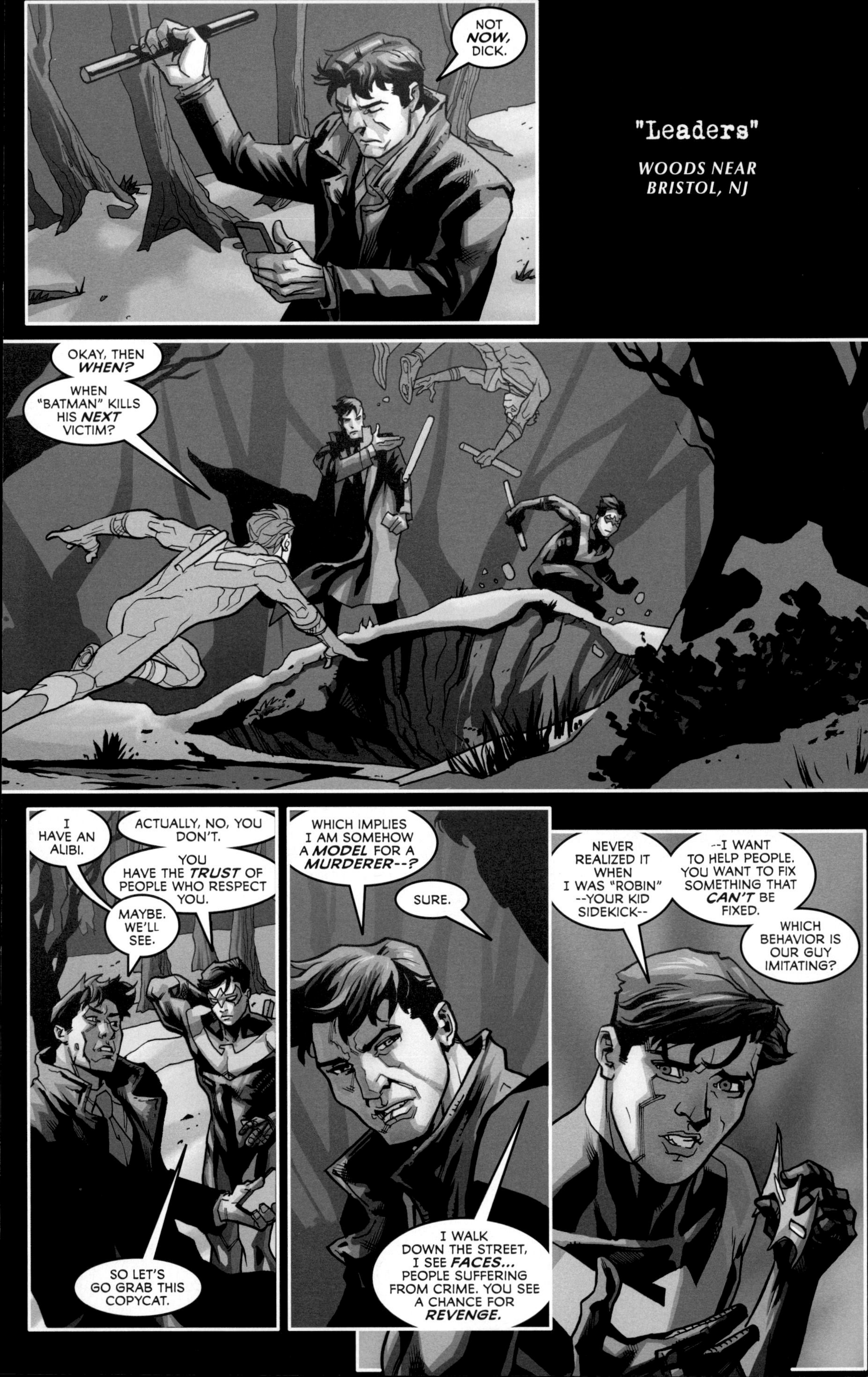
NOT NOW, DICK.
"Leaders"
WOODS NEAR BRISTOL, NJ
OKAY, THEN WHEN?
WHEN "BATMAN" KILLS HIS NEXT VICTIM?
I HAVE AN ALIBI.
ACTUALLY, NO, YOU DON'T.
YOU HAVE THE TRUST OF PEOPLE WHO RESPECT YOU.
MAYBE. WE'LL SEE.
SO LET'S GO GRAB THIS COPYCAT.
WHICH IMPLIES I AM SOMEHOW A MODEL FOR A MURDERER--?
SURE.
I WALK DOWN THE STREET, I SEE FACES... PEOPLE SUFFERING FROM CRIME. YOU SEE A CHANCE FOR REVENGE.
NEVER REALIZED IT WHEN I WAS "ROBIN" --YOUR KID SIDEKICK--
--I WANT TO HELP PEOPLE. YOU WANT TO FIX SOMETHING THAT CAN'T BE FIXED.
WHICH BEHAVIOR IS OUR GUY IMITATING?

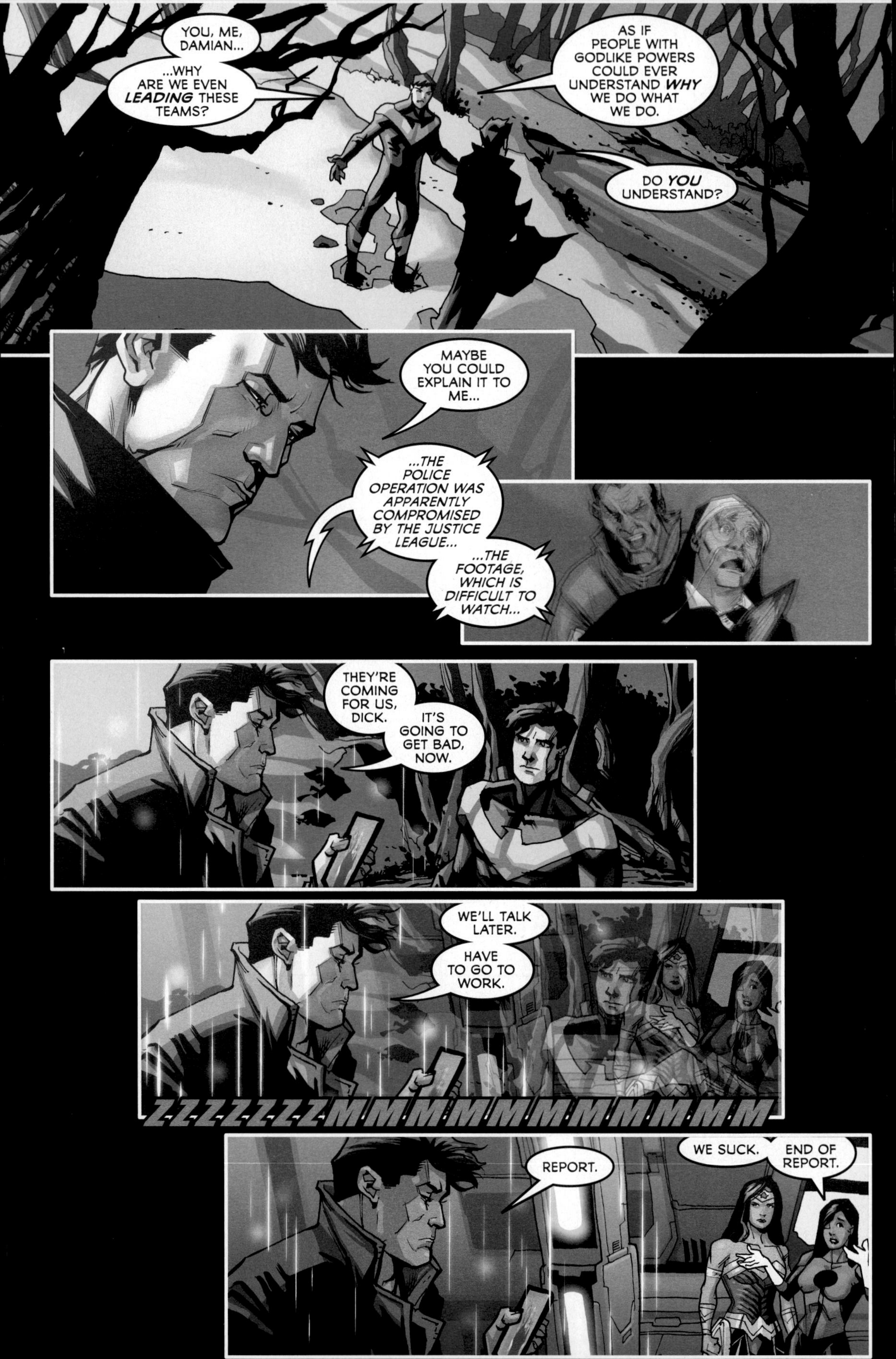
YOU, ME, DAMIAN...
...WHY ARE WE EVEN LEADING THESE TEAMS?
AS IF PEOPLE WITH GODLIKE POWERS COULD EVER UNDERSTAND WHY WE DO WHAT WE DO.
DO YOU UNDERSTAND?
MAYBE YOU COULD EXPLAIN IT TO ME...
...THE POLICE OPERATION WAS APPARENTLY COMPROMISED BY THE JUSTICE LEAGUE...
...THE FOOTAGE, WHICH IS DIFFICULT TO WATCH...
THEY'RE COMING FOR US, DICK.
IT'S GOING TO GET BAD, NOW.
WE'LL TALK LATER.
HAVE TO GO TO WORK.
Z-Z-Z-Z-Z-Z-ZMMMMMMMMMMMMMMMM
REPORT.
WE SUCK.
END OF REPORT.

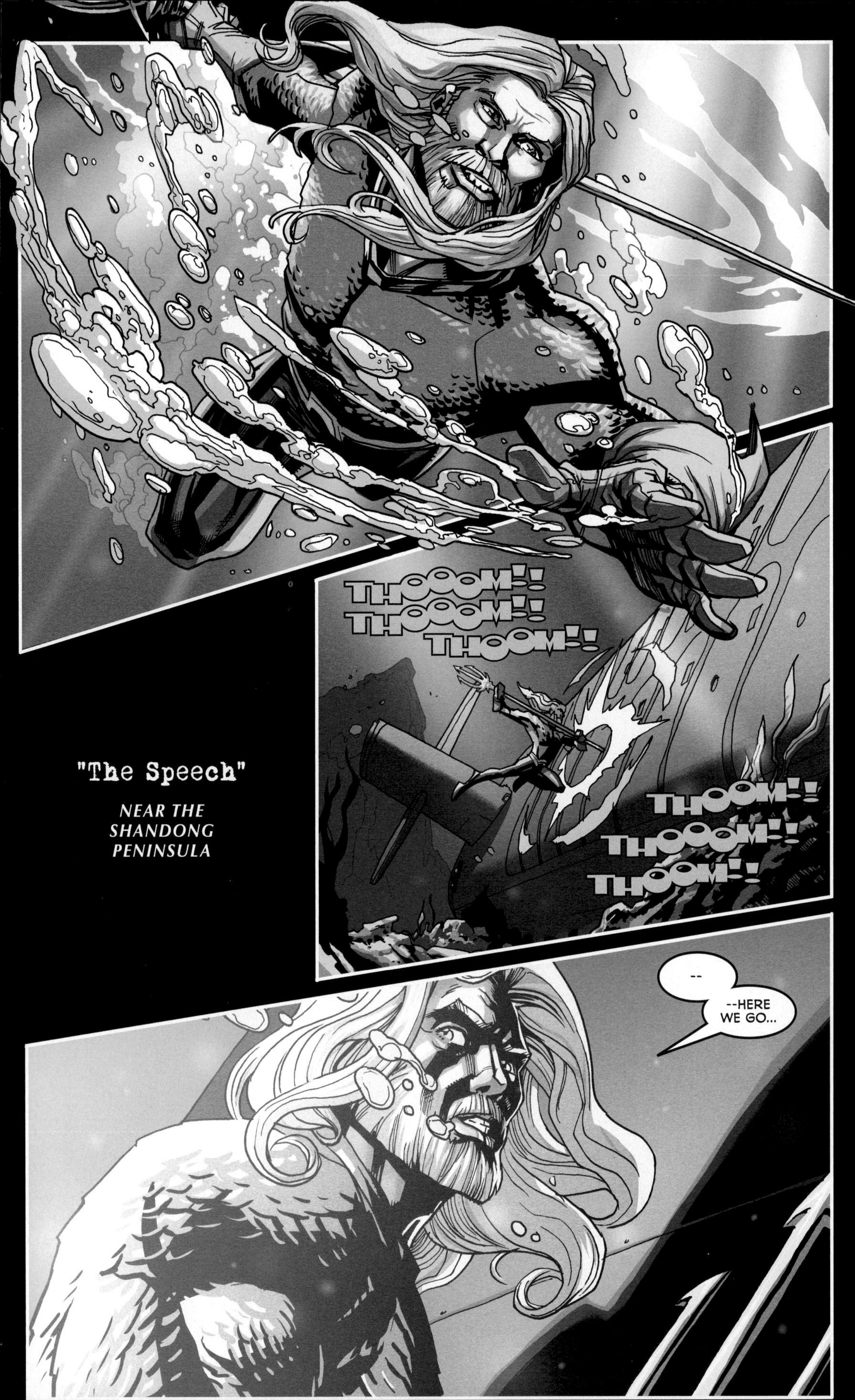
THOOOM!!
THOOOM!!
THOOM!!
"The Speech"
NEAR THE SHANDONG PENINSULA
THOOM!!
THOOOM!!
THOOM!!
--
--HERE WE GO...

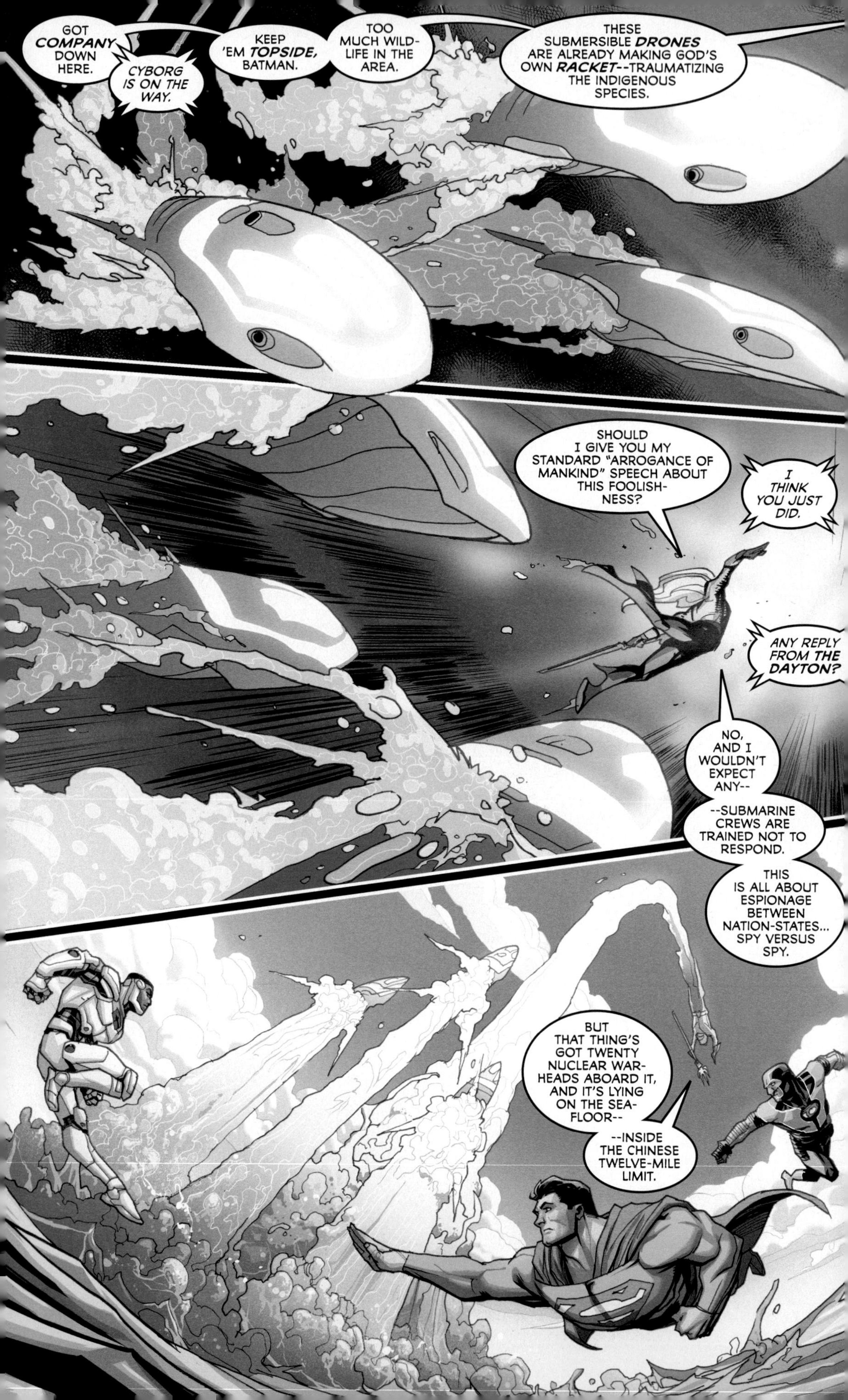
GOT COMPANY DOWN HERE.
CYBORG IS ON THE WAY.
KEEP 'EM TOPSIDE, BATMAN.
TOO MUCH WILD-LIFE IN THE AREA.
THESE SUBMERSIBLE DRONES ARE ALREADY MAKING GOD'S OWN RACKET--TRAUMATIZING THE INDIGENOUS SPECIES.
SHOULD I GIVE YOU MY STANDARD "ARROGANCE OF MANKIND" SPEECH ABOUT THIS FOOLISH-NESS?
I THINK YOU JUST DID.
ANY REPLY FROM THE DAYTON?
NO, AND I WOULDN'T EXPECT ANY--
--SUBMARINE CREWS ARE TRAINED NOT TO RESPOND.
THIS IS ALL ABOUT ESPIONAGE BETWEEN NATION-STATES... SPY VERSUS SPY.
BUT THAT THING'S GOT TWENTY NUCLEAR WAR-HEADS ABOARD IT, AND IT'S LYING ON THE SEA-FLOOR--
--INSIDE THE CHINESE TWELVE-MILE LIMIT.

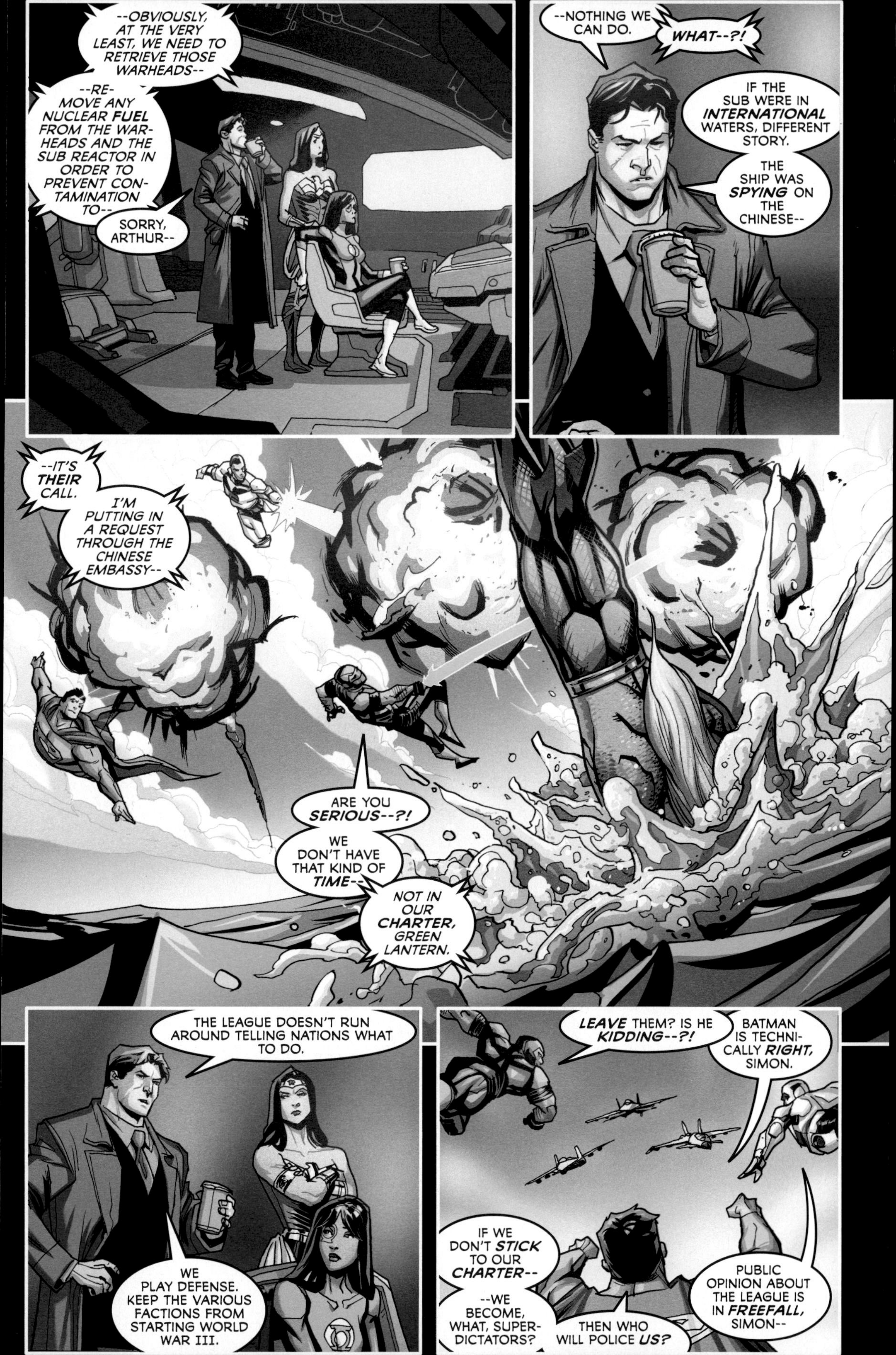
--OBVIOUSLY, AT THE VERY LEAST, WE NEED TO RETRIEVE THOSE WARHEADS--
--RE-MOVE ANY NUCLEAR FUEL FROM THE WAR-HEADS AND THE SUB REACTOR IN ORDER TO PREVENT CON-TAMINATION TO--
SORRY, ARTHUR--
--NOTHING WE CAN DO.
WHAT--?!
IF THE SUB WERE IN INTERNATIONAL WATERS, DIFFERENT STORY.
THE SHIP WAS SPYING ON THE CHINESE--
--IT'S THEIR CALL.
I'M PUTTING IN A REQUEST THROUGH THE CHINESE EMBASSY--
ARE YOU SERIOUS--?!
WE DON'T HAVE THAT KIND OF TIME--
NOT IN OUR CHARTER, GREEN LANTERN.
THE LEAGUE DOESN'T RUN AROUND TELLING NATIONS WHAT TO DO.
WE PLAY DEFENSE. KEEP THE VARIOUS FACTIONS FROM STARTING WORLD WAR III.
LEAVE THEM? IS HE KIDDING--?!
BATMAN IS TECHNI-CALLY RIGHT, SIMON.
IF WE DON'T STICK TO OUR CHARTER--
--WE BECOME, WHAT, SUPER-DICTATORS?
THEN WHO WILL POLICE US?
PUBLIC OPINION ABOUT THE LEAGUE IS IN FREEFALL, SIMON--

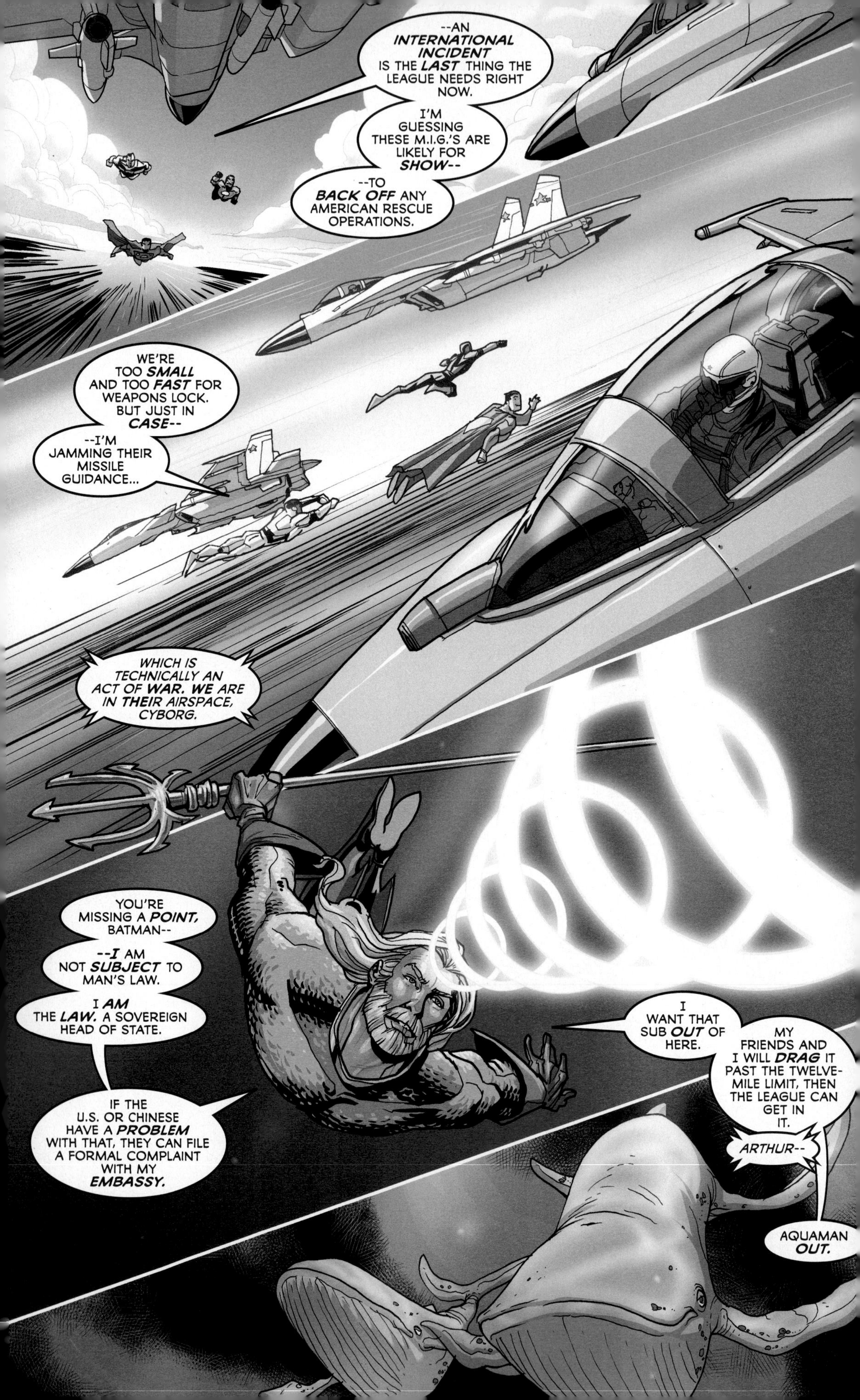
--AN INTERNATIONAL INCIDENT IS THE LAST THING THE LEAGUE NEEDS RIGHT NOW.
I'M GUESSING THESE M.I.G.'S ARE LIKELY FOR SHOW--
--TO BACK OFF ANY AMERICAN RESCUE OPERATIONS.
WE'RE TOO SMALL AND TOO FAST FOR WEAPONS LOCK. BUT JUST IN CASE--
--I'M JAMMING THEIR MISSILE GUIDANCE...
WHICH IS TECHNICALLY AN ACT OF WAR. WE ARE IN THEIR AIRSPACE, CYBORG.
YOU'RE MISSING A POINT, BATMAN--
--I AM NOT SUBJECT TO MAN'S LAW.
I AM THE LAW. A SOVEREIGN HEAD OF STATE.
IF THE U.S. OR CHINESE HAVE A PROBLEM WITH THAT, THEY CAN FILE A FORMAL COMPLAINT WITH MY EMBASSY.
I WANT THAT SUB OUT OF HERE.
MY FRIENDS AND I WILL DRAG IT PAST THE TWELVE-MILE LIMIT, THEN THE LEAGUE CAN GET IN IT.
ARTHUR--
AQUAMAN OUT.

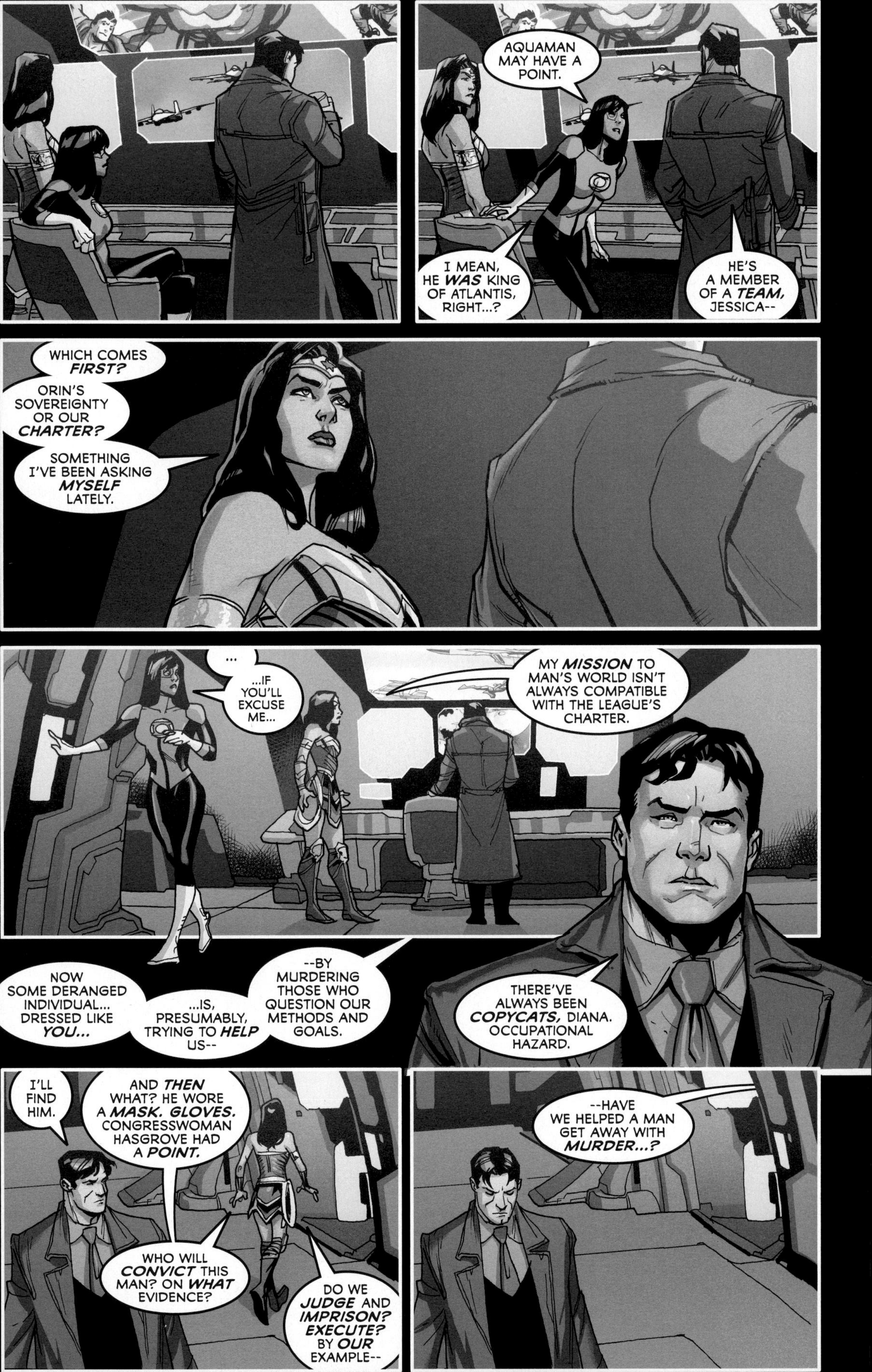
AQUAMAN MAY HAVE A POINT.
I MEAN, HE WAS KING OF ATLANTIS, RIGHT...?
HE'S A MEMBER OF A TEAM, JESSICA--
WHICH COMES FIRST?
ORIN'S SOVEREIGNTY OR OUR CHARTER?
SOMETHING I'VE BEEN ASKING MYSELF LATELY.
...
...IF YOU'LL EXCUSE ME...
MY MISSION TO MAN'S WORLD ISN'T ALWAYS COMPATIBLE WITH THE LEAGUE'S CHARTER.
NOW SOME DERANGED INDIVIDUAL... DRESSED LIKE YOU...
...IS, PRESUMABLY, TRYING TO HELP US--
--BY MURDERING THOSE WHO QUESTION OUR METHODS AND GOALS.
THERE'VE ALWAYS BEEN COPYCATS, DIANA. OCCUPATIONAL HAZARD.
I'LL FIND HIM.
AND THEN WHAT? HE WORE A MASK. GLOVES. CONGRESSWOMAN HASGROVE HAD A POINT.
WHO WILL CONVICT THIS MAN? ON WHAT EVIDENCE?
DO WE JUDGE AND IMPRISON? EXECUTE? BY OUR EXAMPLE--
--HAVE WE HELPED A MAN GET AWAY WITH MURDER...?

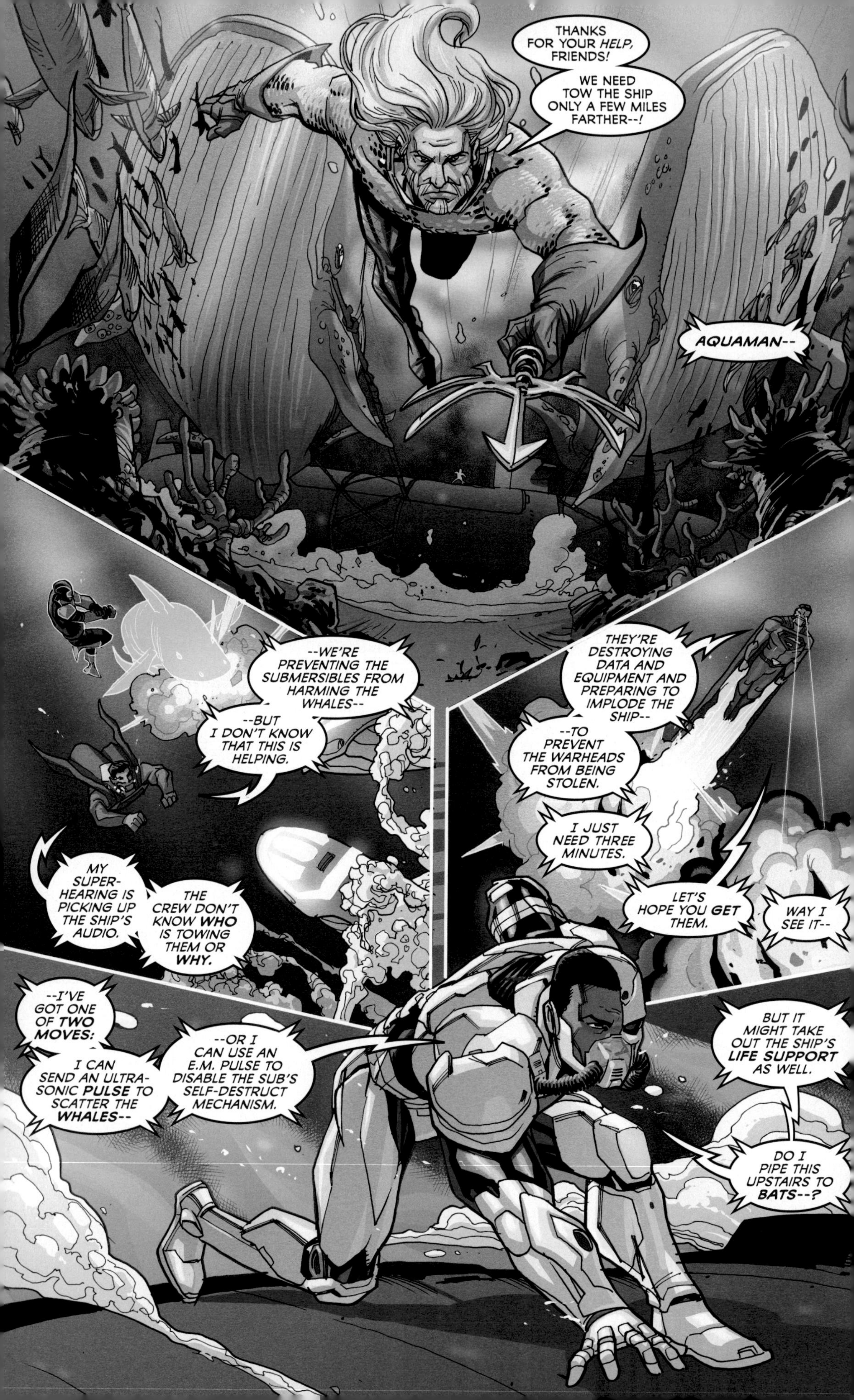
THANKS FOR YOUR *HELP*, FRIENDS!
WE NEED TOW THE SHIP ONLY A FEW MILES FARTHER--!
AQUAMAN--
--WE'RE PREVENTING THE SUBMERSIBLES FROM HARMING THE WHALES--
--BUT I DON'T KNOW THAT THIS IS HELPING.
THEY'RE DESTROYING DATA AND EQUIPMENT AND PREPARING TO IMPLODE THE SHIP--
--TO PREVENT THE WARHEADS FROM BEING STOLEN.
I JUST NEED THREE MINUTES.
MY SUPER-HEARING IS PICKING UP THE SHIP'S AUDIO.
*THE CREW DON'T KNOW **WHO** IS TOWING THEM OR **WHY.***
LET'S HOPE YOU **GET** THEM.
WAY I SEE IT--
*--I'VE GOT ONE OF **TWO MOVES:***
*I CAN SEND AN ULTRA-SONIC **PULSE** TO SCATTER THE **WHALES--***
--OR I CAN USE AN E.M. PULSE TO DISABLE THE SUB'S SELF-DESTRUCT MECHANISM.
*BUT IT MIGHT TAKE OUT THE SHIP'S **LIFE SUPPORT** AS WELL.*
*DO I PIPE THIS UPSTAIRS TO **BATS--?***

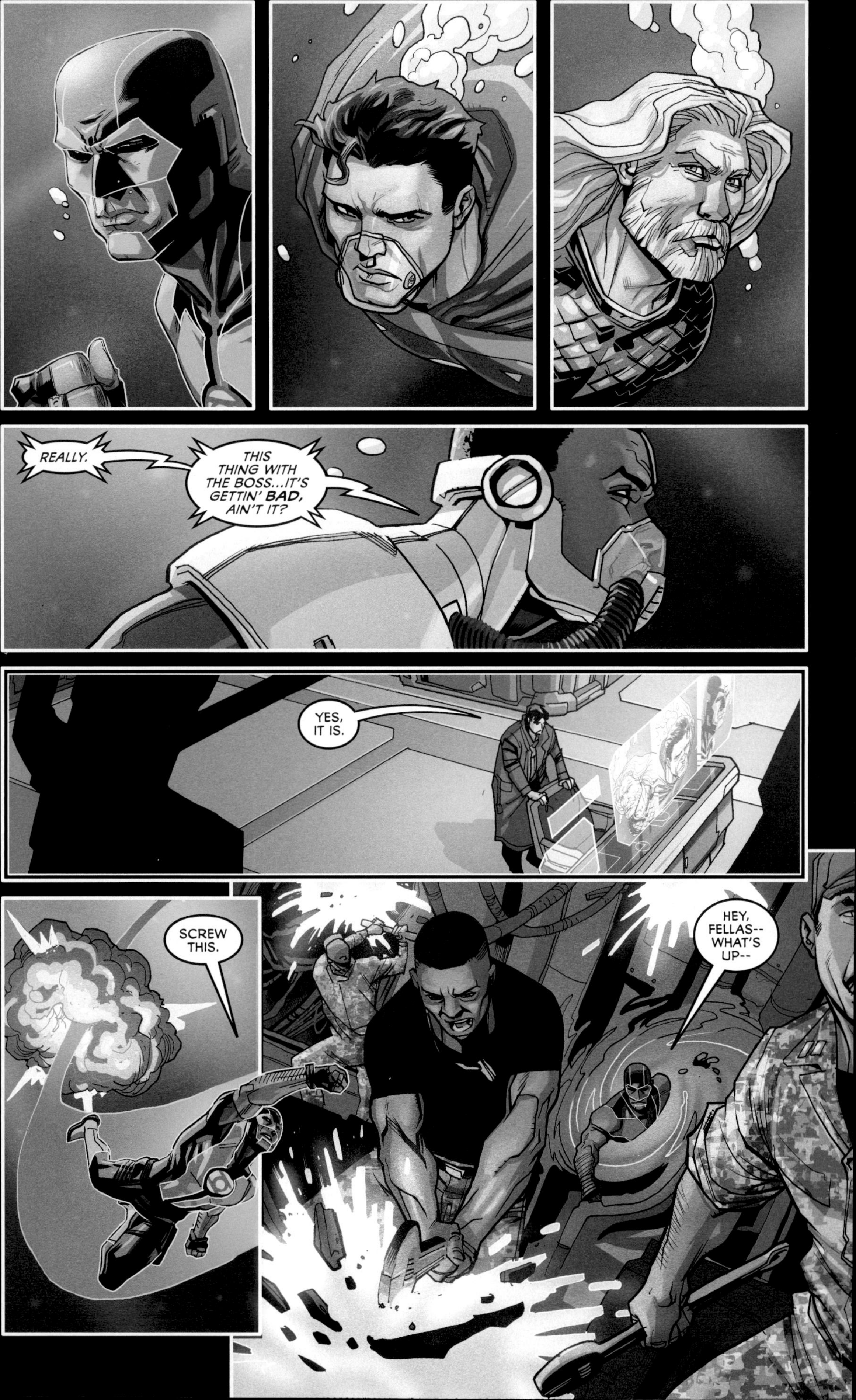
REALLY.
THIS THING WITH THE BOSS...IT'S GETTIN' BAD, AIN'T IT?
YES, IT IS.
SCREW THIS.
HEY, FELLAS-- WHAT'S UP--

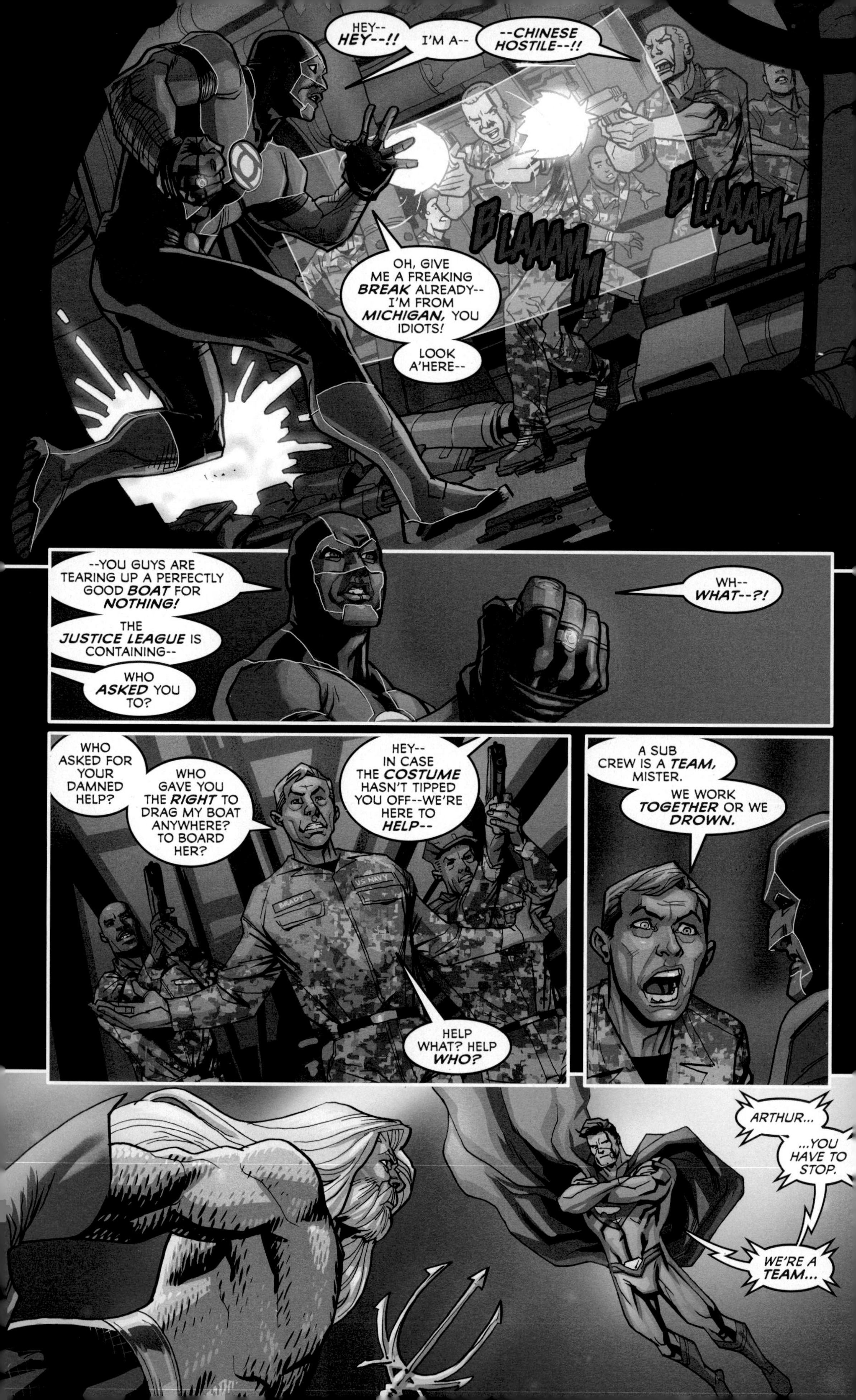
HEY-- HEY--!!
I'M A--
--CHINESE HOSTILE--!!
BLAAAMM
BLAAAMM
OH, GIVE ME A FREAKING BREAK ALREADY-- I'M FROM MICHIGAN, YOU IDIOTS!
LOOK A'HERE--
--YOU GUYS ARE TEARING UP A PERFECTLY GOOD BOAT FOR NOTHING!
THE JUSTICE LEAGUE IS CONTAINING--
WH-- WHAT--?!
WHO ASKED YOU TO?
WHO ASKED FOR YOUR DAMNED HELP?
WHO GAVE YOU THE RIGHT TO DRAG MY BOAT ANYWHERE? TO BOARD HER?
HEY-- IN CASE THE COSTUME HASN'T TIPPED YOU OFF--WE'RE HERE TO HELP--
HELP WHAT? HELP WHO?
A SUB CREW IS A TEAM, MISTER.
WE WORK TOGETHER OR WE DROWN.
ARTHUR...
...YOU HAVE TO STOP.
WE'RE A TEAM...

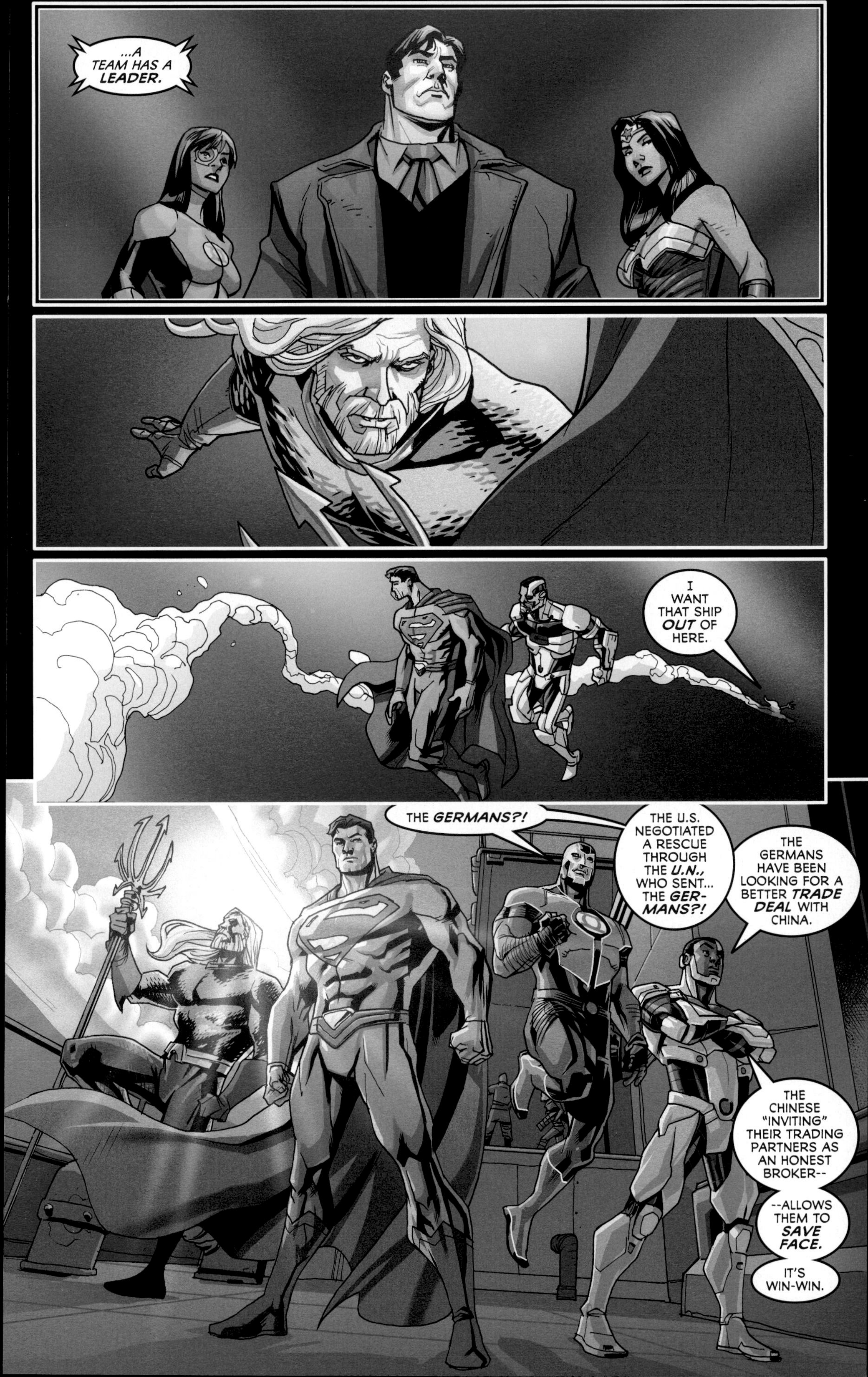

...A TEAM HAS A LEADER.
I WANT THAT SHIP OUT OF HERE.
THE GERMANS?!
THE U.S. NEGOTIATED A RESCUE THROUGH THE U.N., WHO SENT... THE GER-MANS?!
THE GERMANS HAVE BEEN LOOKING FOR A BETTER TRADE DEAL WITH CHINA.
THE CHINESE "INVITING" THEIR TRADING PARTNERS AS AN HONEST BROKER--
--ALLOWS THEM TO SAVE FACE.
IT'S WIN-WIN.

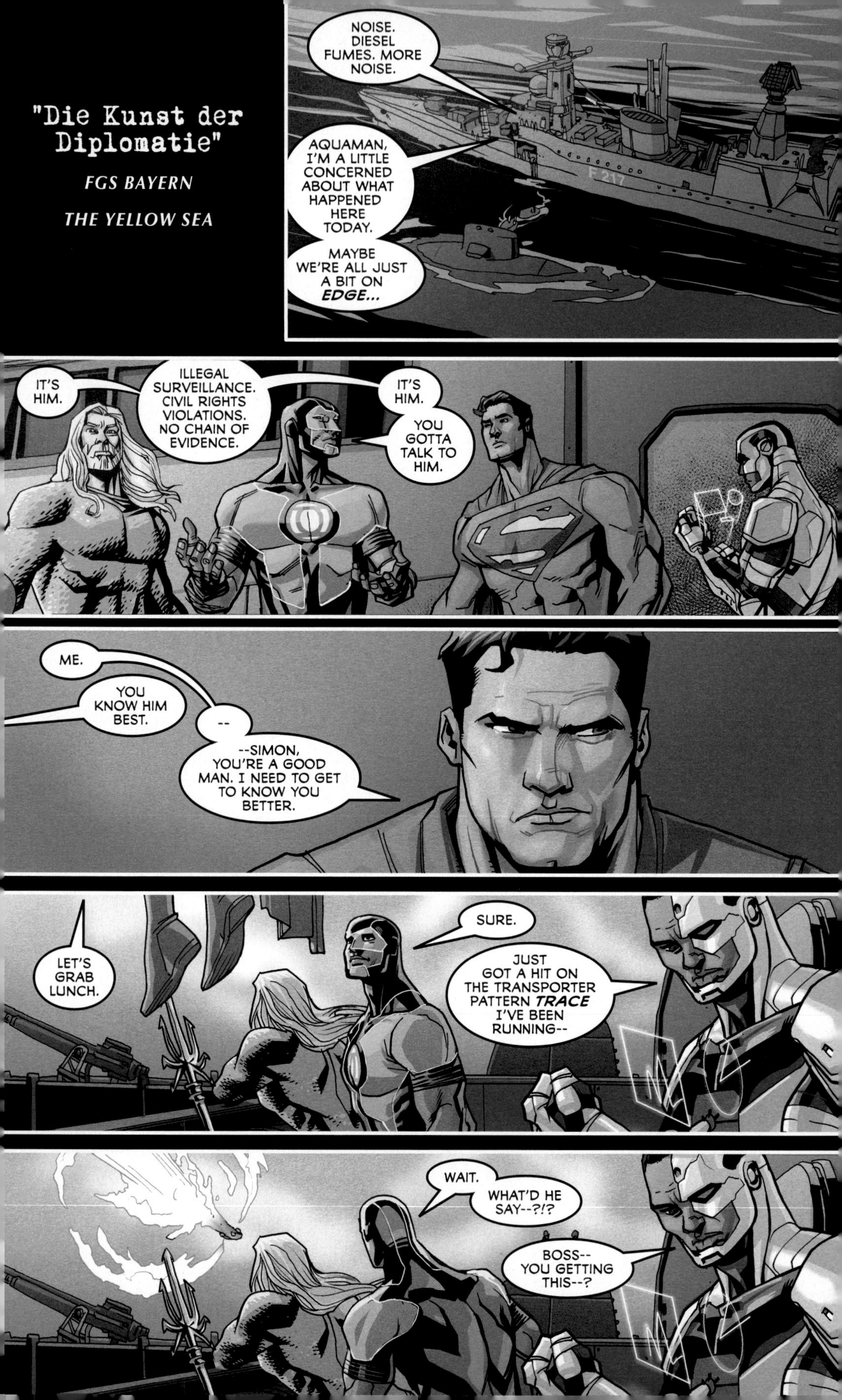
"Die Kunst der Diplomatie"
FGS BAYERN
THE YELLOW SEA
NOISE. DIESEL FUMES. MORE NOISE.
AQUAMAN, I'M A LITTLE CONCERNED ABOUT WHAT HAPPENED HERE TODAY.
MAYBE WE'RE ALL JUST A BIT ON *EDGE...*
F 217
IT'S HIM.
ILLEGAL SURVEILLANCE. CIVIL RIGHTS VIOLATIONS. NO CHAIN OF EVIDENCE.
IT'S HIM.
YOU GOTTA TALK TO HIM.
ME.
YOU KNOW HIM BEST.
--
--SIMON, YOU'RE A GOOD MAN. I NEED TO GET TO KNOW YOU BETTER.
LET'S GRAB LUNCH.
SURE.
JUST GOT A HIT ON THE TRANSPORTER PATTERN *TRACE* I'VE BEEN RUNNING--
WAIT.
WHAT'D HE SAY--?!?
BOSS-- YOU GETTING THIS--?

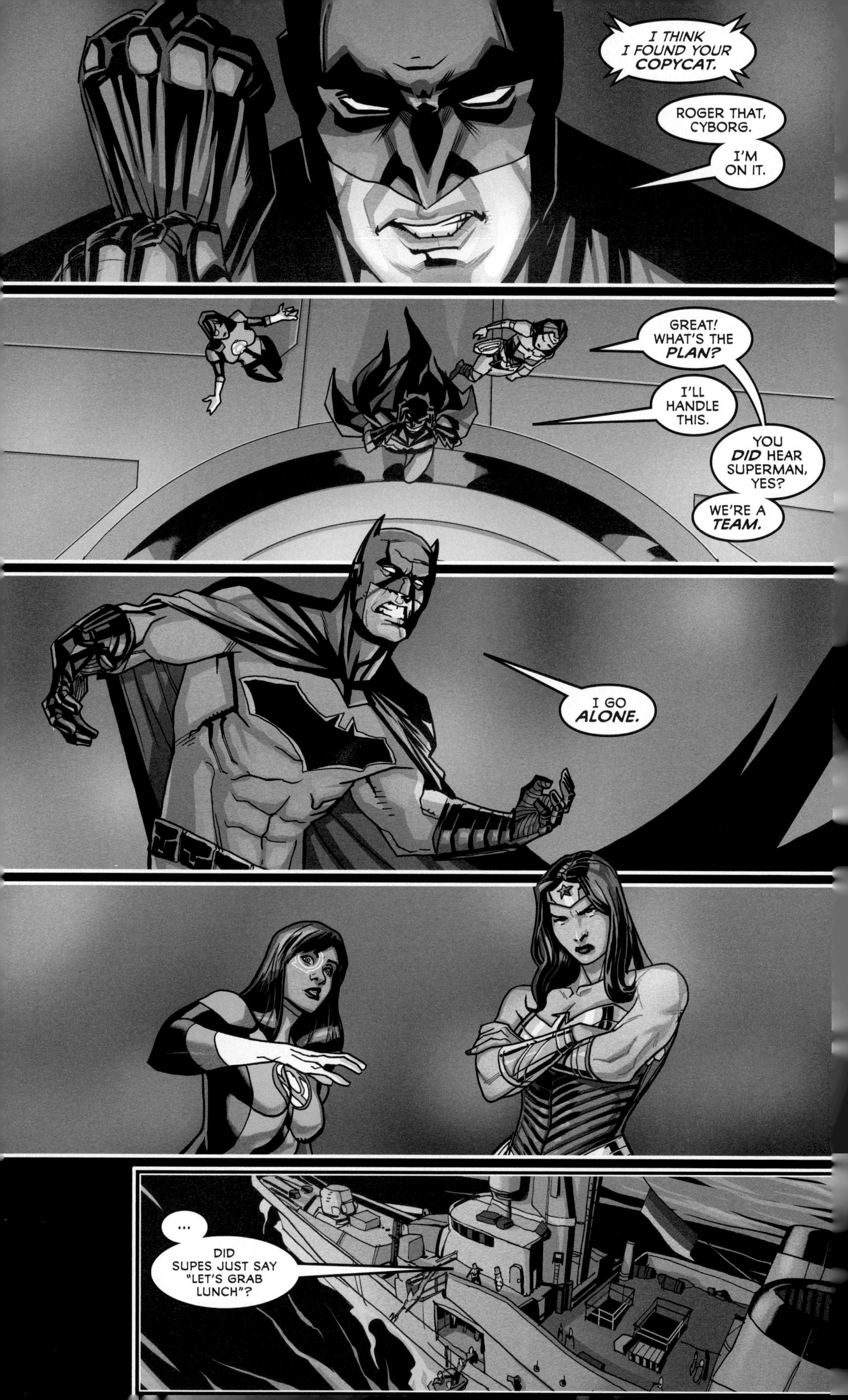
I THINK I FOUND YOUR COPYCAT.
ROGER THAT, CYBORG.
I'M ON IT.
GREAT! WHAT'S THE PLAN?
I'LL HANDLE THIS.
YOU DID HEAR SUPERMAN, YES?
WE'RE A TEAM.
I GO ALONE.
...
DID SUPES JUST SAY "LET'S GRAB LUNCH"?

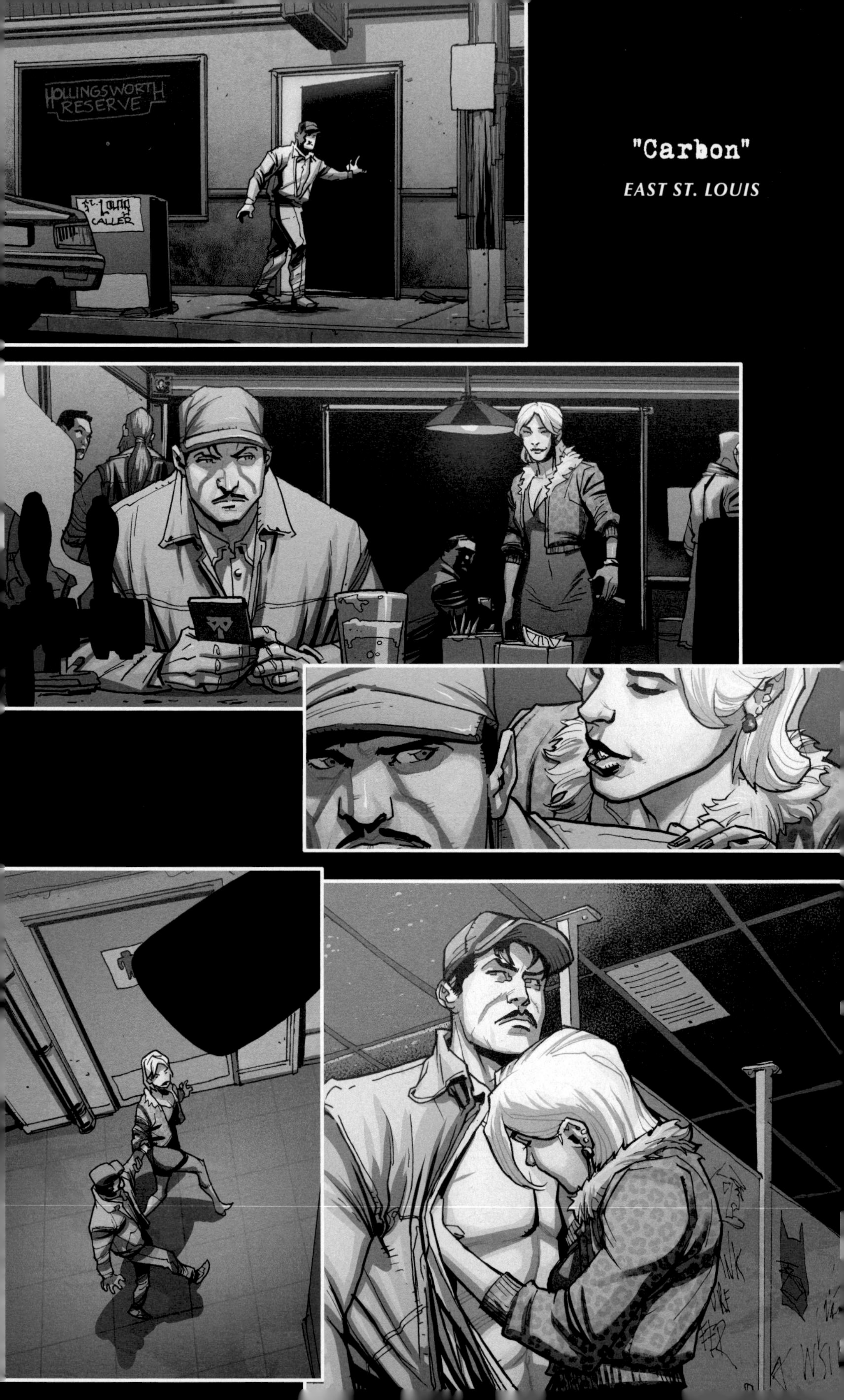
HOLLINGSWORTH RESERVE
St. Louis Caller
"Carbon"
EAST ST. LOUIS

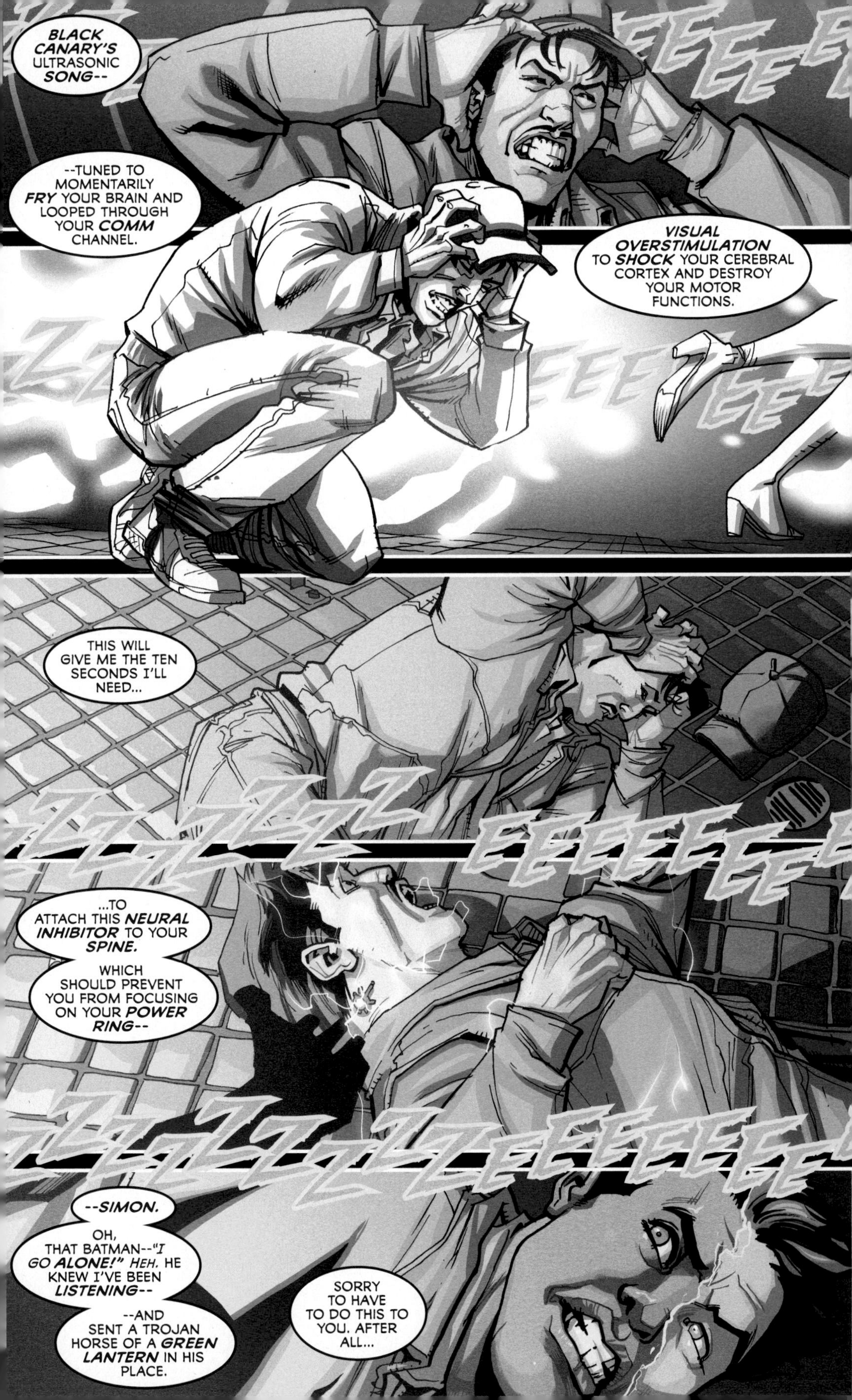
BLACK CANARY'S ULTRASONIC SONG--
--TUNED TO MOMENTARILY FRY YOUR BRAIN AND LOOPED THROUGH YOUR COMM CHANNEL.
VISUAL OVERSTIMULATION TO SHOCK YOUR CEREBRAL CORTEX AND DESTROY YOUR MOTOR FUNCTIONS.
THIS WILL GIVE ME THE TEN SECONDS I'LL NEED...
...TO ATTACH THIS NEURAL INHIBITOR TO YOUR SPINE.
WHICH SHOULD PREVENT YOU FROM FOCUSING ON YOUR POWER RING--
--SIMON.
OH, THAT BATMAN--"I GO ALONE!" HEH. HE KNEW I'VE BEEN LISTENING--
--AND SENT A TROJAN HORSE OF A GREEN LANTERN IN HIS PLACE.
SORRY TO HAVE TO DO THIS TO YOU. AFTER ALL...

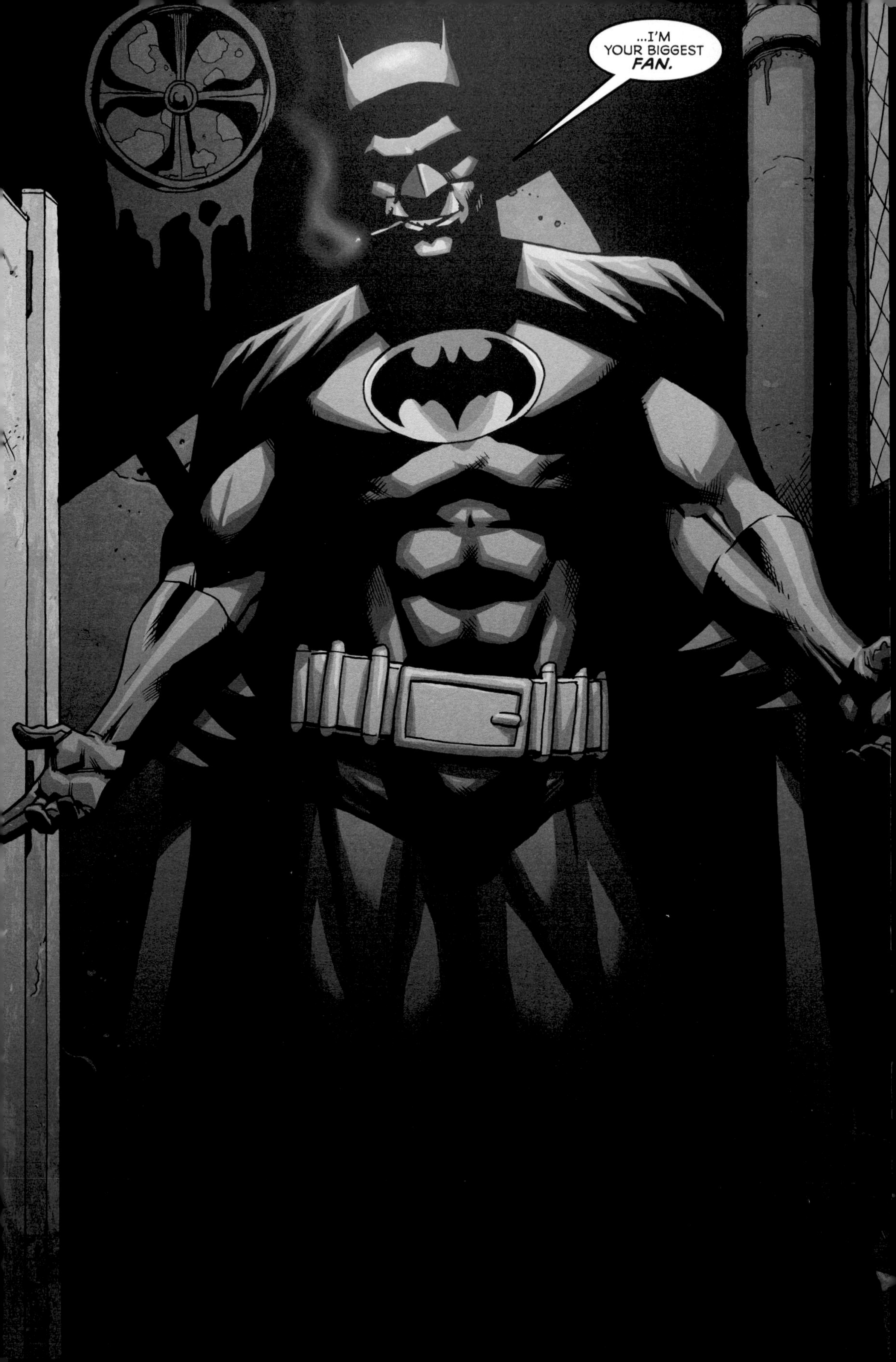
...I'M YOUR BIGGEST FAN.

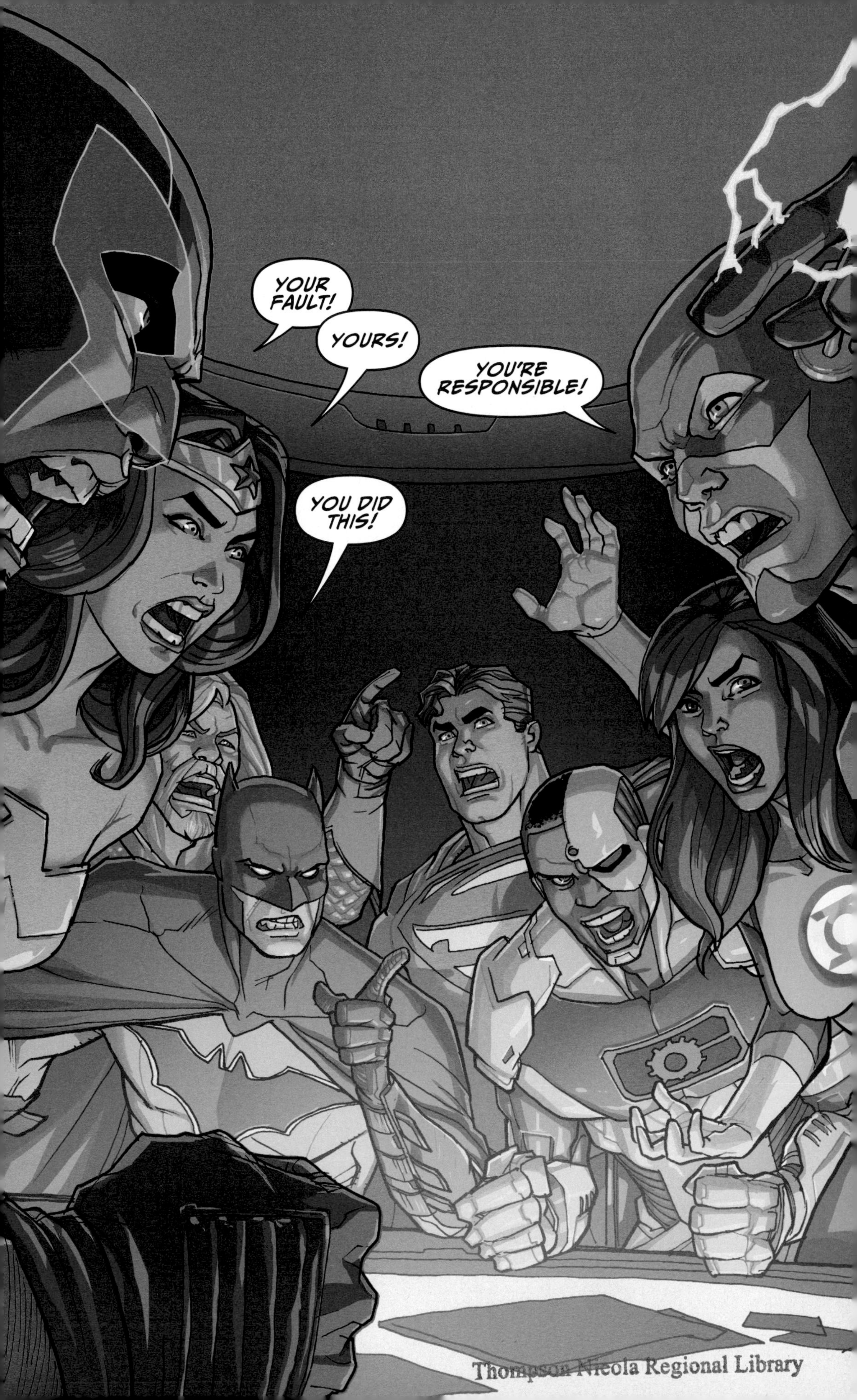
YOUR FAULT!
YOURS!
YOU'RE RESPONSIBLE!
YOU DID THIS!

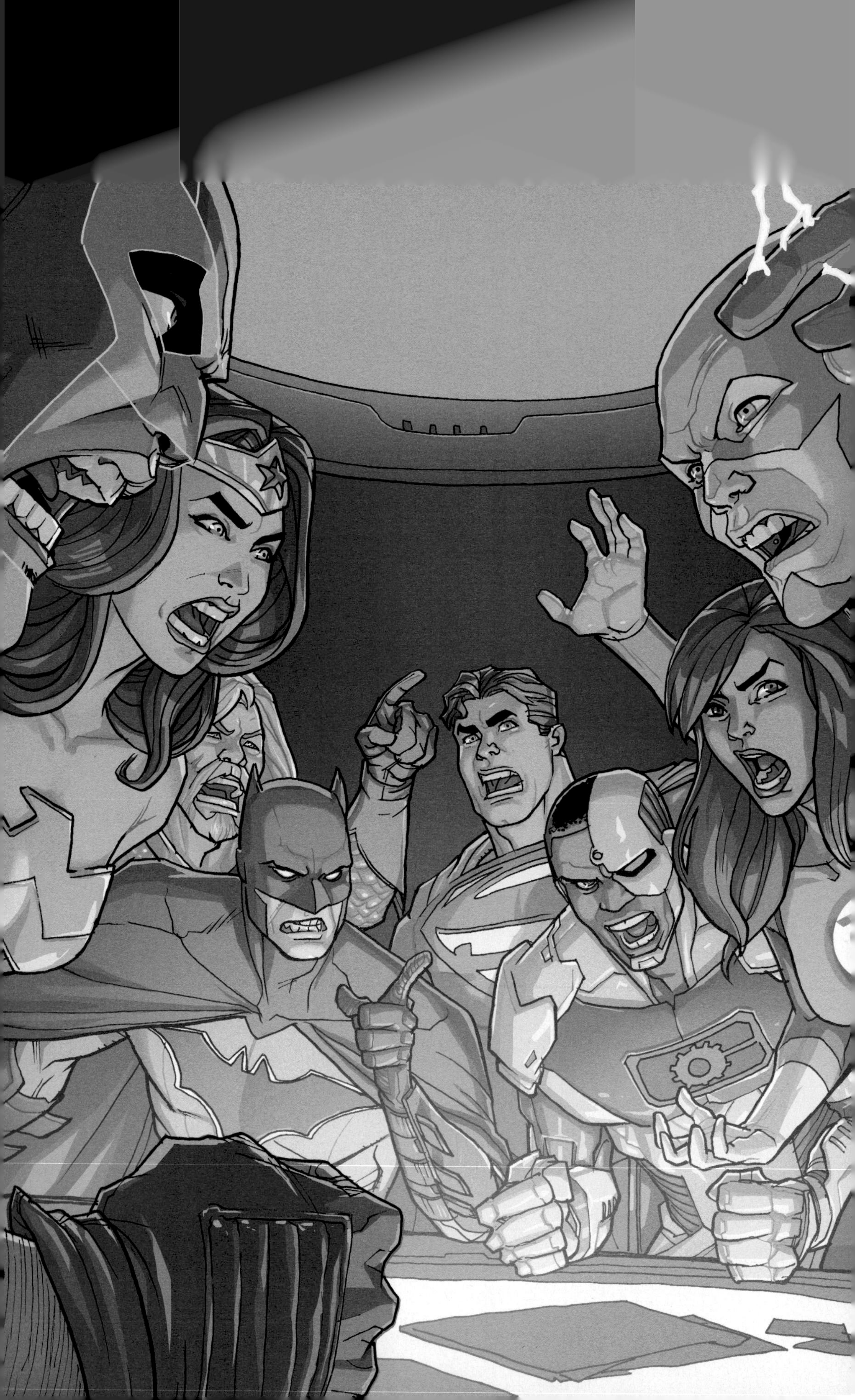

...NO RESPONSE FROM THE JUSTICE LEAGUE REGARDING THESE MURDER ACCUSATIONS...

...THE LEAGUE DOES NOT APPEAR TO *HAVE* AN OFFICIAL SPOKESMAN...

BAT-MURDERER?

"Identity Crisis"

...ALTHOUGH GOTHAM CITY'S COMMISSIONER GORDON VEHEMENTLY DEFENDS THE CAPED CRUSADER...

--RIDICULOUS.

I CAN STATE *CATEGORICALLY*-- THAT WAS *NOT* THE BATMAN.

SIONER GORDON

BUT HOW CAN *ANYONE* KNOW FOR SURE WHO IS BEHIND THAT MASK...

...OR HOW MANY BATMEN ARE *OUT* THERE?

THE RECENT CONGRESSIONAL HEARING...

BAT-MURDERER?

AND... THE *MASKS*, SIR...

HOW DO YOU SUBPOENA A *WRAITH?*

HON. D. HASGROVE

PREVIOUSLY RECORDED

I DON'T HAVE A GOOD ANSWER FOR THAT, MADAM CHAIRPERSON.

I CAN ONLY ASSURE YOU, AND THE AMERICAN PUBLIC, THAT THE LEAGUE IS COMPOSED OF MEN AND WOMEN OF *GOOD WILL*--

SUPERMAN

REVIOUSLY RECORDED

--WHO CHOOSE ANONYMITY OUT OF AN ABUNDANCE OF *CAUTION*--

--AND CONCERN FOR THEIR FAMILIES AND COMMUNITIES...

...WHO MIGHT BE AT RISK SHOULD THOSE *TRUE* IDENTITIES BECOME KNOWN...

SUPERMAN

PREVIOUSLY RECORDED

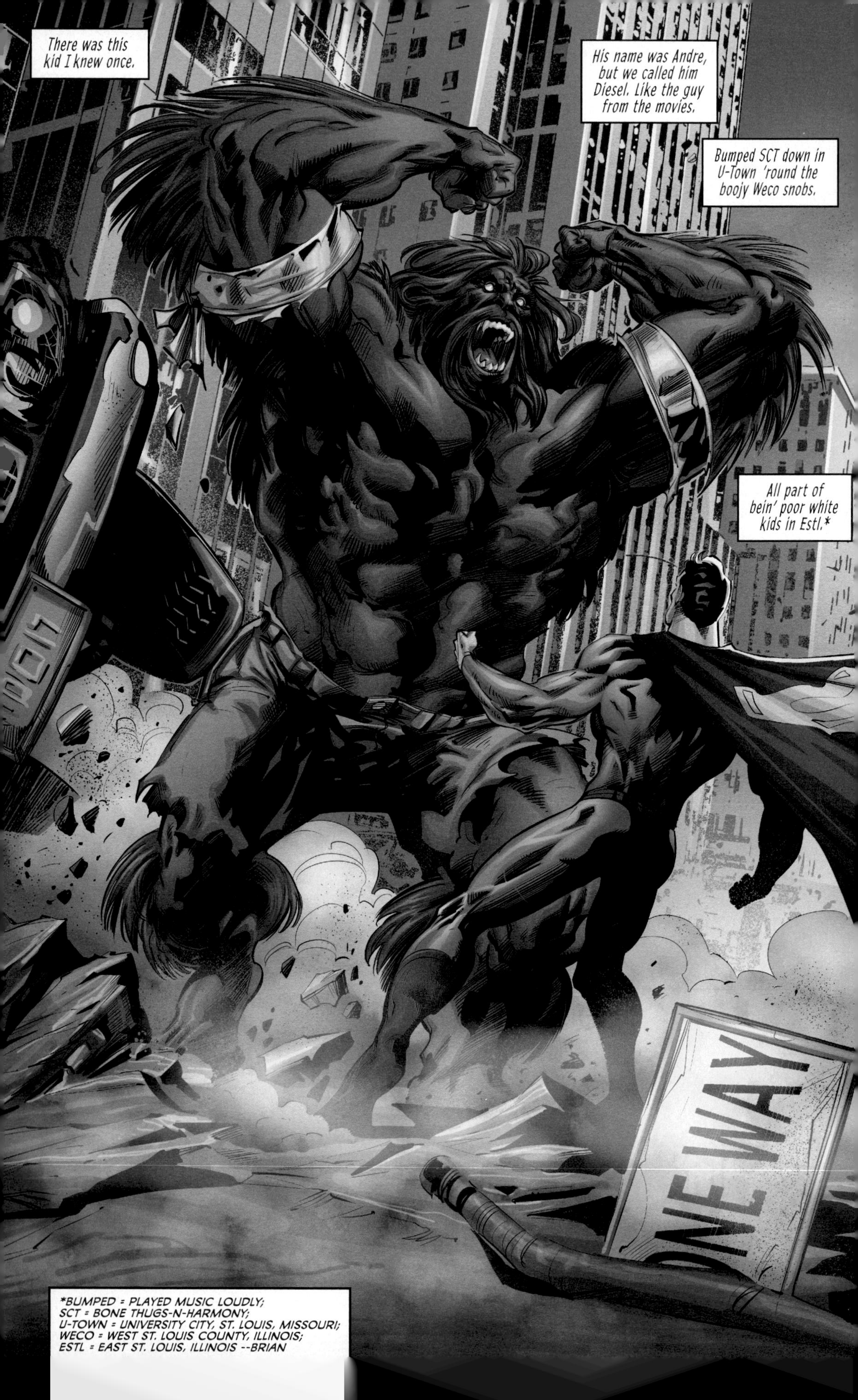
There was this kid I knew once.
His name was Andre, but we called him Diesel. Like the guy from the movies.
Bumped SCT down in U-Town 'round the boojy Weco snobs.
All part of bein' poor white kids in Estl.*
*BUMPED = PLAYED MUSIC LOUDLY; SCT = BONE THUGS-N-HARMONY; U-TOWN = UNIVERSITY CITY, ST. LOUIS, MISSOURI; WECO = WEST ST. LOUIS COUNTY, ILLINOIS; ESTL = EAST ST. LOUIS, ILLINOIS --BRIAN

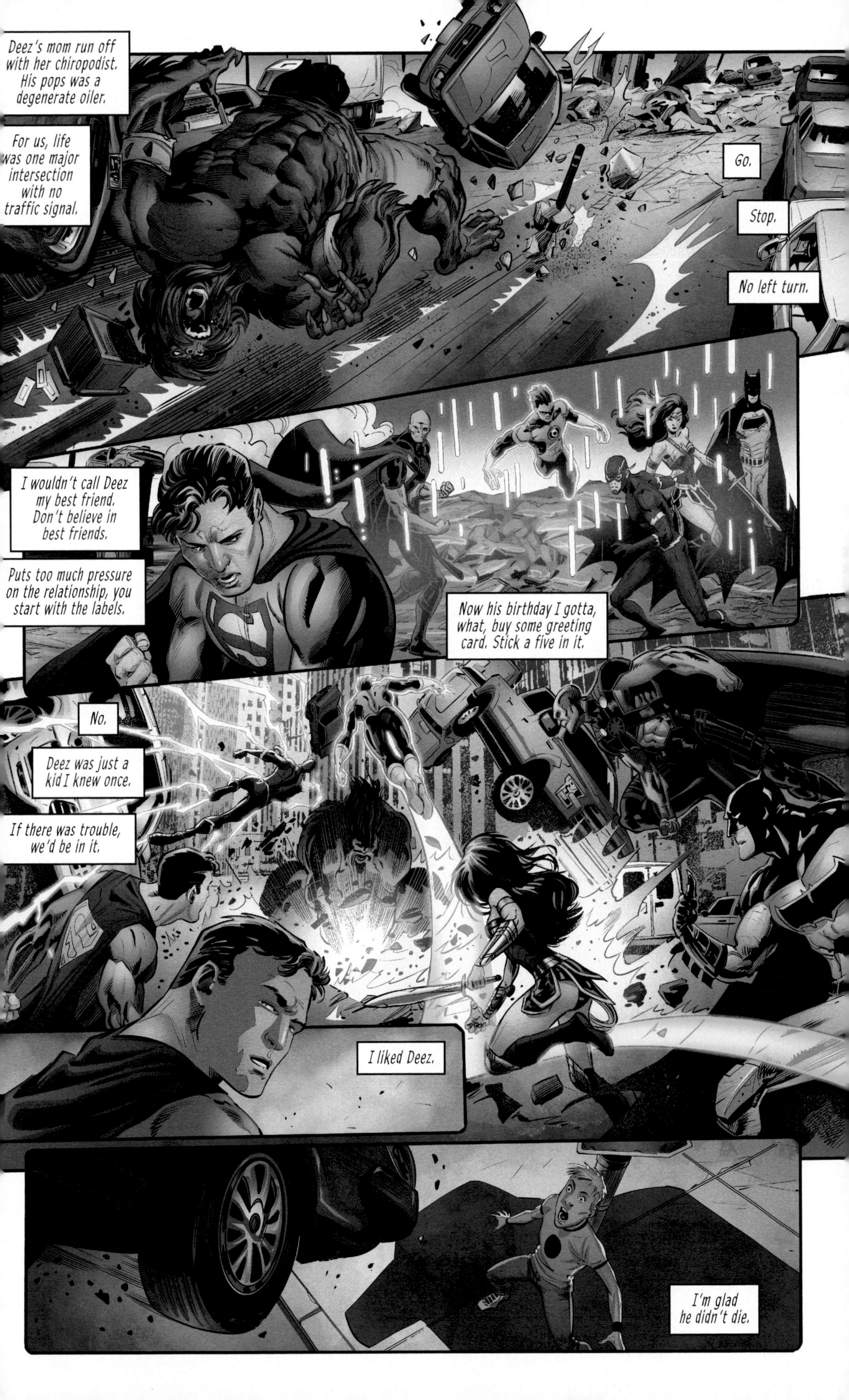
Deez's mom run off with her chiropodist. His pops was a degenerate oiler.
For us, life was one major intersection with no traffic signal.
Go.
Stop.
No left turn.
I wouldn't call Deez my best friend. Don't believe in best friends.
Puts too much pressure on the relationship, you start with the labels.
Now his birthday I gotta, what, buy some greeting card. Stick a five in it.
No.
Deez was just a kid I knew once.
If there was trouble, we'd be in it.
I liked Deez.
I'm glad he didn't die.

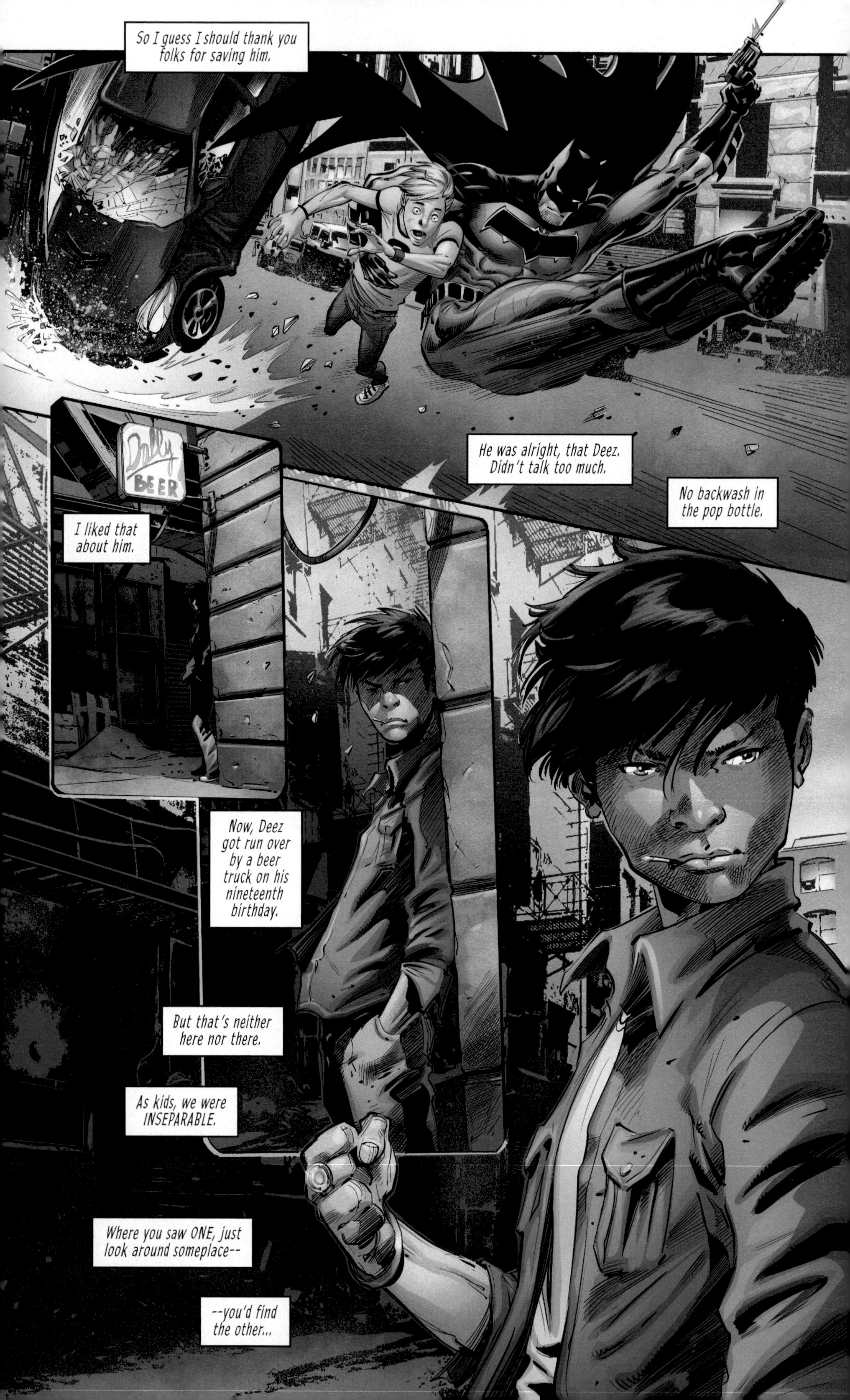
So I guess I should thank you folks for saving him.
He was alright, that Deez. Didn't talk too much.
No backwash in the pop bottle.
I liked that about him.
Dolly BEER
Now, Deez got run over by a beer truck on his nineteenth birthday.
But that's neither here nor there.
As kids, we were INSEPARABLE.
Where you saw ONE, just look around someplace--
--you'd find the other...

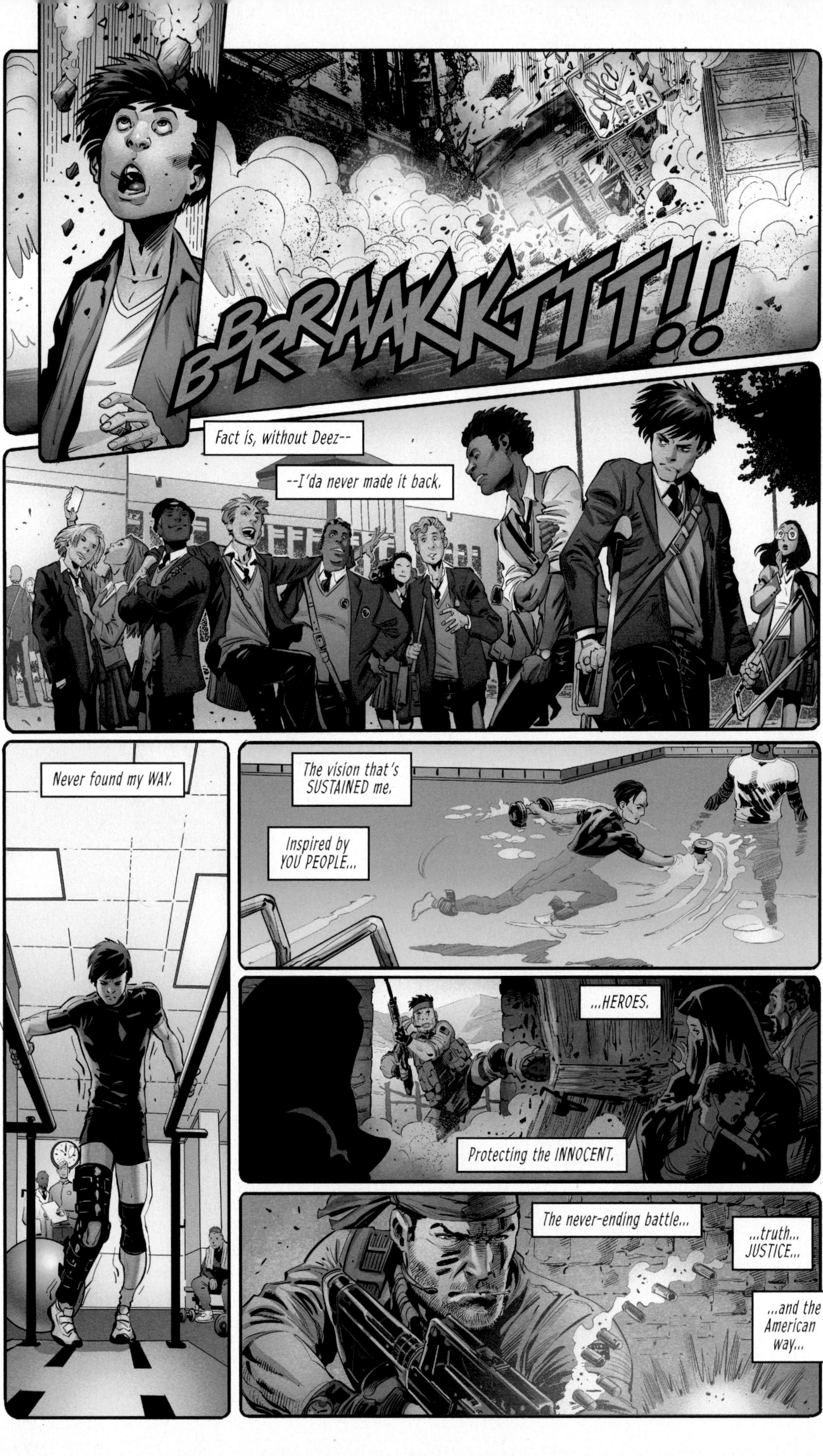
BBRRAAKKTTT!!
Fact is, without Deez--
--I'da never made it back.
Never found my WAY.
The vision that's SUSTAINED me.
Inspired by YOU PEOPLE...
...HEROES.
Protecting the INNOCENT.
The never-ending battle...
...truth... JUSTICE...
...and the American way...

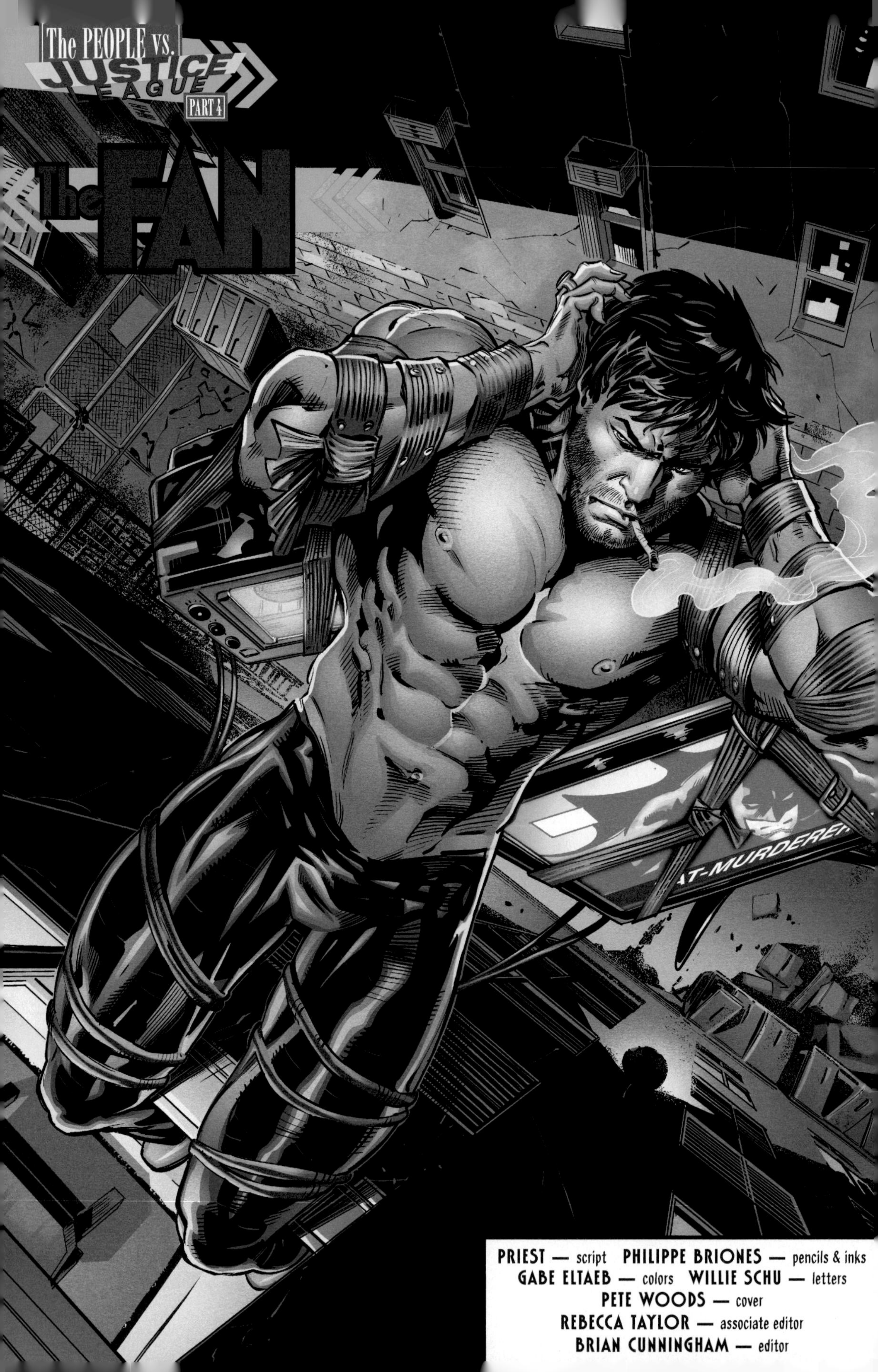
The PEOPLE vs. JUSTICE LEAGUE
PART 4
The FAN
PRIEST — script PHILIPPE BRIONES — pencils & inks
GABE ELTAEB — colors WILLIE SCHU — letters
PETE WOODS — cover
REBECCA TAYLOR — associate editor
BRIAN CUNNINGHAM — editor

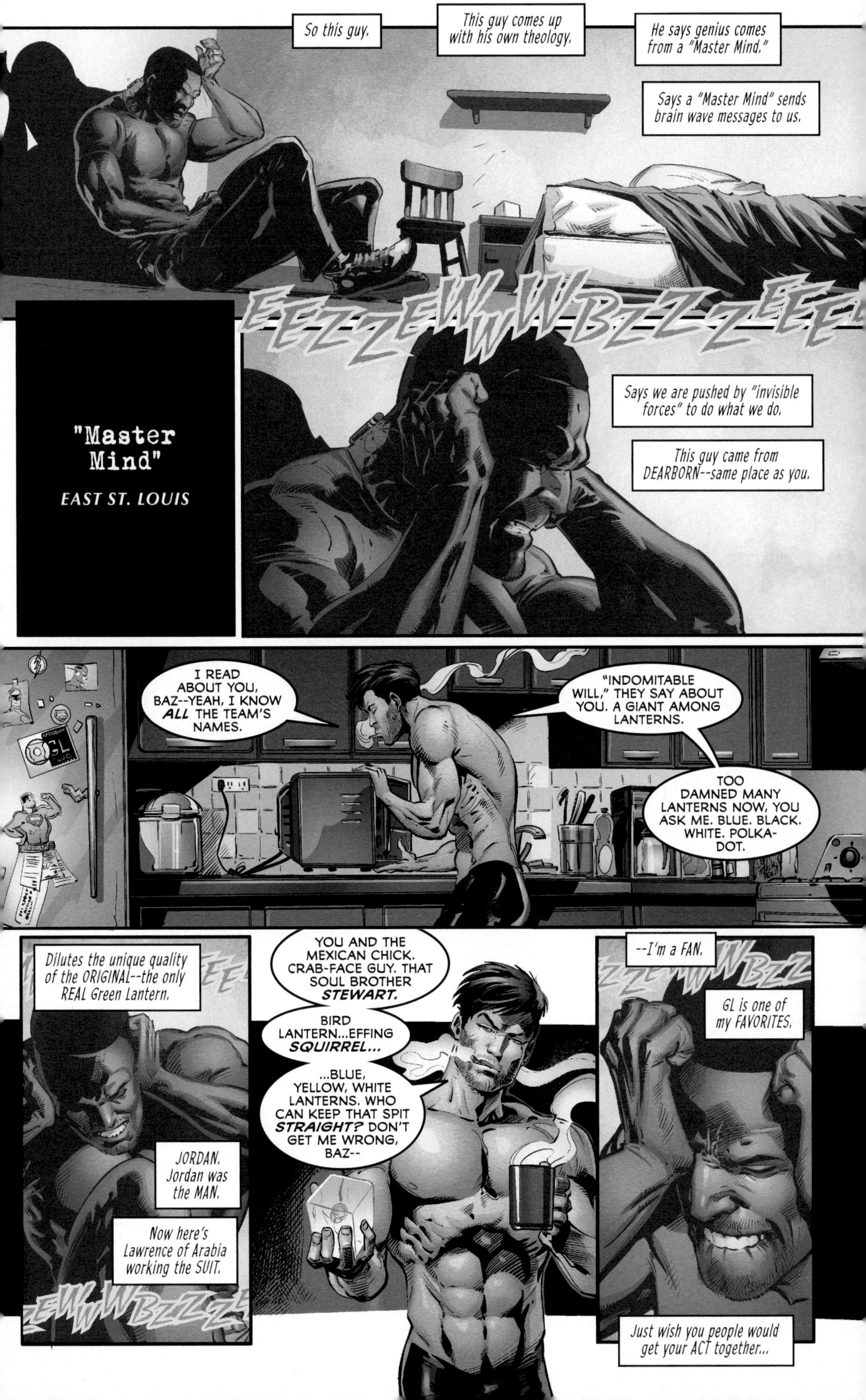

So this guy.
This guy comes up with his own theology.
He says genius comes from a "Master Mind."
Says a "Master Mind" sends brain wave messages to us.
EEZZZEWWWWBZZZZEEEE
"Master Mind"
EAST ST. LOUIS
Says we are pushed by "invisible forces" to do what we do.
This guy came from DEARBORN--same place as you.
I READ ABOUT YOU, BAZ--YEAH, I KNOW ALL THE TEAM'S NAMES.
"INDOMITABLE WILL," THEY SAY ABOUT YOU. A GIANT AMONG LANTERNS.
TOO DAMNED MANY LANTERNS NOW, YOU ASK ME. BLUE. BLACK. WHITE. POLKA-DOT.
Dilutes the unique quality of the ORIGINAL--the only REAL Green Lantern.
JORDAN. Jordan was the MAN.
Now here's Lawrence of Arabia working the SUIT.
ZEWWWBZZZZE
YOU AND THE MEXICAN CHICK. CRAB-FACE GUY. THAT SOUL BROTHER STEWART.
BIRD LANTERN...EFFING SQUIRREL...
...BLUE, YELLOW, WHITE LANTERNS. WHO CAN KEEP THAT SPIT STRAIGHT? DON'T GET ME WRONG, BAZ--
--I'm a FAN.
ZZEWWWBZZ
GL is one of my FAVORITES.
Just wish you people would get your ACT together...

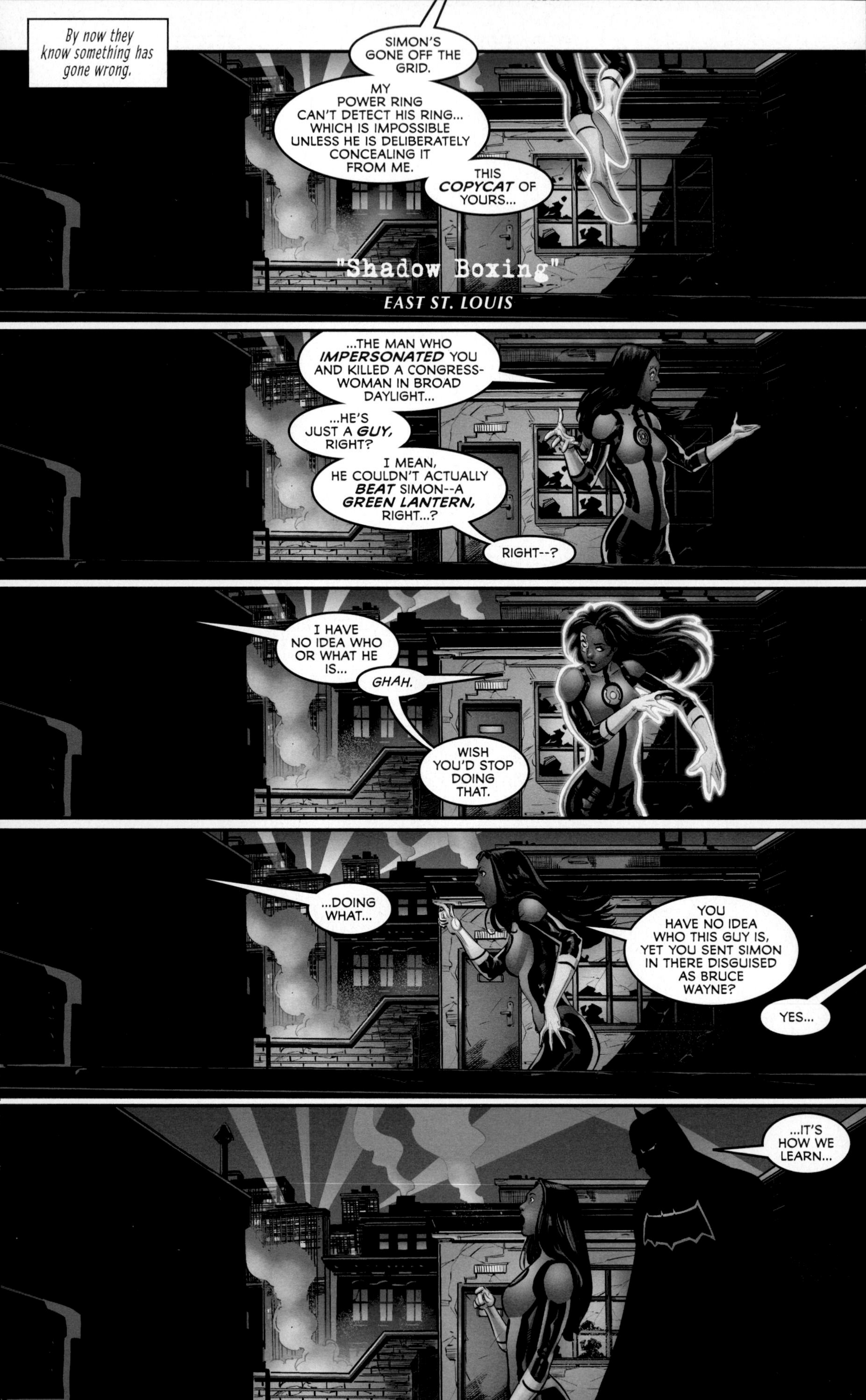
By now they know something has gone wrong.
SIMON'S GONE OFF THE GRID.
MY POWER RING CAN'T DETECT HIS RING... WHICH IS IMPOSSIBLE UNLESS HE IS DELIBERATELY CONCEALING IT FROM ME.
THIS COPYCAT OF YOURS...
"Shadow Boxing"
EAST ST. LOUIS
...THE MAN WHO IMPERSONATED YOU AND KILLED A CONGRESS-WOMAN IN BROAD DAYLIGHT...
...HE'S JUST A GUY, RIGHT?
I MEAN, HE COULDN'T ACTUALLY BEAT SIMON--A GREEN LANTERN, RIGHT...?
RIGHT--?
I HAVE NO IDEA WHO OR WHAT HE IS...
GHAH.
WISH YOU'D STOP DOING THAT.
...DOING WHAT...
YOU HAVE NO IDEA WHO THIS GUY IS, YET YOU SENT SIMON IN THERE DISGUISED AS BRUCE WAYNE?
YES...
...IT'S HOW WE LEARN...

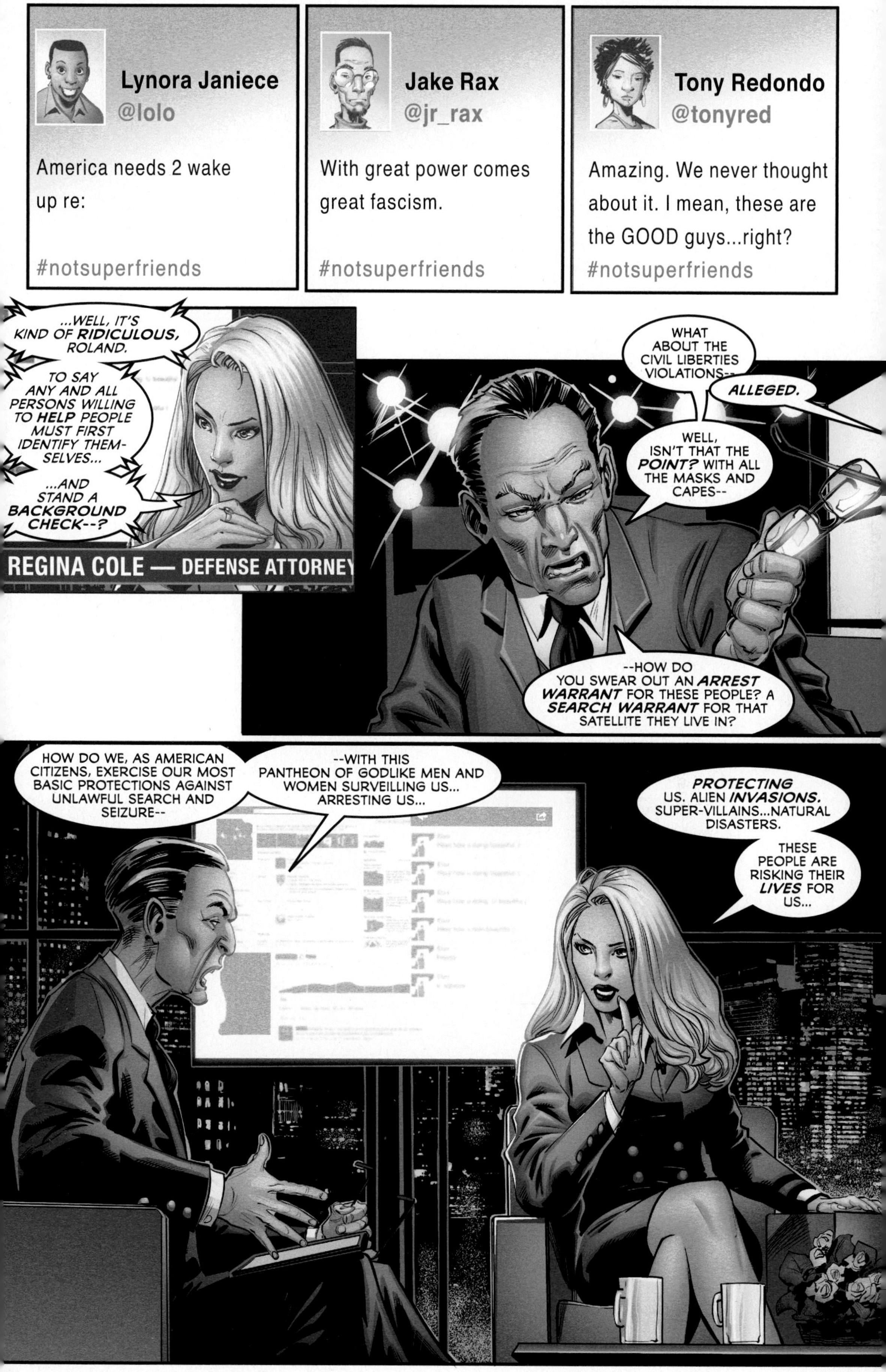
Lynora Janiece
@lolo
America needs 2 wake up re:
#notsuperfriends
Jake Rax
@jr_rax
With great power comes great fascism.
#notsuperfriends
Tony Redondo
@tonyred
Amazing. We never thought about it. I mean, these are the GOOD guys...right?
#notsuperfriends
...WELL, IT'S KIND OF RIDICULOUS, ROLAND.
TO SAY ANY AND ALL PERSONS WILLING TO HELP PEOPLE MUST FIRST IDENTIFY THEMSELVES...
...AND STAND A BACKGROUND CHECK--?
REGINA COLE — DEFENSE ATTORNEY
WHAT ABOUT THE CIVIL LIBERTIES VIOLATIONS--
ALLEGED.
WELL, ISN'T THAT THE POINT? WITH ALL THE MASKS AND CAPES--
--HOW DO YOU SWEAR OUT AN ARREST WARRANT FOR THESE PEOPLE? A SEARCH WARRANT FOR THAT SATELLITE THEY LIVE IN?
HOW DO WE, AS AMERICAN CITIZENS, EXERCISE OUR MOST BASIC PROTECTIONS AGAINST UNLAWFUL SEARCH AND SEIZURE--
--WITH THIS PANTHEON OF GODLIKE MEN AND WOMEN SURVEILLING US... ARRESTING US...
PROTECTING US. ALIEN INVASIONS. SUPER-VILLAINS...NATURAL DISASTERS.
THESE PEOPLE ARE RISKING THEIR LIVES FOR US...

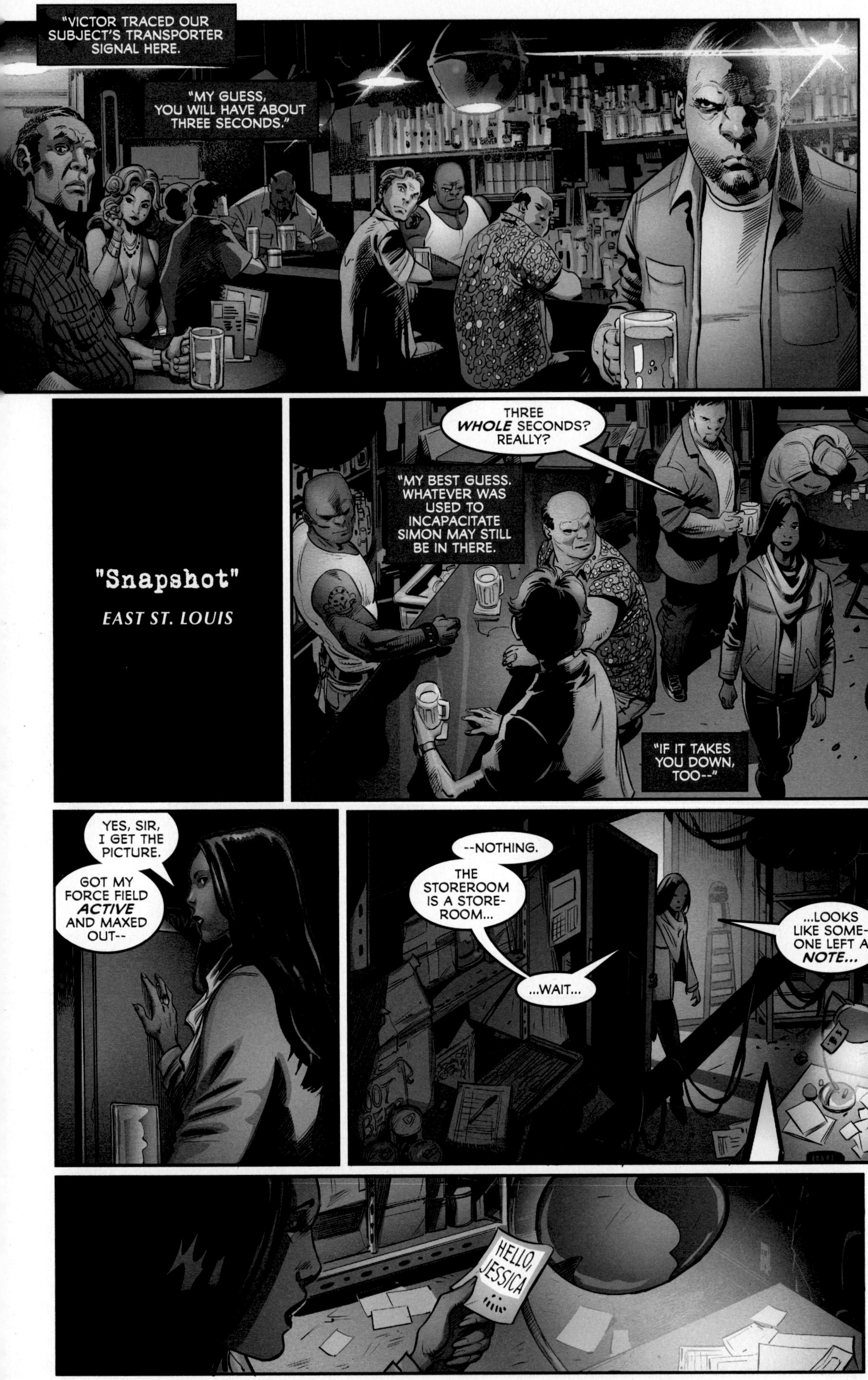
"VICTOR TRACED OUR SUBJECT'S TRANSPORTER SIGNAL HERE.
"MY GUESS, YOU WILL HAVE ABOUT THREE SECONDS."
"Snapshot"
EAST ST. LOUIS
THREE *WHOLE* SECONDS? REALLY?
"MY BEST GUESS. WHATEVER WAS USED TO INCAPACITATE SIMON MAY STILL BE IN THERE.
"IF IT TAKES YOU DOWN, TOO--"
YES, SIR, I GET THE PICTURE.
GOT MY FORCE FIELD *ACTIVE* AND MAXED OUT--
--NOTHING.
THE STOREROOM IS A STORE-ROOM...
...WAIT...
...LOOKS LIKE SOME-ONE LEFT A *NOTE*...
HELLO, JESSICA

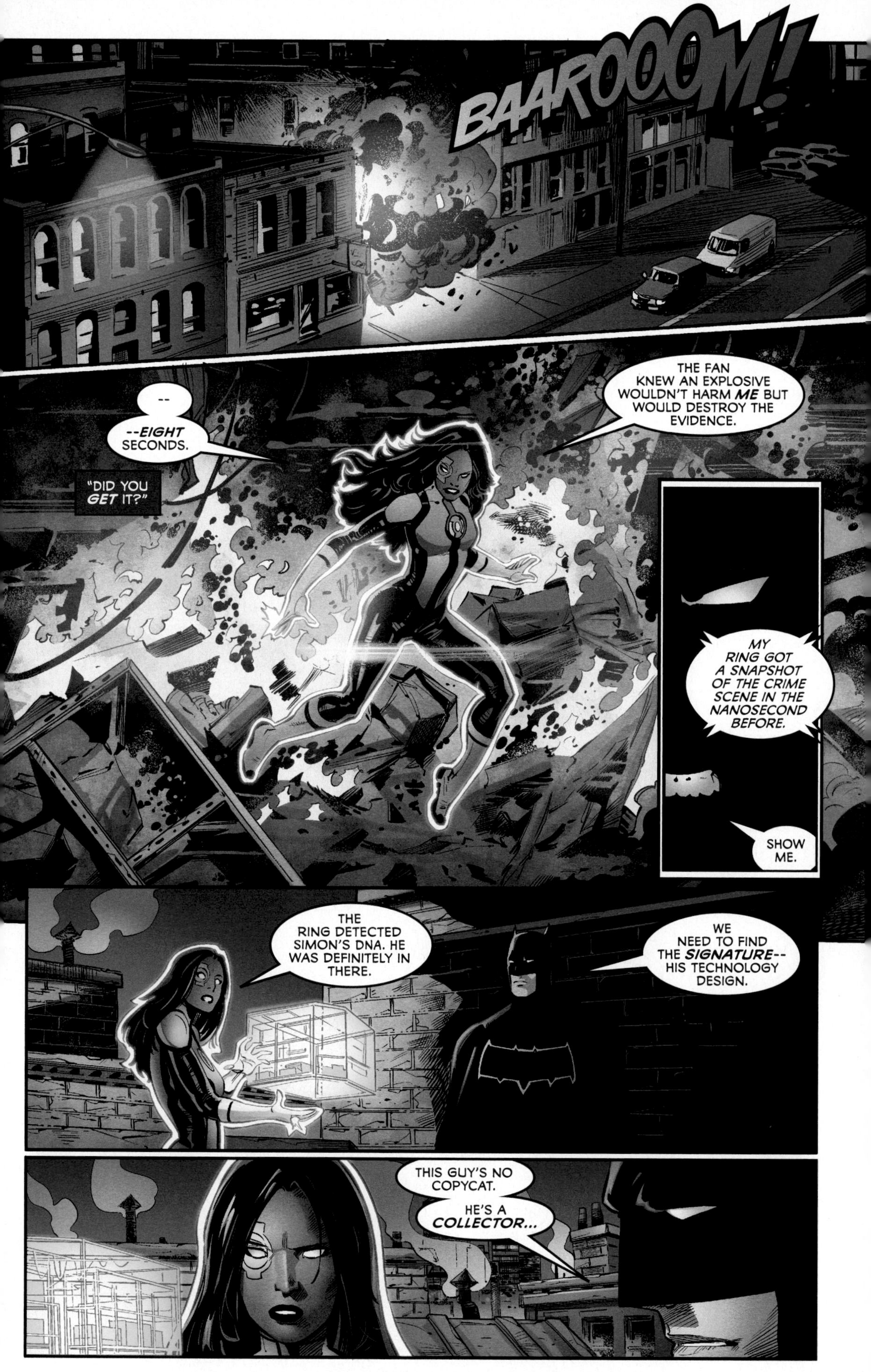
BAAROOOM!
--
--EIGHT SECONDS.
"DID YOU GET IT?"
THE FAN KNEW AN EXPLOSIVE WOULDN'T HARM ME BUT WOULD DESTROY THE EVIDENCE.
MY RING GOT A SNAPSHOT OF THE CRIME SCENE IN THE NANOSECOND BEFORE.
SHOW ME.
THE RING DETECTED SIMON'S DNA. HE WAS DEFINITELY IN THERE.
WE NEED TO FIND THE SIGNATURE-- HIS TECHNOLOGY DESIGN.
THIS GUY'S NO COPYCAT.
HE'S A COLLECTOR...

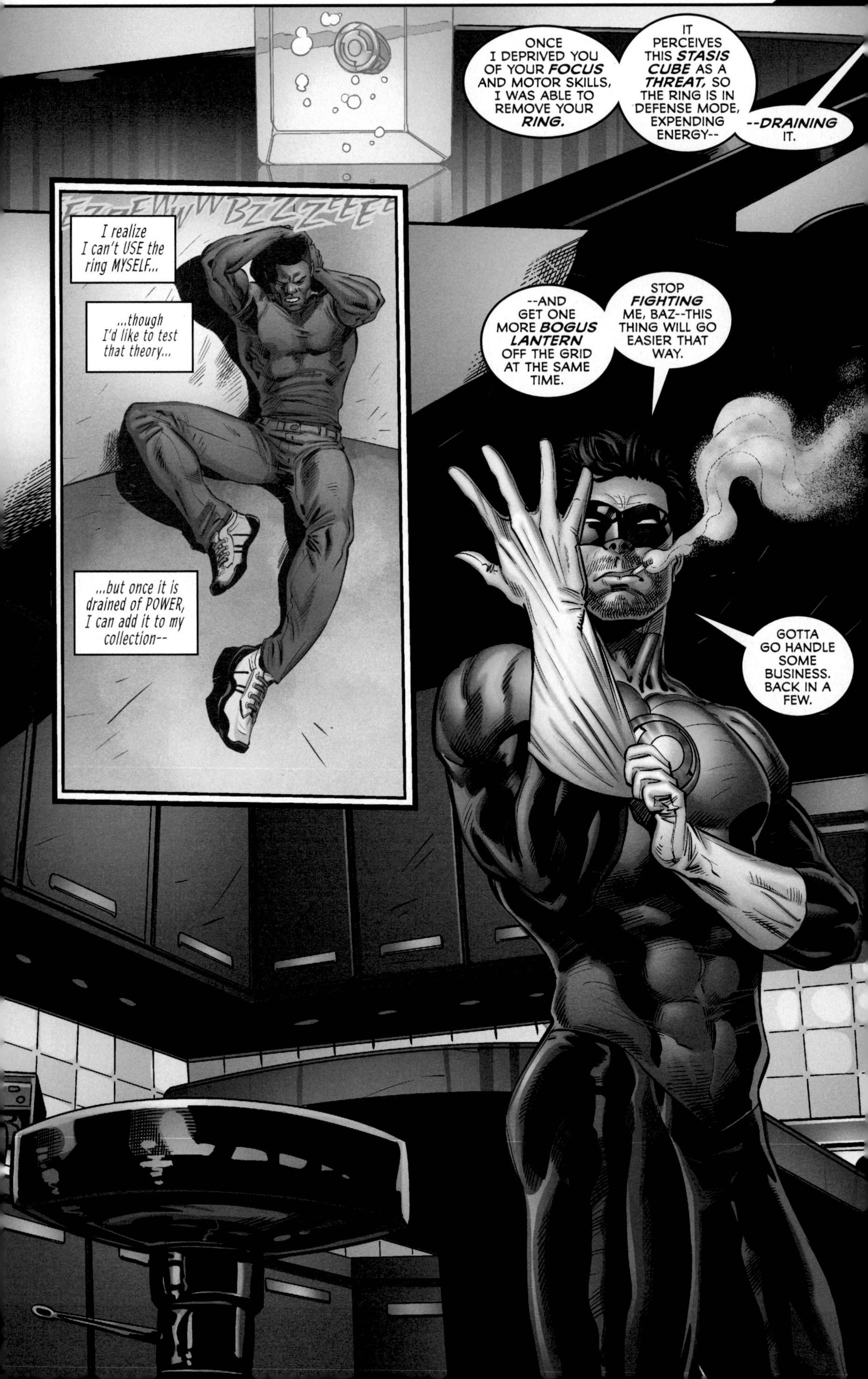
ONCE I DEPRIVED YOU OF YOUR FOCUS AND MOTOR SKILLS, I WAS ABLE TO REMOVE YOUR RING.
IT PERCEIVES THIS STASIS CUBE AS A THREAT, SO THE RING IS IN DEFENSE MODE, EXPENDING ENERGY--
--DRAINING IT.
I realize I can't USE the ring MYSELF...
...though I'd like to test that theory...
...but once it is drained of POWER, I can add it to my collection--
--AND GET ONE MORE BOGUS LANTERN OFF THE GRID AT THE SAME TIME.
STOP FIGHTING ME, BAZ--THIS THING WILL GO EASIER THAT WAY.
GOTTA GO HANDLE SOME BUSINESS. BACK IN A FEW.

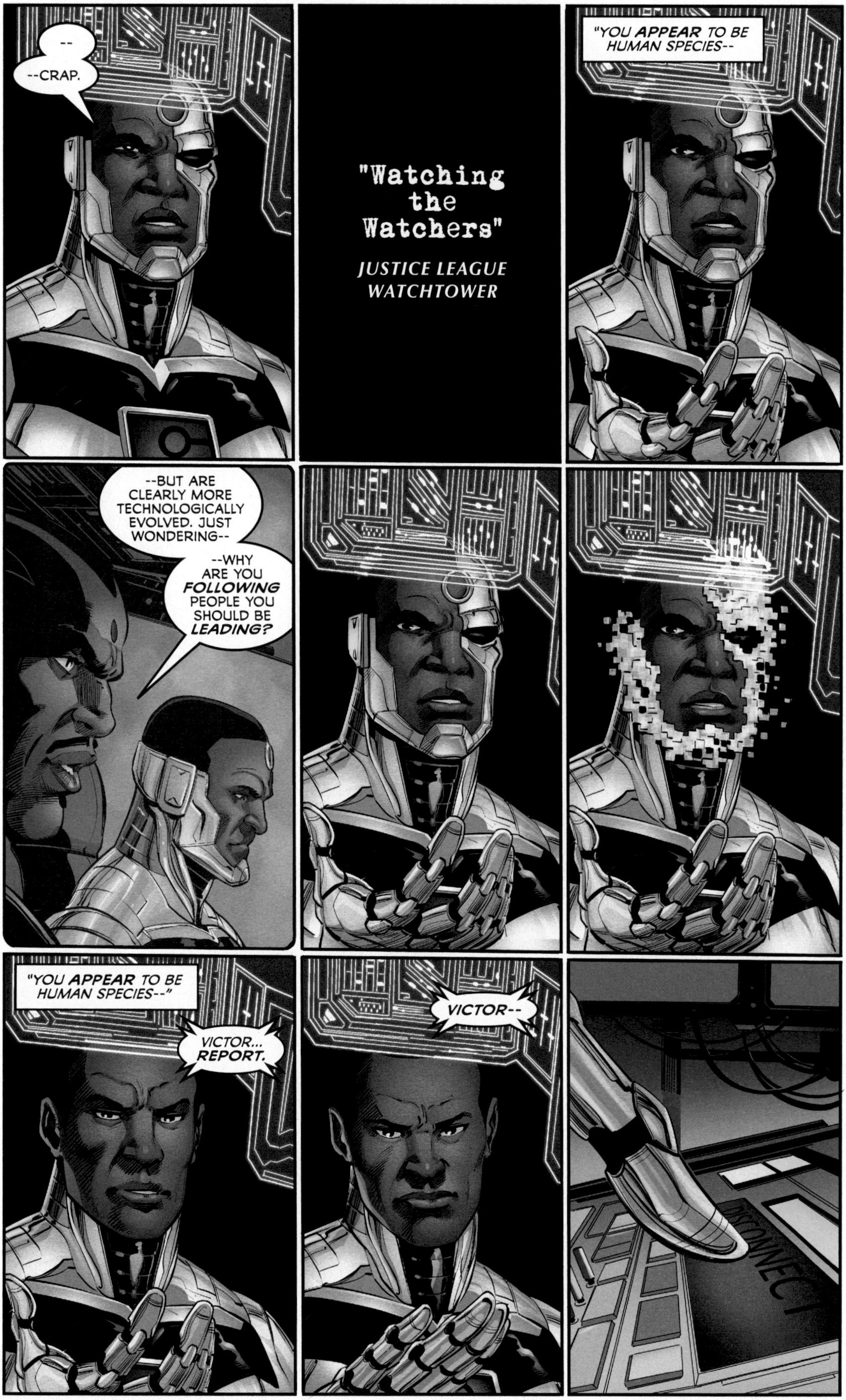
--
--CRAP.
"Watching the Watchers"
JUSTICE LEAGUE WATCHTOWER
"YOU APPEAR TO BE HUMAN SPECIES--
--BUT ARE CLEARLY MORE TECHNOLOGICALLY EVOLVED. JUST WONDERING--
--WHY ARE YOU FOLLOWING PEOPLE YOU SHOULD BE LEADING?
"YOU APPEAR TO BE HUMAN SPECIES--"
VICTOR... REPORT.
VICTOR--
DISCONNECT

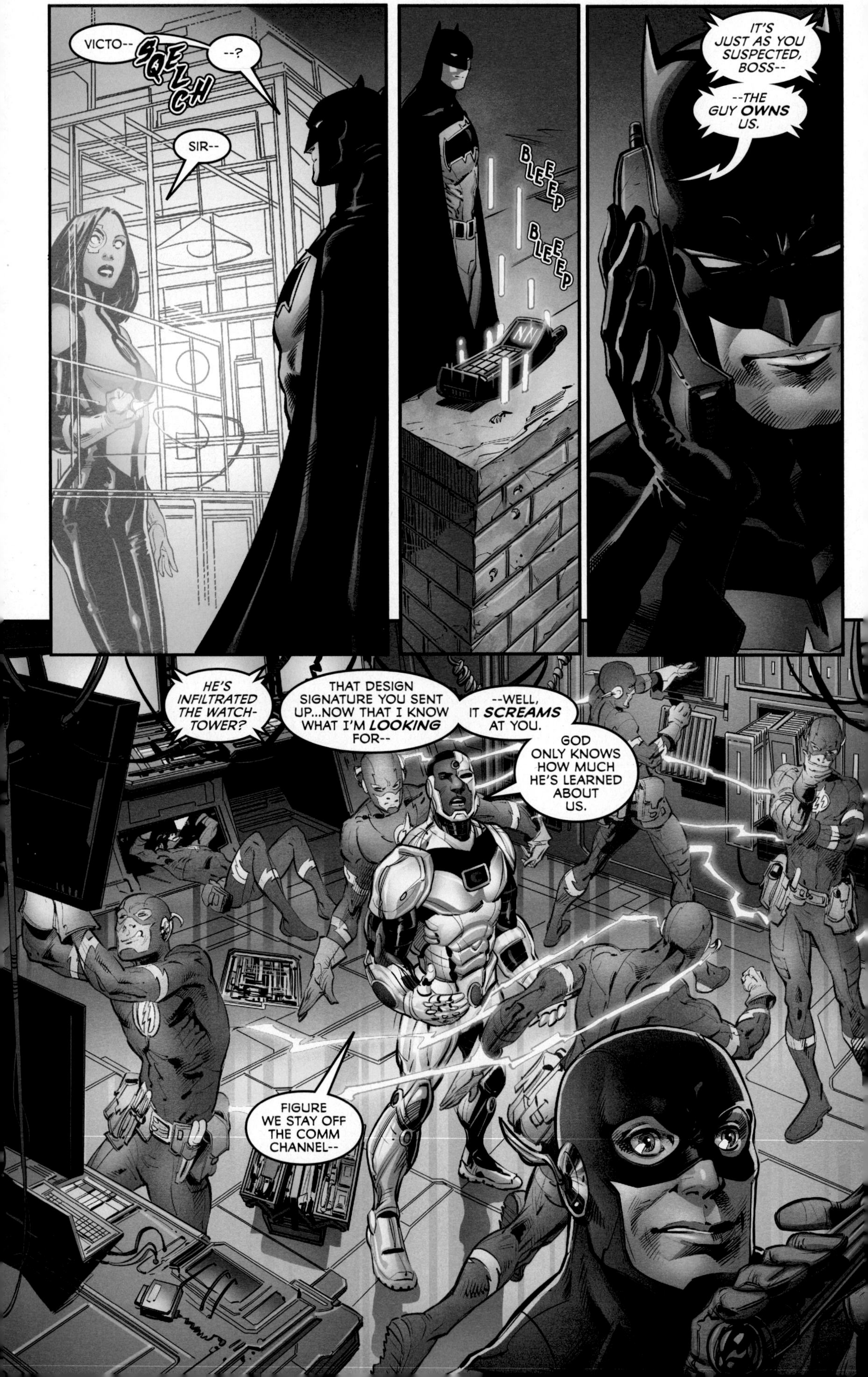
VICTO--
SQELCH
--?
SIR--
BLEEEP
BLEEEP
IT'S JUST AS YOU SUSPECTED, BOSS--
--THE GUY OWNS US.
HE'S INFILTRATED THE WATCH-TOWER?
THAT DESIGN SIGNATURE YOU SENT UP...NOW THAT I KNOW WHAT I'M LOOKING FOR--
--WELL, IT SCREAMS AT YOU.
GOD ONLY KNOWS HOW MUCH HE'S LEARNED ABOUT US.
FIGURE WE STAY OFF THE COMM CHANNEL--

--WHICH CRIPPLES OUR ABILITY TO CO-ORDINATE.

HOWEVER, THIS LEVEL OF PENETRATION IS ITSELF A BIG CLUE TO THE PERP--

BLEEP

--VICTOR? VICTOR--

NOT A46-- A26.

SORRY.

WALK AWAY FROM ME.

EEEZWWZZ

CAN'T... THINK... CAN'T...

ZLEEEEWBZZE

AAAACCKK--!!

...OFF...

...GET... INHIBITOR...

WHUMP!

...BETTER...

...FOCUS ON...PAIN...

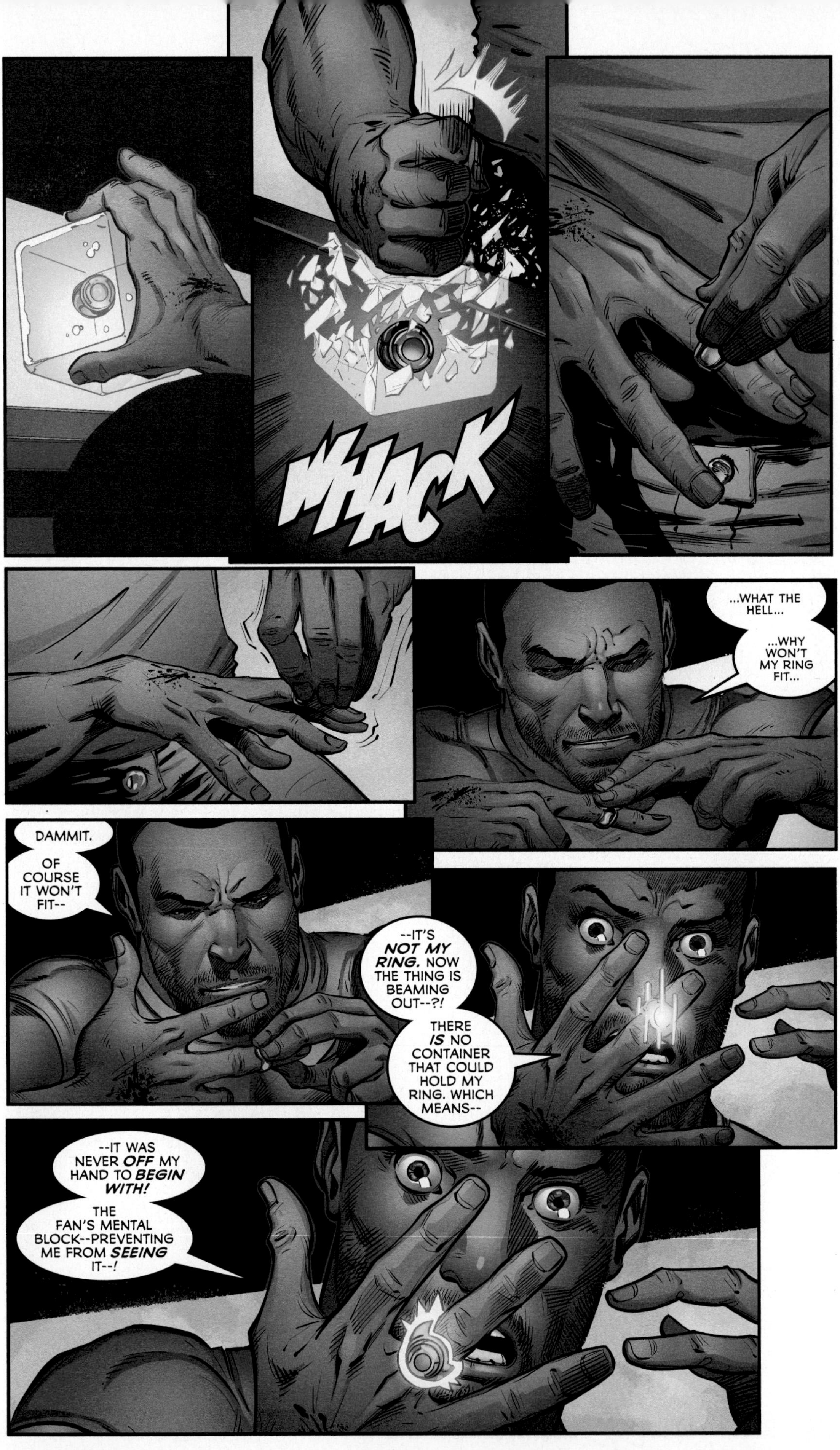
WHACK
...WHAT THE HELL...
...WHY WON'T MY RING FIT...
DAMMIT.
OF COURSE IT WON'T FIT--
--IT'S NOT MY RING. NOW THE THING IS BEAMING OUT--?!
THERE IS NO CONTAINER THAT COULD HOLD MY RING. WHICH MEANS--
--IT WAS NEVER OFF MY HAND TO BEGIN WITH!
THE FAN'S MENTAL BLOCK--PREVENTING ME FROM SEEING IT--!

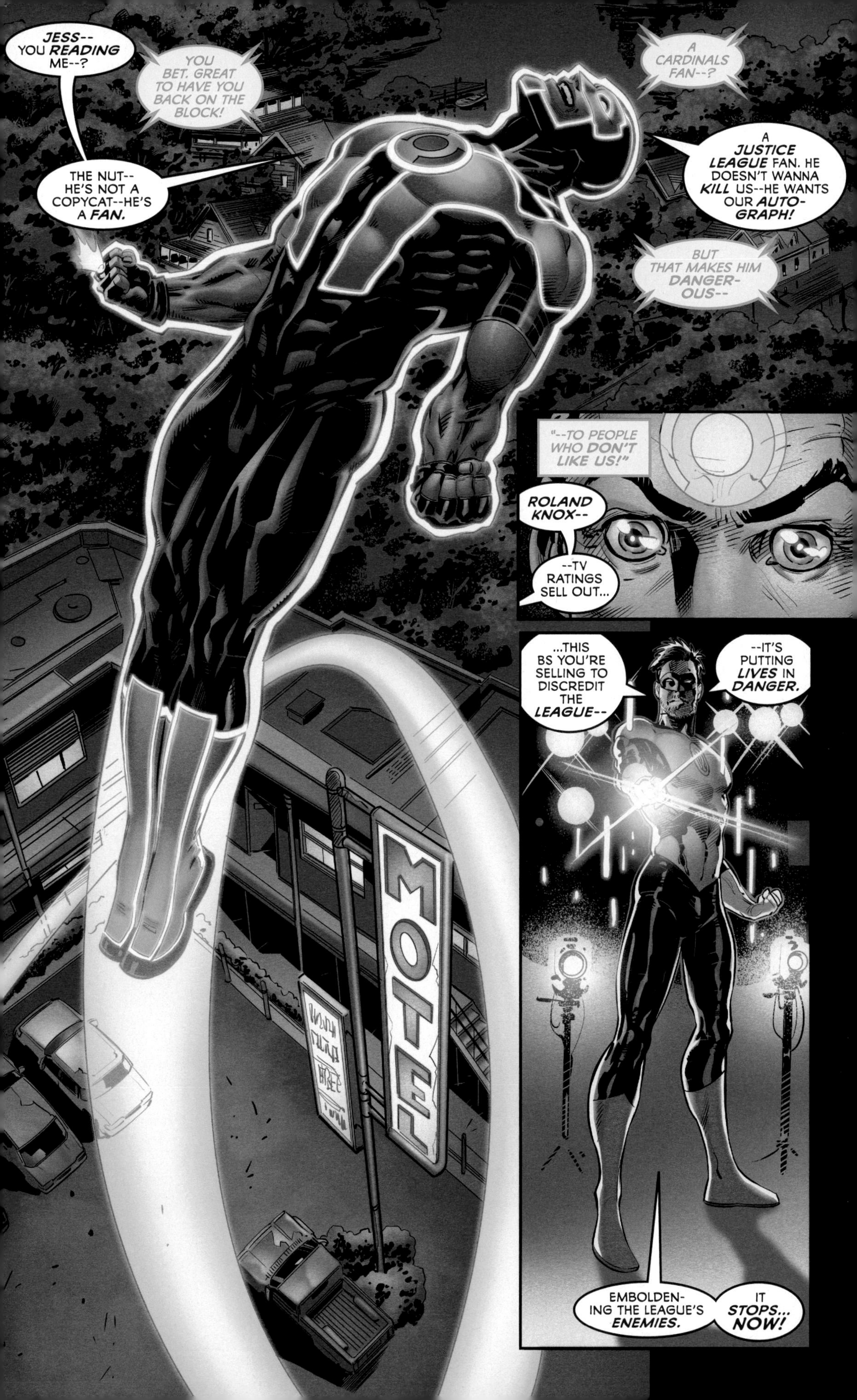
JESS-- YOU READING ME--?
YOU BET. GREAT TO HAVE YOU BACK ON THE BLOCK!
THE NUT-- HE'S NOT A COPYCAT--HE'S A FAN.
A CARDINALS FAN--?
A JUSTICE LEAGUE FAN. HE DOESN'T WANNA KILL US--HE WANTS OUR AUTO-GRAPH!
BUT THAT MAKES HIM DANGER-OUS--
MOTEL
"--TO PEOPLE WHO DON'T LIKE US!"
ROLAND KNOX--
--TV RATINGS SELL OUT...
...THIS BS YOU'RE SELLING TO DISCREDIT THE LEAGUE--
--IT'S PUTTING LIVES IN DANGER.
EMBOLDEN-ING THE LEAGUE'S ENEMIES.
IT STOPS... NOW!

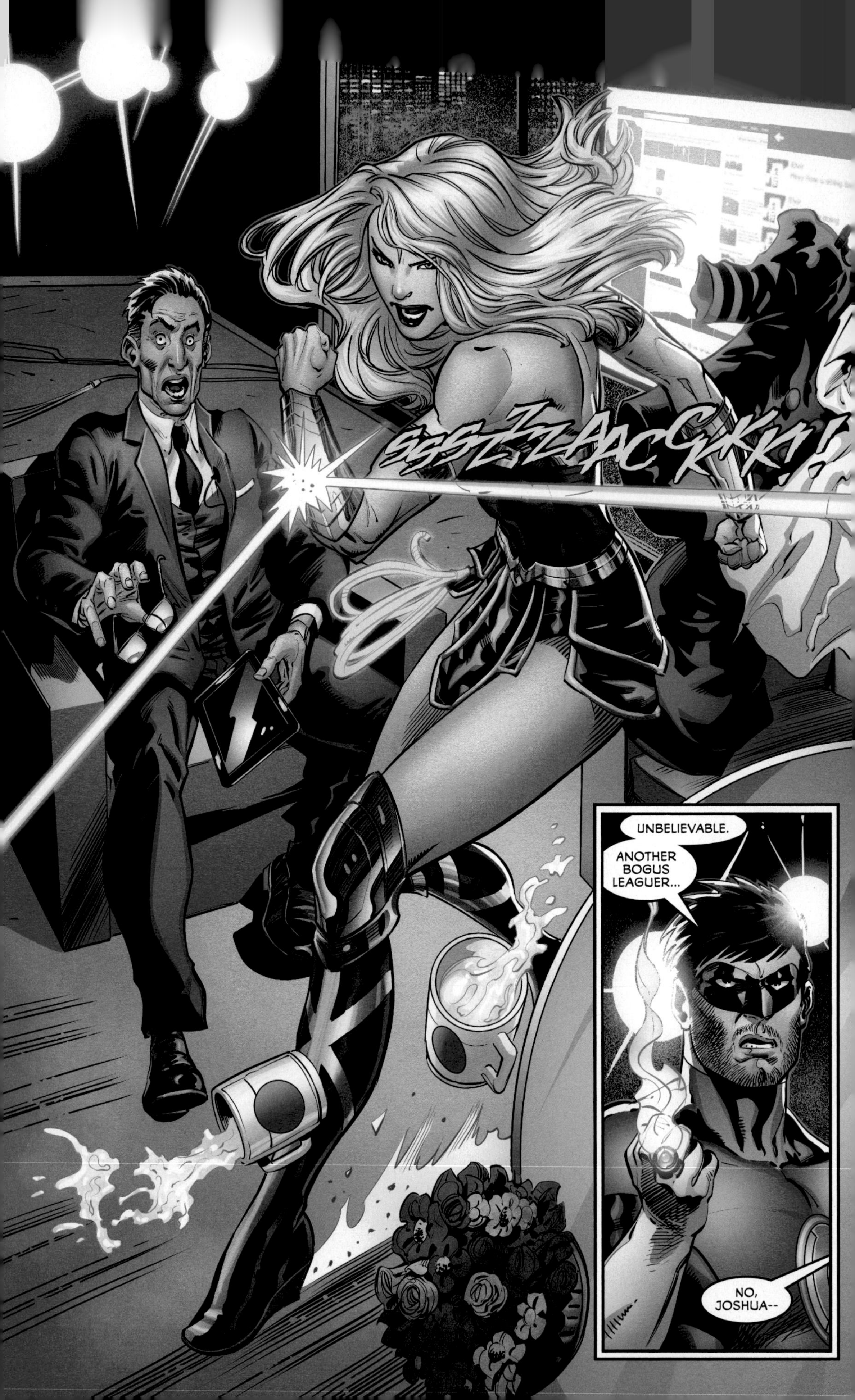
SSSZZZZAACCKKK!!
UNBELIEVABLE.
ANOTHER BOGUS LEAGUER...
NO, JOSHUA--

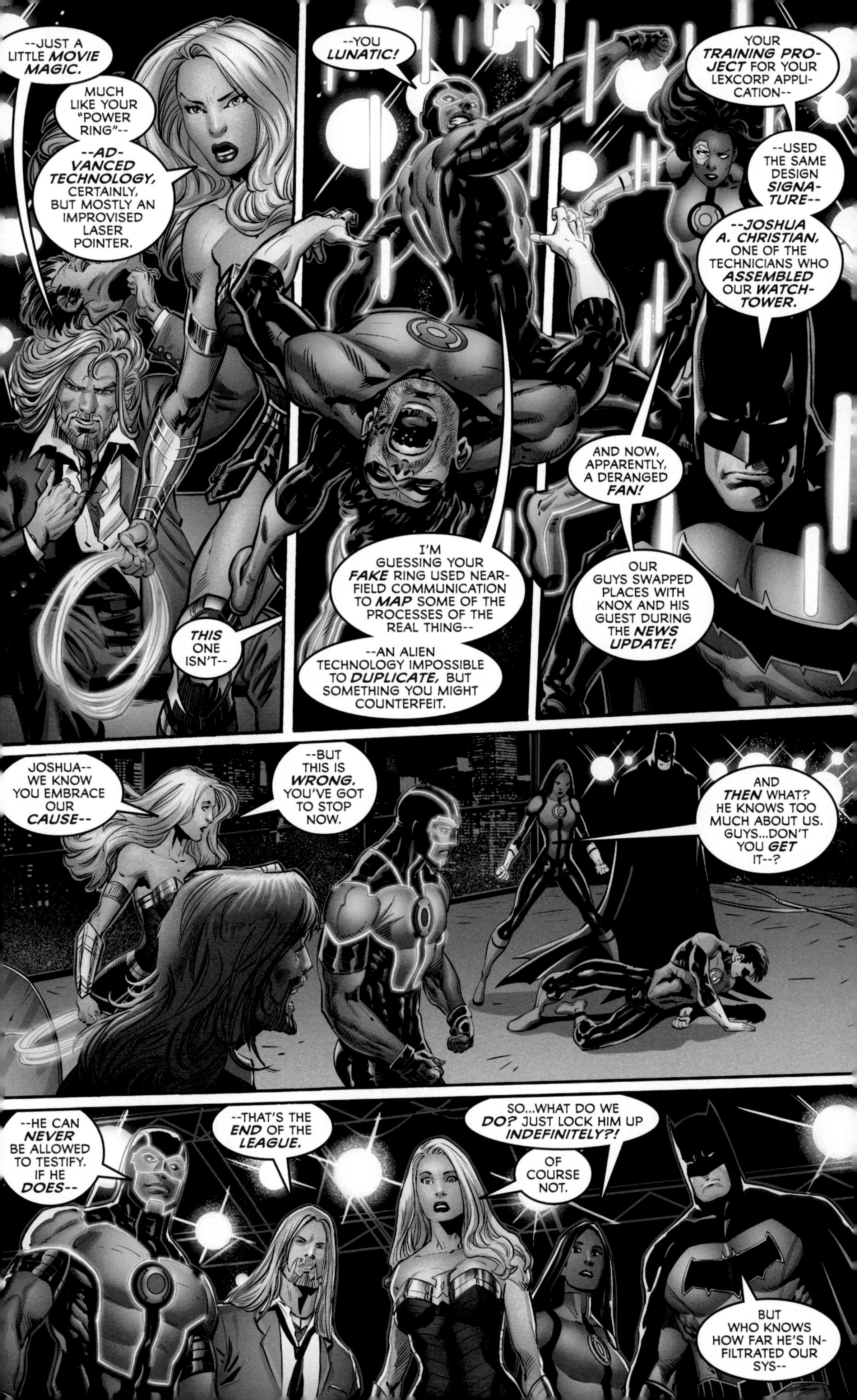
--JUST A LITTLE MOVIE MAGIC.
MUCH LIKE YOUR "POWER RING"--
--ADVANCED TECHNOLOGY, CERTAINLY, BUT MOSTLY AN IMPROVISED LASER POINTER.
THIS ONE ISN'T--
--YOU LUNATIC!
I'M GUESSING YOUR FAKE RING USED NEAR-FIELD COMMUNICATION TO MAP SOME OF THE PROCESSES OF THE REAL THING--
--AN ALIEN TECHNOLOGY IMPOSSIBLE TO DUPLICATE, BUT SOMETHING YOU MIGHT COUNTERFEIT.
YOUR TRAINING PROJECT FOR YOUR LEXCORP APPLICATION--
--USED THE SAME DESIGN SIGNATURE--
--JOSHUA A. CHRISTIAN, ONE OF THE TECHNICIANS WHO ASSEMBLED OUR WATCHTOWER.
AND NOW, APPARENTLY, A DERANGED FAN!
OUR GUYS SWAPPED PLACES WITH KNOX AND HIS GUEST DURING THE NEWS UPDATE!
JOSHUA-- WE KNOW YOU EMBRACE OUR CAUSE--
--BUT THIS IS WRONG. YOU'VE GOT TO STOP NOW.
AND THEN WHAT? HE KNOWS TOO MUCH ABOUT US. GUYS...DON'T YOU GET IT--?
--HE CAN NEVER BE ALLOWED TO TESTIFY. IF HE DOES--
--THAT'S THE END OF THE LEAGUE.
SO...WHAT DO WE DO? JUST LOCK HIM UP INDEFINITELY?!
OF COURSE NOT.
BUT WHO KNOWS HOW FAR HE'S INFILTRATED OUR SYS--

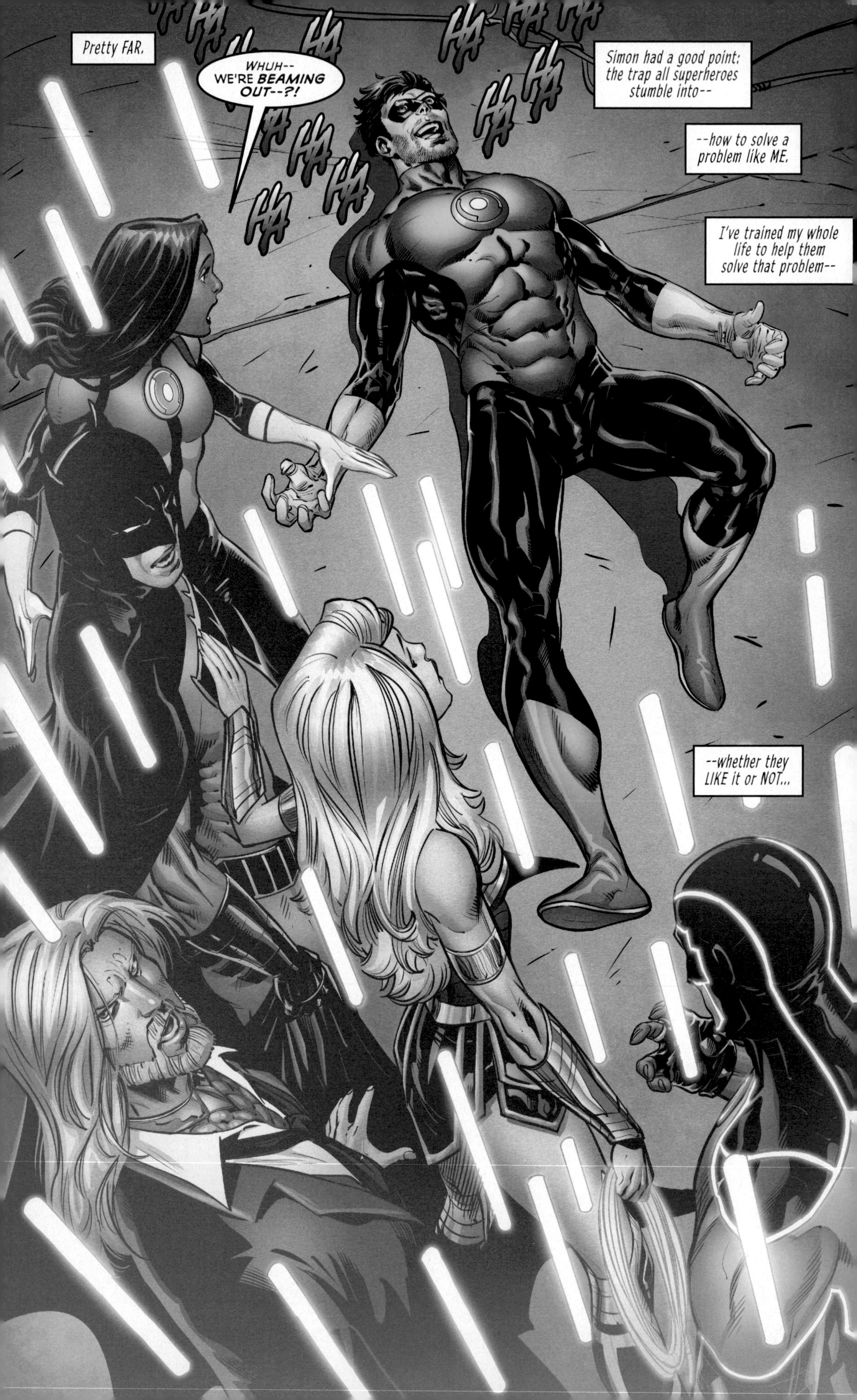
Pretty FAR.
WHUH-- WE'RE BEAMING OUT--?!
HA HA HA HA HA HA HA HA HA HA HA HA HA HA HA HA
Simon had a good point: the trap all superheroes stumble into--
--how to solve a problem like ME.
I've trained my whole life to help them solve that problem--
--whether they LIKE it or NOT...

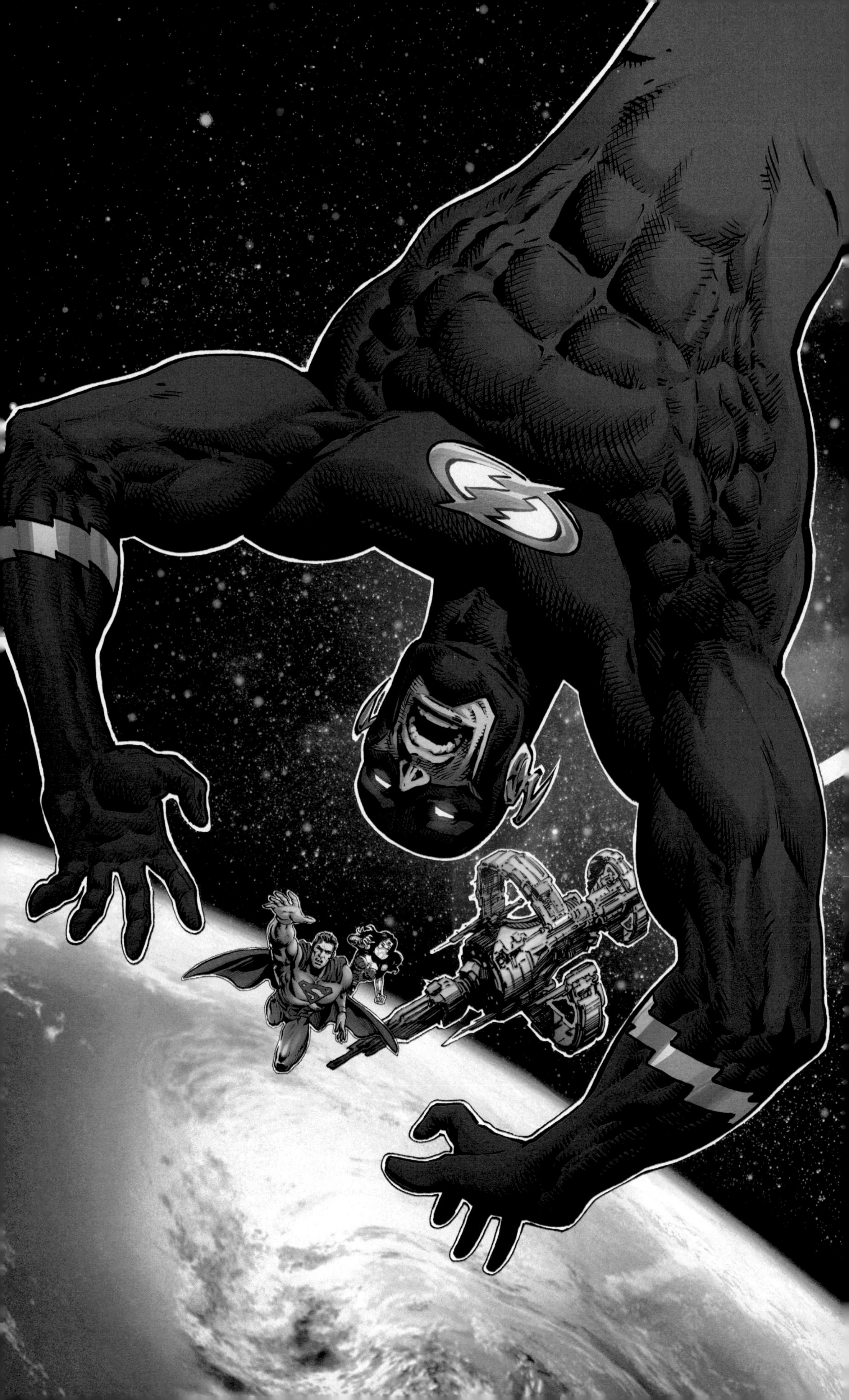

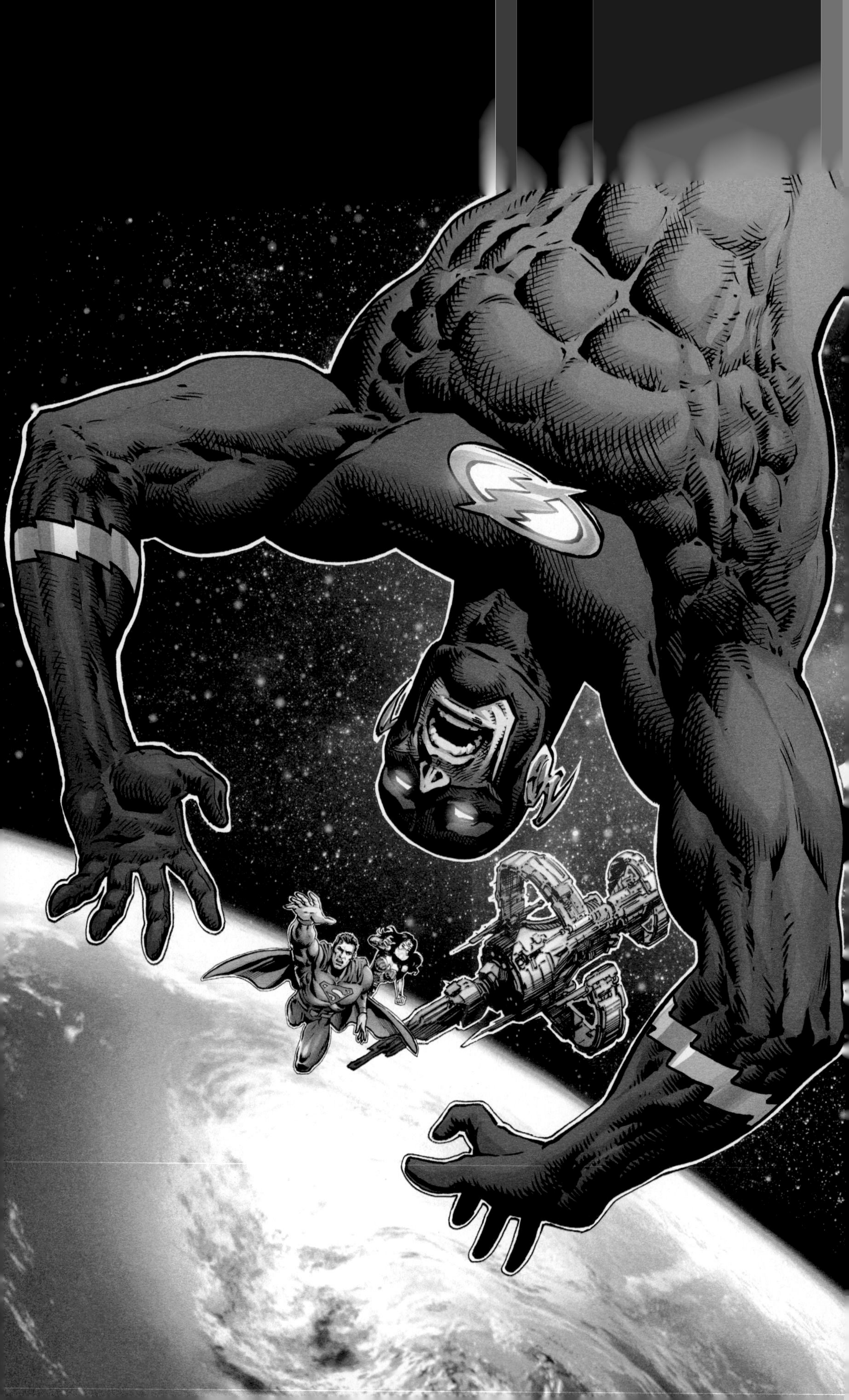

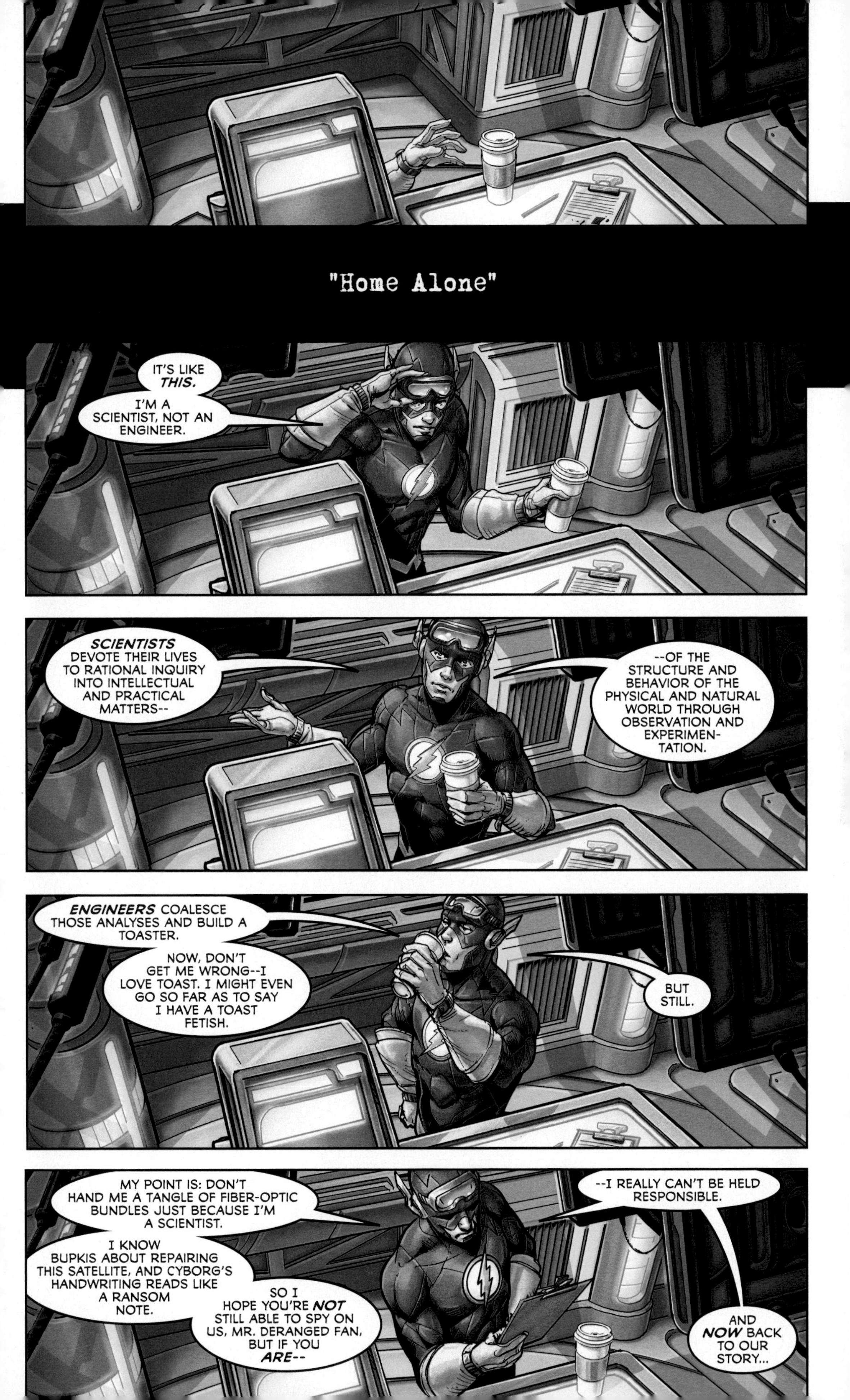
"Home Alone"
IT'S LIKE *THIS.*
I'M A SCIENTIST, NOT AN ENGINEER.
SCIENTISTS DEVOTE THEIR LIVES TO RATIONAL INQUIRY INTO INTELLECTUAL AND PRACTICAL MATTERS--
--OF THE STRUCTURE AND BEHAVIOR OF THE PHYSICAL AND NATURAL WORLD THROUGH OBSERVATION AND EXPERIMEN-TATION.
ENGINEERS COALESCE THOSE ANALYSES AND BUILD A TOASTER.
NOW, DON'T GET ME WRONG--I LOVE TOAST. I MIGHT EVEN GO SO FAR AS TO SAY I HAVE A TOAST FETISH.
BUT STILL.
MY POINT IS: DON'T HAND ME A TANGLE OF FIBER-OPTIC BUNDLES JUST BECAUSE I'M A SCIENTIST.
I KNOW BUPKIS ABOUT REPAIRING THIS SATELLITE, AND CYBORG'S HANDWRITING READS LIKE A RANSOM NOTE.
SO I HOPE YOU'RE *NOT* STILL ABLE TO SPY ON US, MR. DERANGED FAN, BUT IF YOU *ARE*--
--I REALLY CAN'T BE HELD RESPONSIBLE.
AND *NOW* BACK TO OUR STORY...

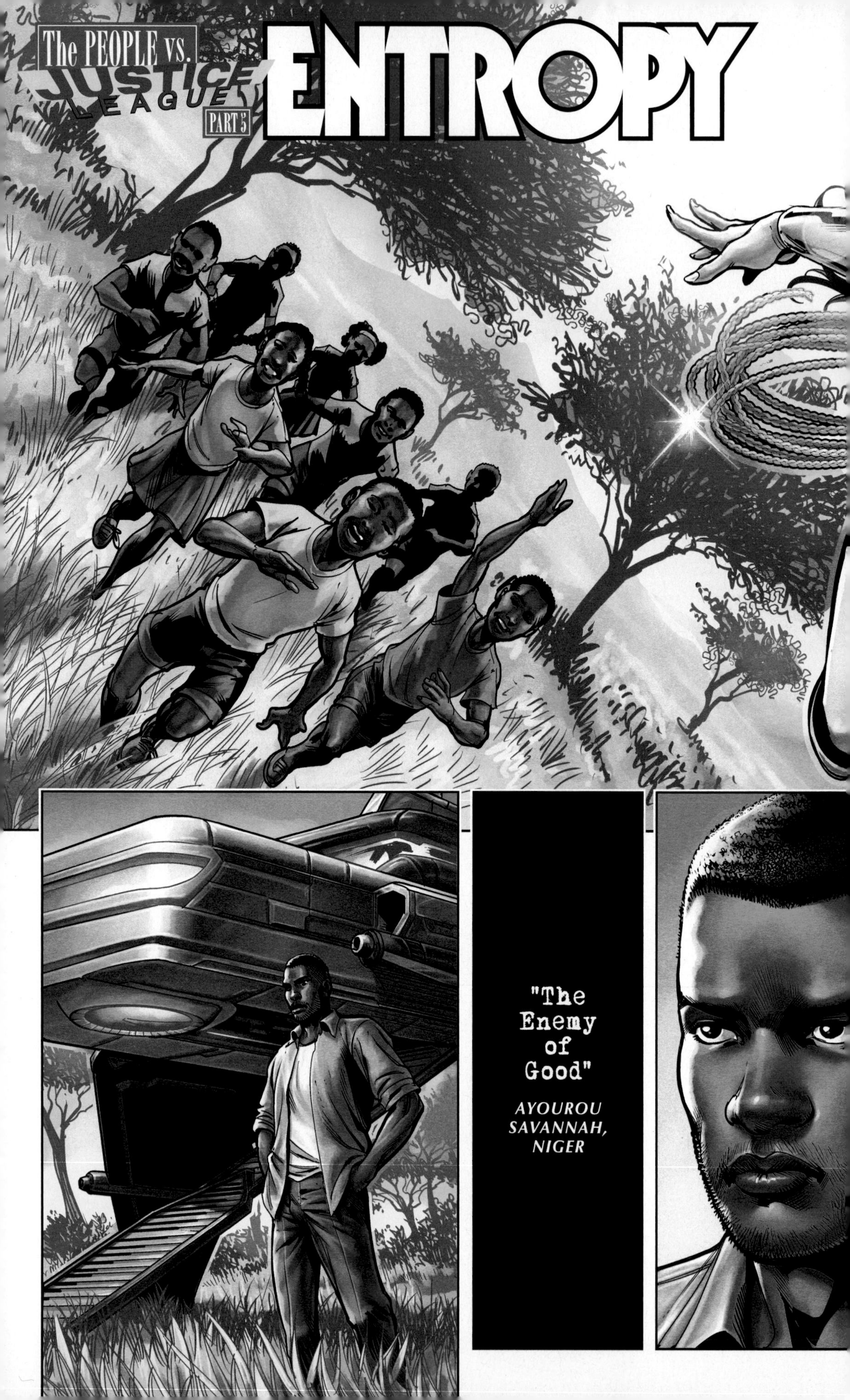

The PEOPLE vs. JUSTICE LEAGUE PART 5
ENTROPY
"The Enemy of Good"
AYOUROU SAVANNAH, NIGER

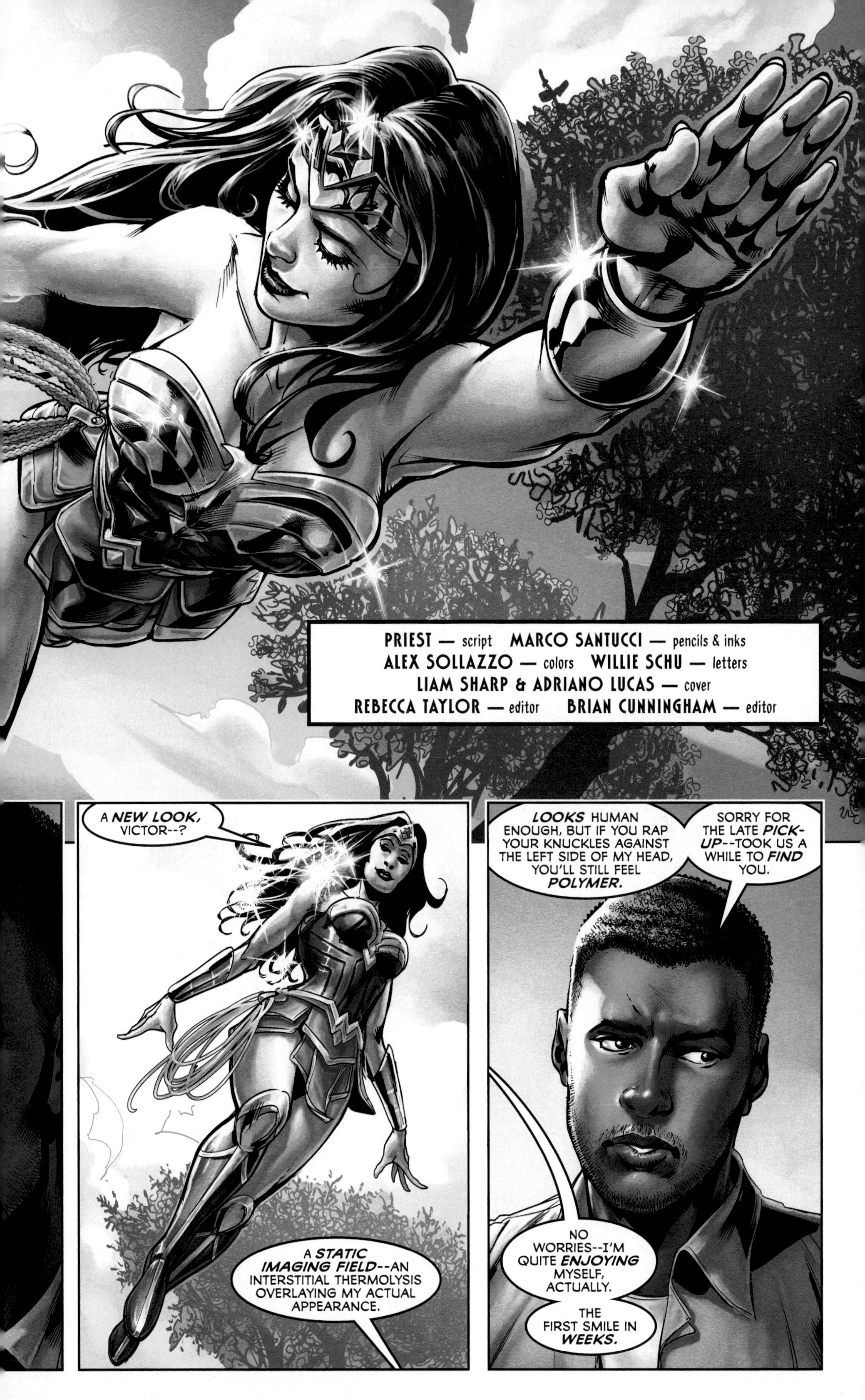
PRIEST — script MARCO SANTUCCI — pencils & inks
ALEX SOLLAZZO — colors WILLIE SCHU — letters
LIAM SHARP & ADRIANO LUCAS — cover
REBECCA TAYLOR — editor BRIAN CUNNINGHAM — editor
A NEW LOOK, VICTOR--?
A STATIC IMAGING FIELD--AN INTERSTITIAL THERMOLYSIS OVERLAYING MY ACTUAL APPEARANCE.
LOOKS HUMAN ENOUGH, BUT IF YOU RAP YOUR KNUCKLES AGAINST THE LEFT SIDE OF MY HEAD, YOU'LL STILL FEEL POLYMER.
SORRY FOR THE LATE PICK-UP--TOOK US A WHILE TO FIND YOU.
NO WORRIES--I'M QUITE ENJOYING MYSELF, ACTUALLY.
THE FIRST SMILE IN WEEKS.

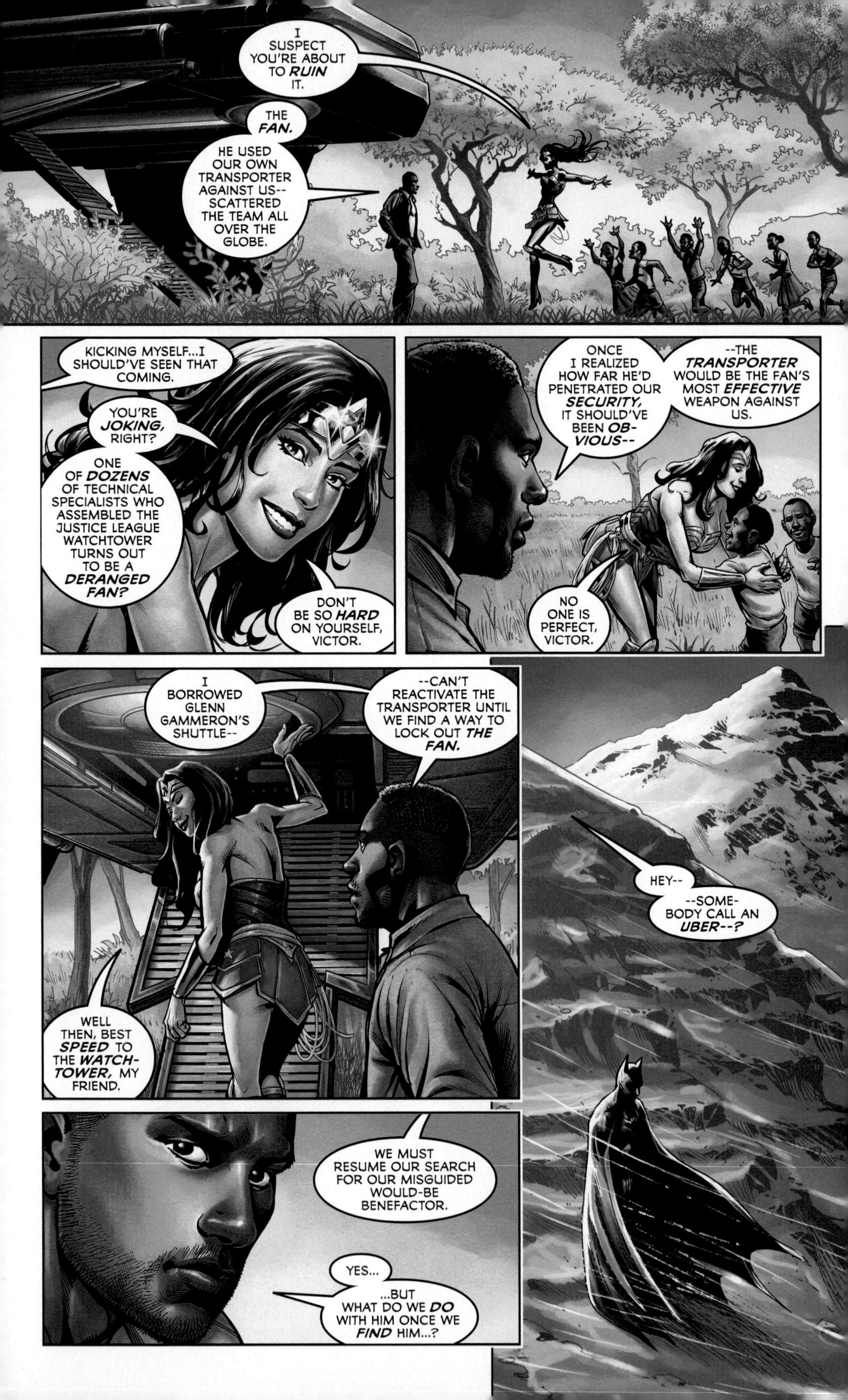
I SUSPECT YOU'RE ABOUT TO *RUIN* IT.
THE *FAN.*
HE USED OUR OWN TRANSPORTER AGAINST US--SCATTERED THE TEAM ALL OVER THE GLOBE.
KICKING MYSELF...I SHOULD'VE SEEN THAT COMING.
YOU'RE *JOKING,* RIGHT?
ONE OF *DOZENS* OF TECHNICAL SPECIALISTS WHO ASSEMBLED THE JUSTICE LEAGUE WATCHTOWER TURNS OUT TO BE A *DERANGED FAN?*
DON'T BE SO *HARD* ON YOURSELF, VICTOR.
ONCE I REALIZED HOW FAR HE'D PENETRATED OUR *SECURITY,* IT SHOULD'VE BEEN *OB-VIOUS--*
--THE *TRANSPORTER* WOULD BE THE FAN'S MOST *EFFECTIVE* WEAPON AGAINST US.
NO ONE IS PERFECT, VICTOR.
I BORROWED GLENN GAMMERON'S SHUTTLE--
--CAN'T REACTIVATE THE TRANSPORTER UNTIL WE FIND A WAY TO LOCK OUT *THE FAN.*
WELL THEN, BEST *SPEED* TO THE *WATCH-TOWER,* MY FRIEND.
WE MUST RESUME OUR SEARCH FOR OUR MISGUIDED WOULD-BE BENEFACTOR.
YES...
...BUT WHAT DO WE *DO* WITH HIM ONCE WE *FIND* HIM...?
HEY--
--SOME-BODY CALL AN *UBER--?*

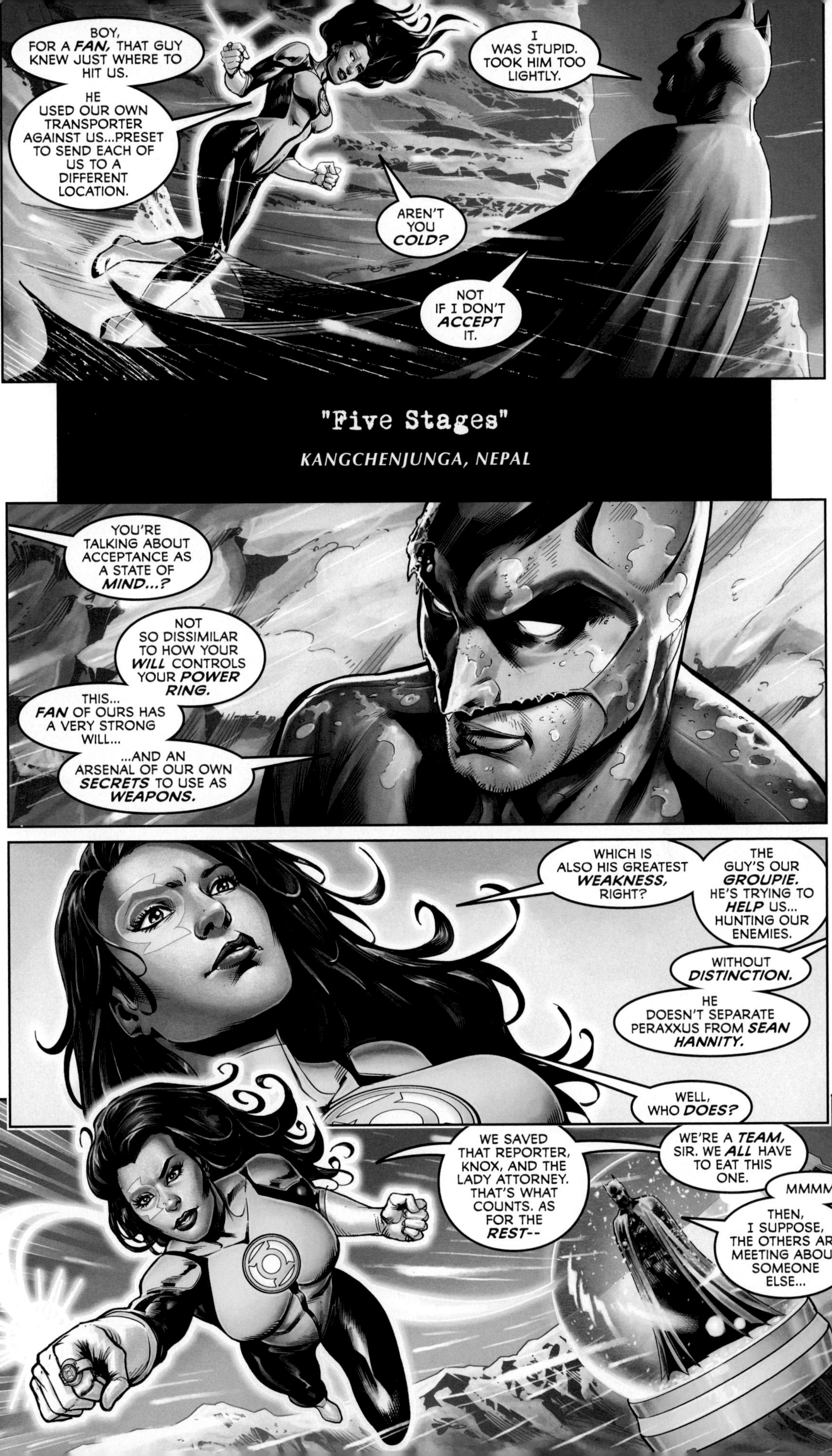
BOY, FOR A FAN, THAT GUY KNEW JUST WHERE TO HIT US.
HE USED OUR OWN TRANSPORTER AGAINST US...PRESET TO SEND EACH OF US TO A DIFFERENT LOCATION.
I WAS STUPID. TOOK HIM TOO LIGHTLY.
AREN'T YOU COLD?
NOT IF I DON'T ACCEPT IT.
"Five Stages"
KANGCHENJUNGA, NEPAL
YOU'RE TALKING ABOUT ACCEPTANCE AS A STATE OF MIND...?
NOT SO DISSIMILAR TO HOW YOUR WILL CONTROLS YOUR POWER RING.
THIS... FAN OF OURS HAS A VERY STRONG WILL...
...AND AN ARSENAL OF OUR OWN SECRETS TO USE AS WEAPONS.
WHICH IS ALSO HIS GREATEST WEAKNESS, RIGHT?
THE GUY'S OUR GROUPIE. HE'S TRYING TO HELP US... HUNTING OUR ENEMIES.
WITHOUT DISTINCTION.
HE DOESN'T SEPARATE PERAXXUS FROM SEAN HANNITY.
WELL, WHO DOES?
WE SAVED THAT REPORTER, KNOX, AND THE LADY ATTORNEY. THAT'S WHAT COUNTS. AS FOR THE REST--
WE'RE A TEAM, SIR. WE ALL HAVE TO EAT THIS ONE.
MMMM.
THEN, I SUPPOSE, THE OTHERS ARE MEETING ABOUT SOMEONE ELSE...

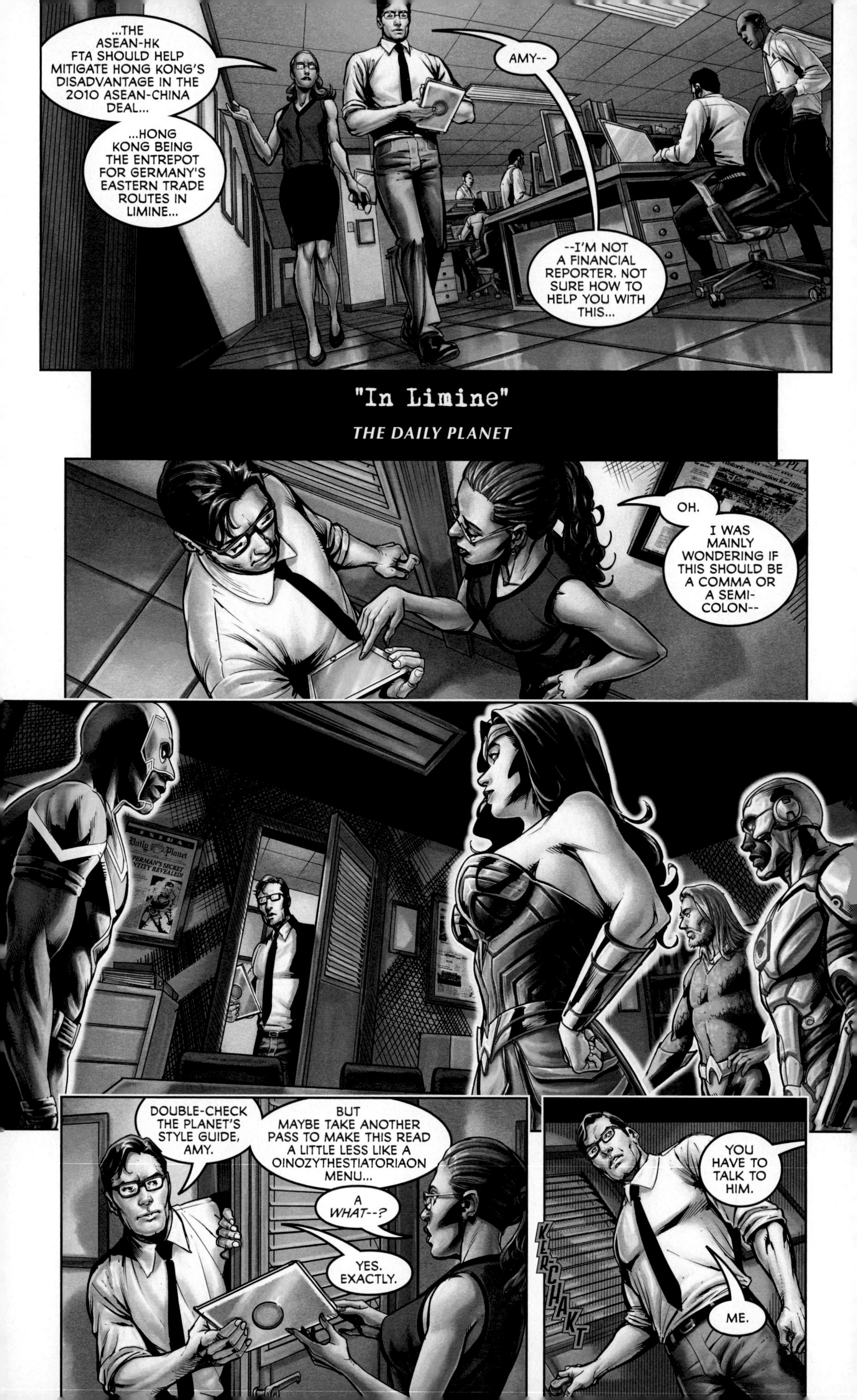
...THE ASEAN-HK FTA SHOULD HELP MITIGATE HONG KONG'S DISADVANTAGE IN THE 2010 ASEAN-CHINA DEAL...
...HONG KONG BEING THE ENTREPOT FOR GERMANY'S EASTERN TRADE ROUTES IN LIMINE...
AMY--
--I'M NOT A FINANCIAL REPORTER. NOT SURE HOW TO HELP YOU WITH THIS...
"In Limine"
THE DAILY PLANET
OH.
I WAS MAINLY WONDERING IF THIS SHOULD BE A COMMA OR A SEMI-COLON--
DOUBLE-CHECK THE PLANET'S STYLE GUIDE, AMY.
BUT MAYBE TAKE ANOTHER PASS TO MAKE THIS READ A LITTLE LESS LIKE A OINOZYTHESTIATORIAON MENU...
A WHAT--?
YES. EXACTLY.
KER-CHAKT
YOU HAVE TO TALK TO HIM.
ME.

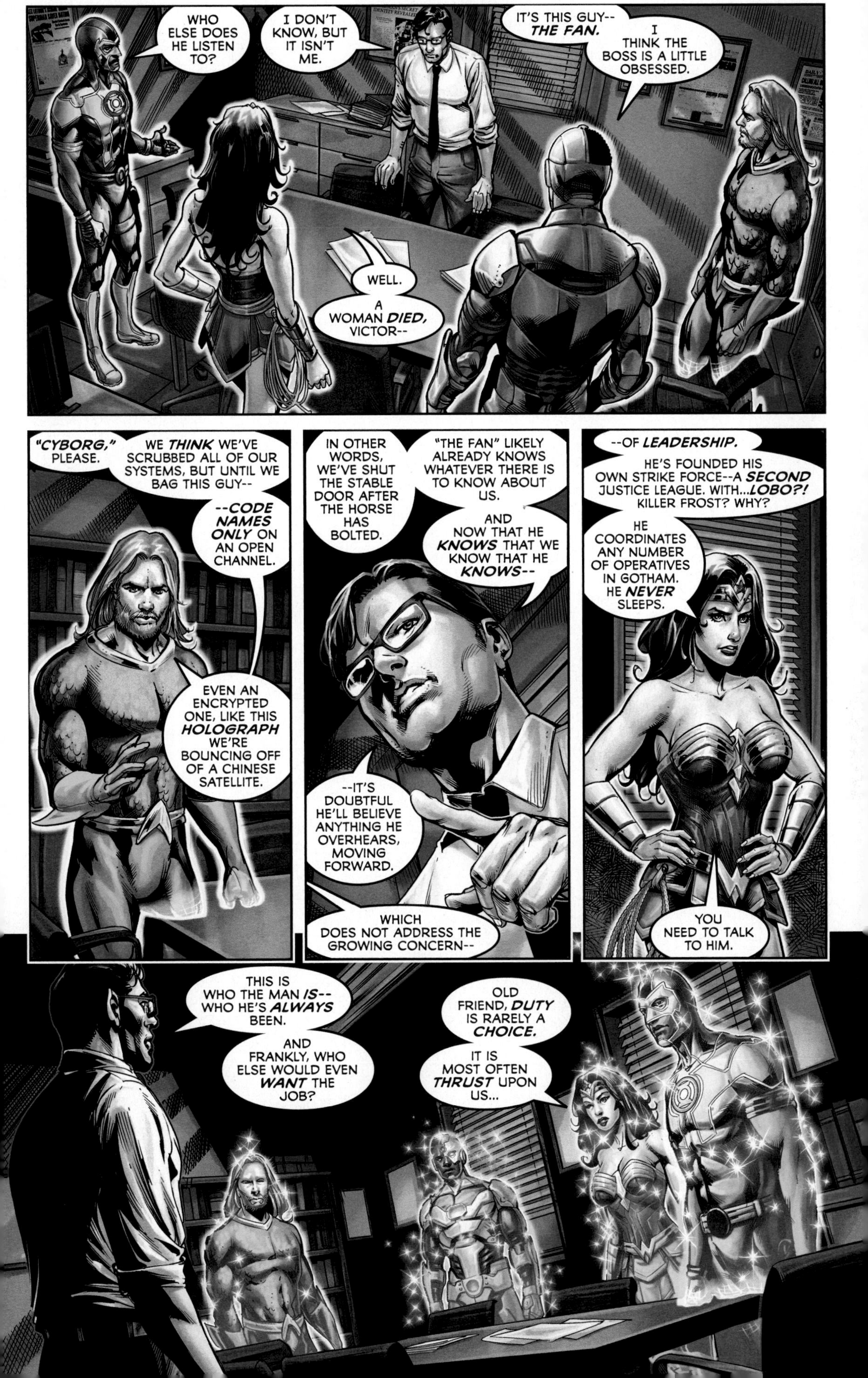
WHO ELSE DOES HE LISTEN TO?
I DON'T KNOW, BUT IT ISN'T ME.
IT'S THIS GUY-- THE FAN.
I THINK THE BOSS IS A LITTLE OBSESSED.
WELL.
A WOMAN DIED, VICTOR--
"CYBORG," PLEASE.
WE THINK WE'VE SCRUBBED ALL OF OUR SYSTEMS, BUT UNTIL WE BAG THIS GUY--
--CODE NAMES ONLY ON AN OPEN CHANNEL.
EVEN AN ENCRYPTED ONE, LIKE THIS HOLOGRAPH WE'RE BOUNCING OFF OF A CHINESE SATELLITE.
IN OTHER WORDS, WE'VE SHUT THE STABLE DOOR AFTER THE HORSE HAS BOLTED.
"THE FAN" LIKELY ALREADY KNOWS WHATEVER THERE IS TO KNOW ABOUT US.
AND NOW THAT HE KNOWS THAT WE KNOW THAT HE KNOWS--
--IT'S DOUBTFUL HE'LL BELIEVE ANYTHING HE OVERHEARS, MOVING FORWARD.
WHICH DOES NOT ADDRESS THE GROWING CONCERN--
--OF LEADERSHIP.
HE'S FOUNDED HIS OWN STRIKE FORCE--A SECOND JUSTICE LEAGUE. WITH...LOBO?! KILLER FROST? WHY?
HE COORDINATES ANY NUMBER OF OPERATIVES IN GOTHAM. HE NEVER SLEEPS.
YOU NEED TO TALK TO HIM.
THIS IS WHO THE MAN IS-- WHO HE'S ALWAYS BEEN.
AND FRANKLY, WHO ELSE WOULD EVEN WANT THE JOB?
OLD FRIEND, DUTY IS RARELY A CHOICE.
IT IS MOST OFTEN THRUST UPON US...

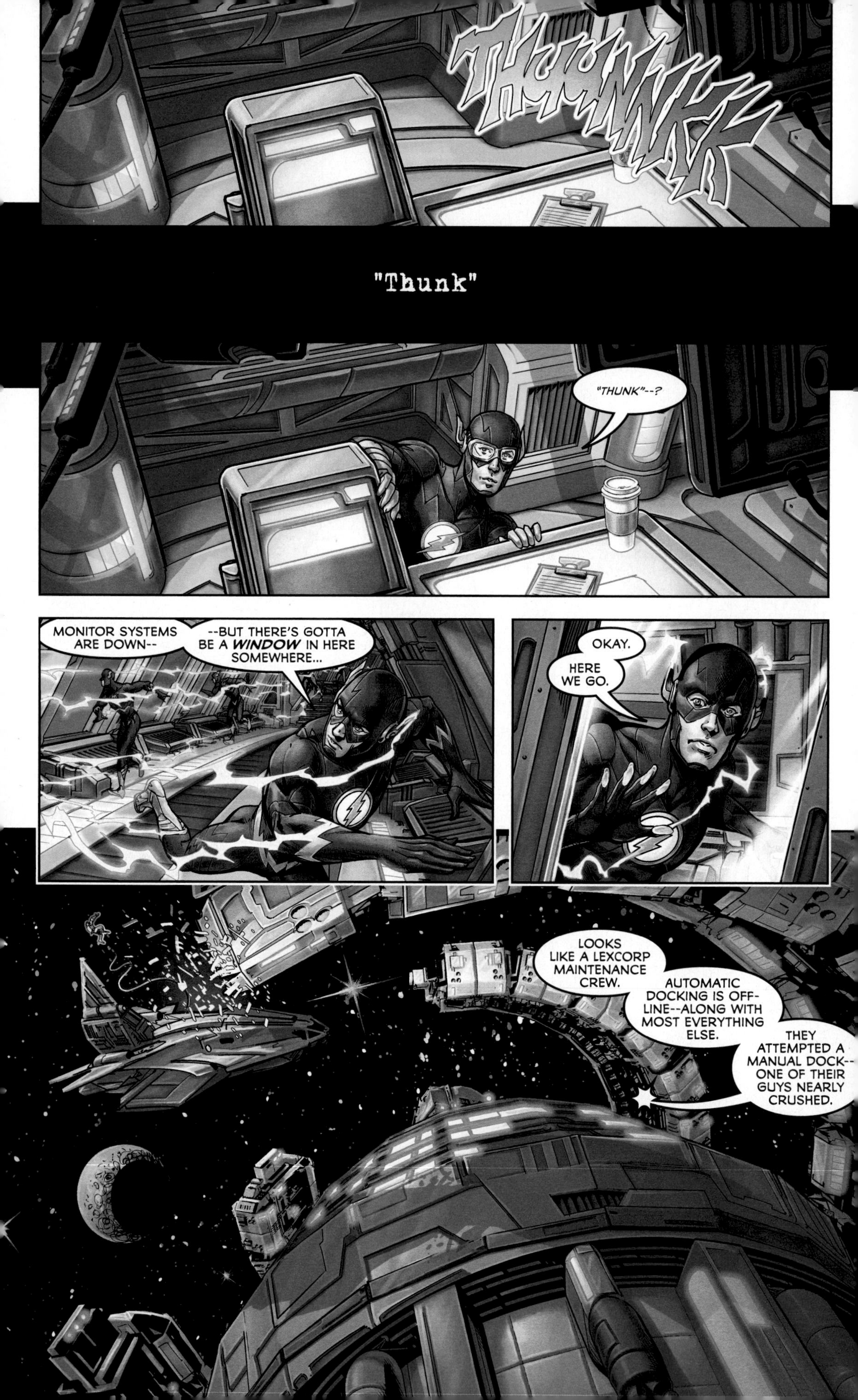

THUNNNKK
"Thunk"
"THUNK"--?
MONITOR SYSTEMS ARE DOWN--
--BUT THERE'S GOTTA BE A *WINDOW* IN HERE SOMEWHERE...
OKAY.
HERE WE GO.
LOOKS LIKE A LEXCORP MAINTENANCE CREW.
AUTOMATIC DOCKING IS OFF-LINE--ALONG WITH MOST EVERYTHING ELSE.
THEY ATTEMPTED A MANUAL DOCK--ONE OF THEIR GUYS NEARLY CRUSHED.

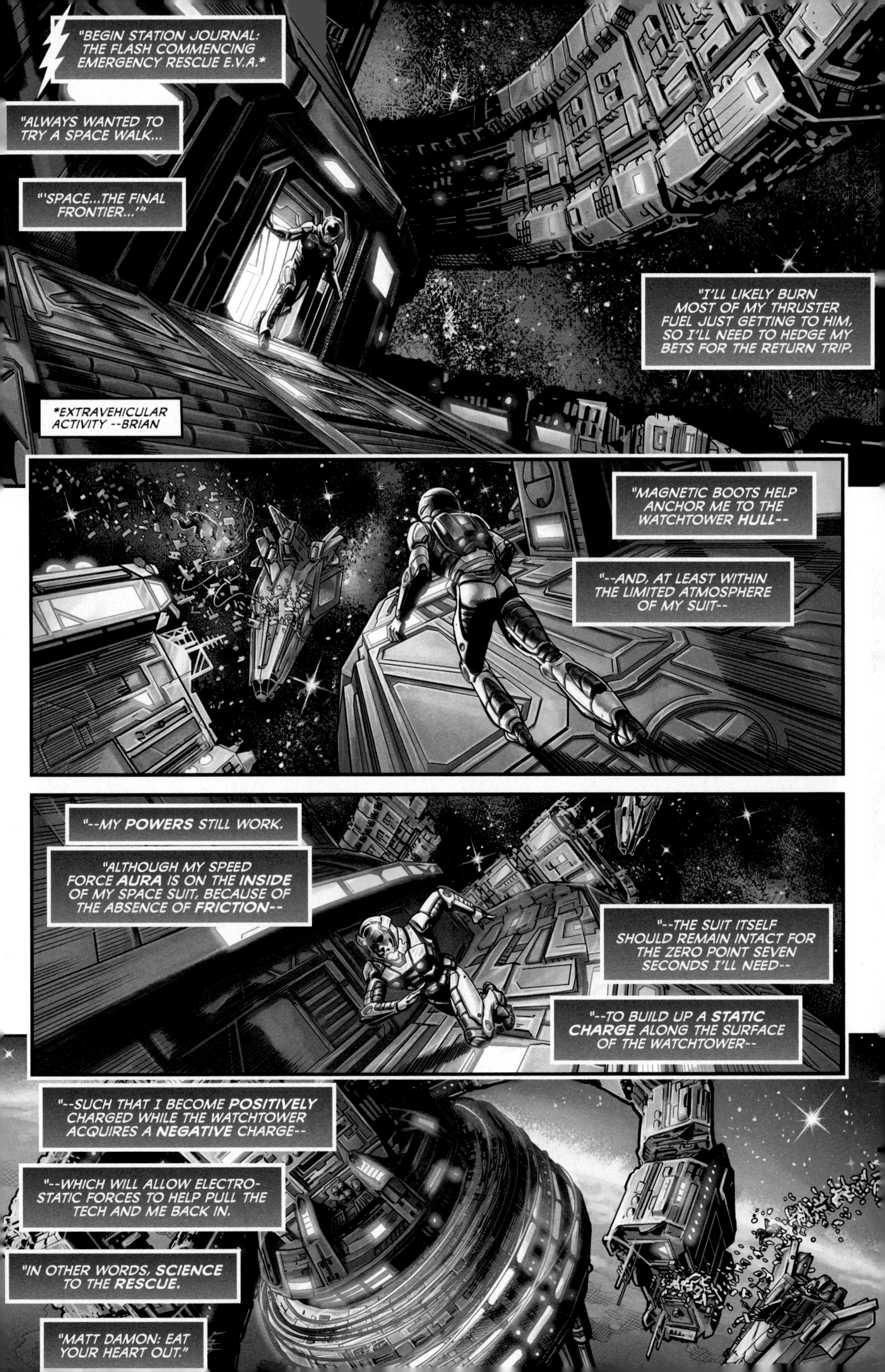
"BEGIN STATION JOURNAL: THE FLASH COMMENCING EMERGENCY RESCUE E.V.A.*
"ALWAYS WANTED TO TRY A SPACE WALK...
"'SPACE...THE FINAL FRONTIER...'"
"I'LL LIKELY BURN MOST OF MY THRUSTER FUEL JUST GETTING TO HIM, SO I'LL NEED TO HEDGE MY BETS FOR THE RETURN TRIP.
*EXTRAVEHICULAR ACTIVITY --BRIAN
"MAGNETIC BOOTS HELP ANCHOR ME TO THE WATCHTOWER HULL--
"--AND, AT LEAST WITHIN THE LIMITED ATMOSPHERE OF MY SUIT--
"--MY POWERS STILL WORK.
"ALTHOUGH MY SPEED FORCE AURA IS ON THE INSIDE OF MY SPACE SUIT, BECAUSE OF THE ABSENCE OF FRICTION--
"--THE SUIT ITSELF SHOULD REMAIN INTACT FOR THE ZERO POINT SEVEN SECONDS I'LL NEED--
"--TO BUILD UP A STATIC CHARGE ALONG THE SURFACE OF THE WATCHTOWER--
"--SUCH THAT I BECOME POSITIVELY CHARGED WHILE THE WATCHTOWER ACQUIRES A NEGATIVE CHARGE--
"--WHICH WILL ALLOW ELECTRO-STATIC FORCES TO HELP PULL THE TECH AND ME BACK IN.
"IN OTHER WORDS, SCIENCE TO THE RESCUE.
"MATT DAMON: EAT YOUR HEART OUT."

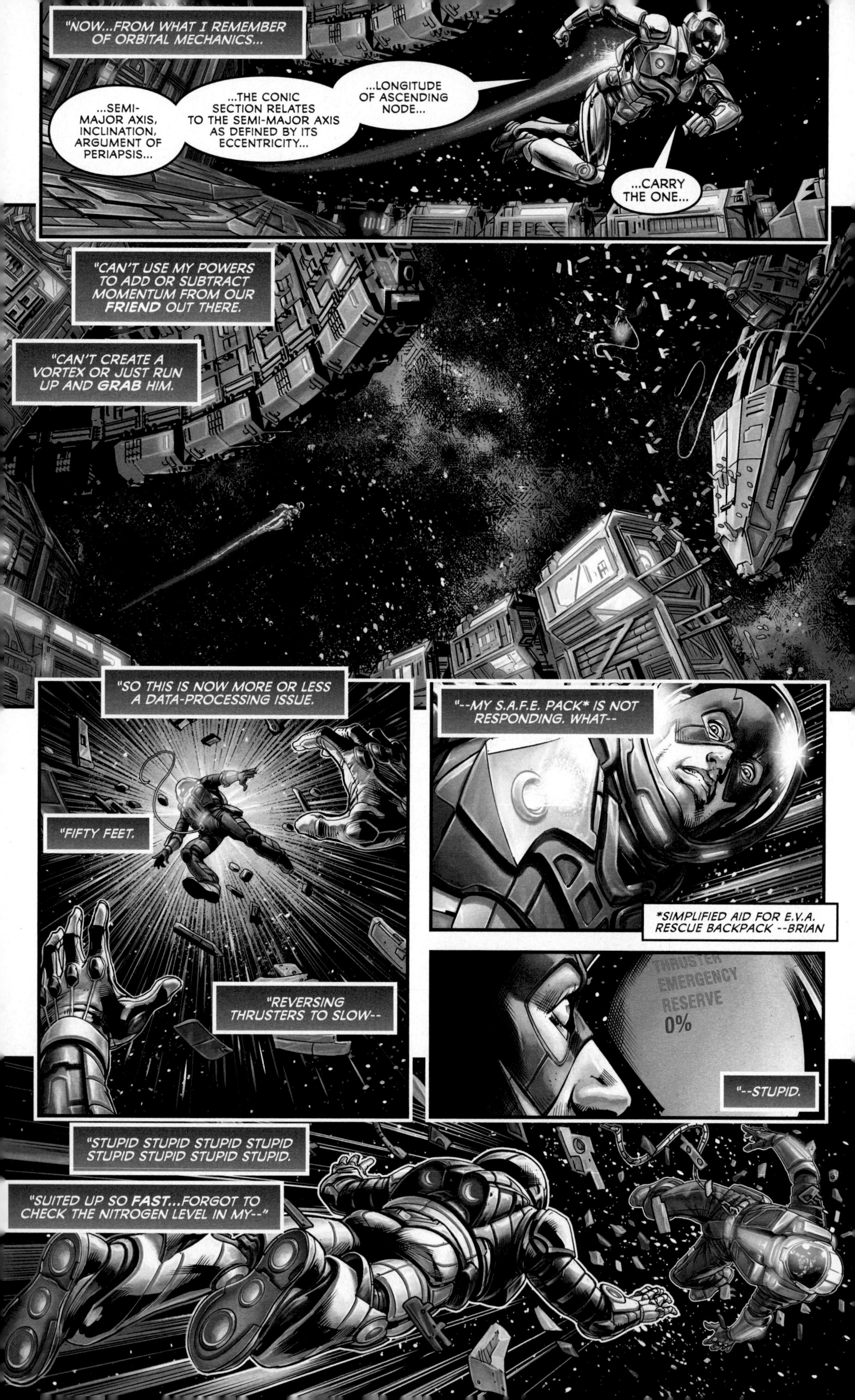

"NOW...FROM WHAT I REMEMBER OF ORBITAL MECHANICS...
...SEMI-MAJOR AXIS, INCLINATION, ARGUMENT OF PERIAPSIS...
...THE CONIC SECTION RELATES TO THE SEMI-MAJOR AXIS AS DEFINED BY ITS ECCENTRICITY...
...LONGITUDE OF ASCENDING NODE...
...CARRY THE ONE...
"CAN'T USE MY POWERS TO ADD OR SUBTRACT MOMENTUM FROM OUR FRIEND OUT THERE.
"CAN'T CREATE A VORTEX OR JUST RUN UP AND GRAB HIM.
"SO THIS IS NOW MORE OR LESS A DATA-PROCESSING ISSUE.
"FIFTY FEET.
"REVERSING THRUSTERS TO SLOW--
"--MY S.A.F.E. PACK* IS NOT RESPONDING. WHAT--
*SIMPLIFIED AID FOR E.V.A. RESCUE BACKPACK --BRIAN
THRUSTER EMERGENCY RESERVE 0%
"--STUPID.
"STUPID STUPID STUPID STUPID STUPID STUPID STUPID STUPID.
"SUITED UP SO FAST...FORGOT TO CHECK THE NITROGEN LEVEL IN MY--"

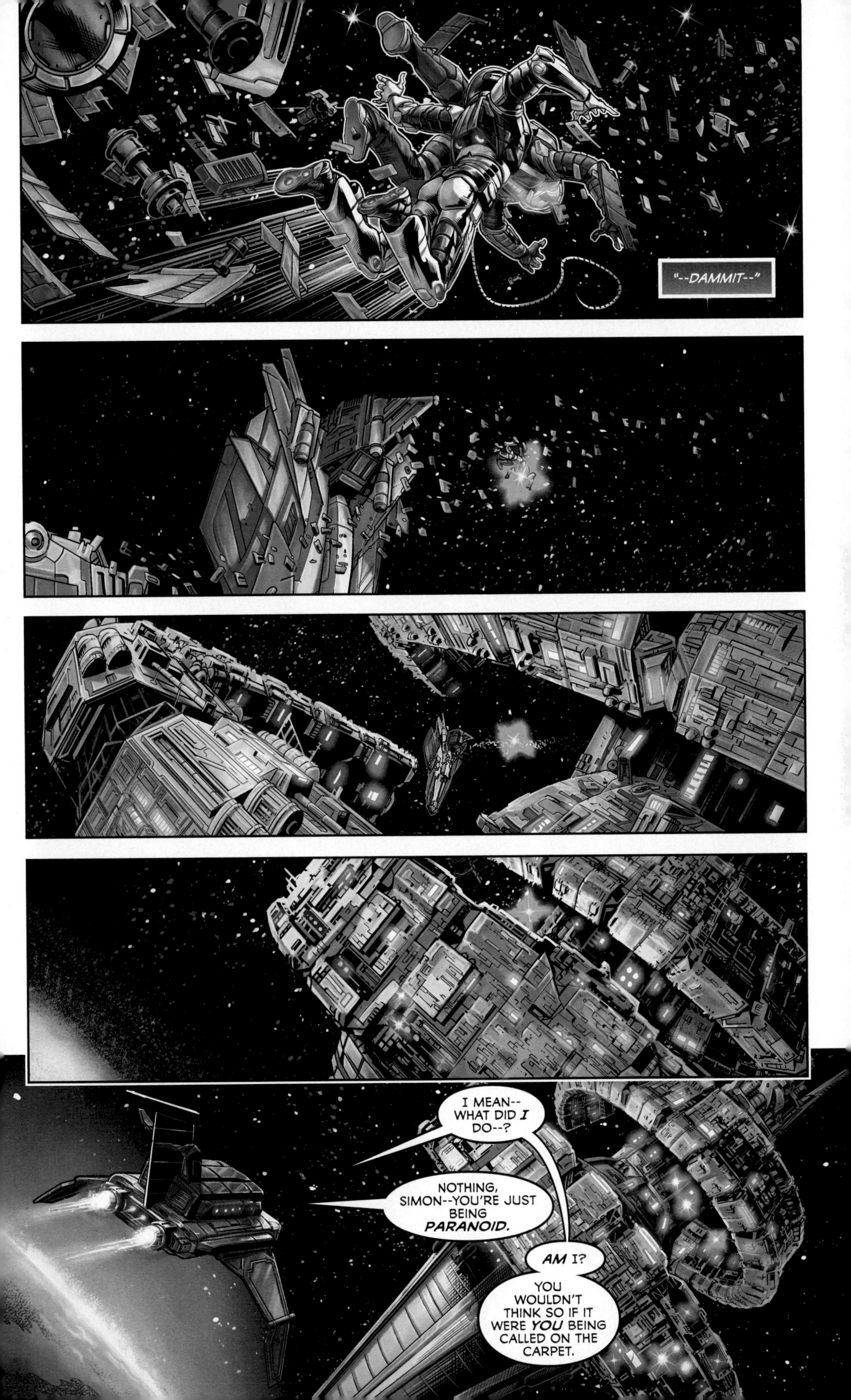
"--DAMMIT--"
I MEAN-- WHAT DID *I* DO--?
NOTHING, SIMON--YOU'RE JUST BEING *PARANOID.*
AM I?
YOU WOULDN'T THINK SO IF IT WERE *YOU* BEING CALLED ON THE CARPET.

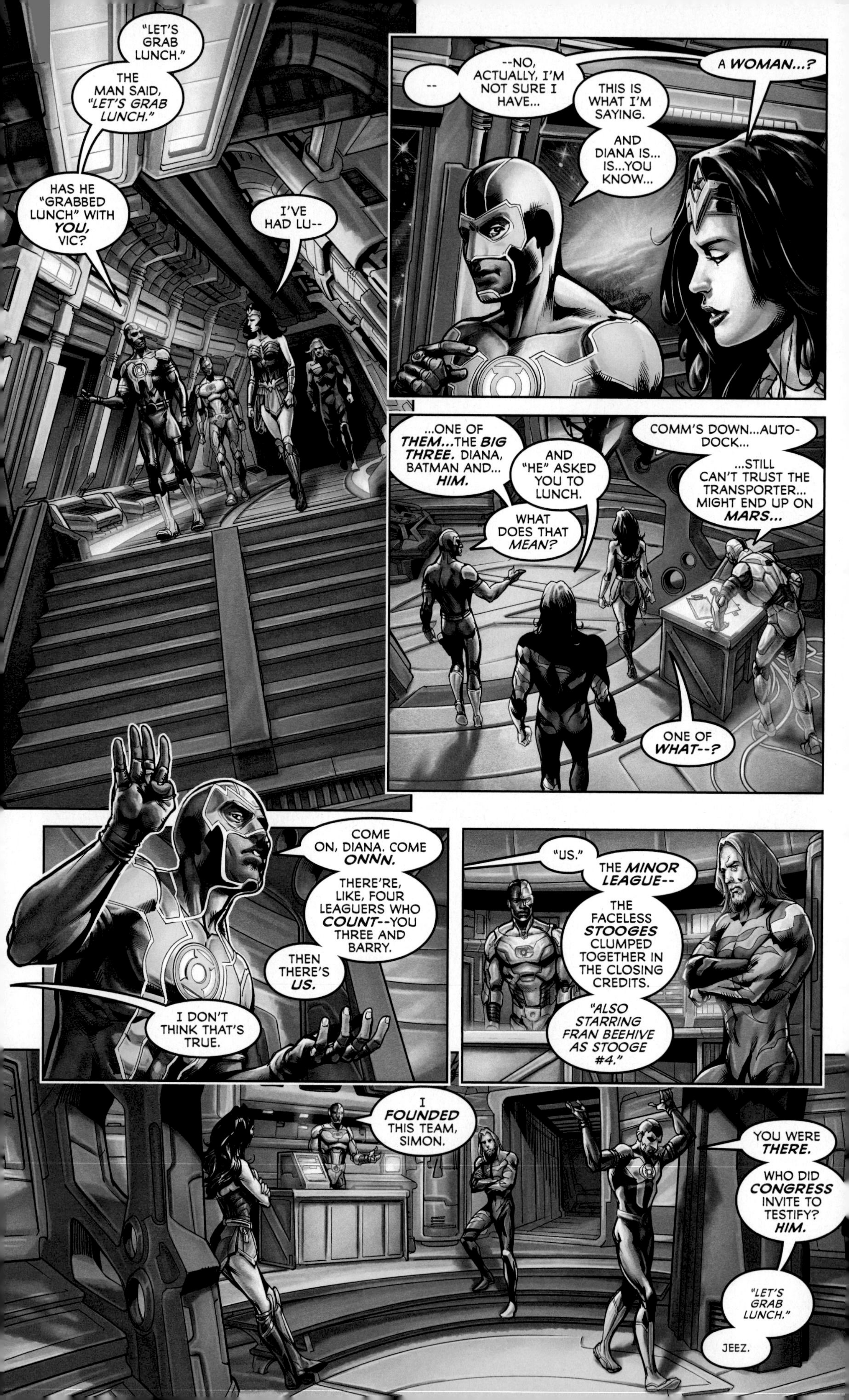
"LET'S GRAB LUNCH."
THE MAN SAID, "LET'S GRAB LUNCH."
HAS HE "GRABBED LUNCH" WITH YOU, VIC?
I'VE HAD LU--
--
--NO, ACTUALLY, I'M NOT SURE I HAVE...
A WOMAN...?
THIS IS WHAT I'M SAYING.
AND DIANA IS... IS...YOU KNOW...
...ONE OF THEM...THE BIG THREE. DIANA, BATMAN AND... HIM.
AND "HE" ASKED YOU TO LUNCH.
WHAT DOES THAT MEAN?
COMM'S DOWN...AUTO-DOCK...
...STILL CAN'T TRUST THE TRANSPORTER... MIGHT END UP ON MARS...
ONE OF WHAT--?
COME ON, DIANA. COME ONNN.
THERE'RE, LIKE, FOUR LEAGUERS WHO COUNT--YOU THREE AND BARRY.
THEN THERE'S US.
I DON'T THINK THAT'S TRUE.
"US."
THE MINOR LEAGUE--
THE FACELESS STOOGES CLUMPED TOGETHER IN THE CLOSING CREDITS.
"ALSO STARRING FRAN BEEHIVE AS STOOGE #4."
I FOUNDED THIS TEAM, SIMON.
YOU WERE THERE.
WHO DID CONGRESS INVITE TO TESTIFY? HIM.
"LET'S GRAB LUNCH."
JEEZ.

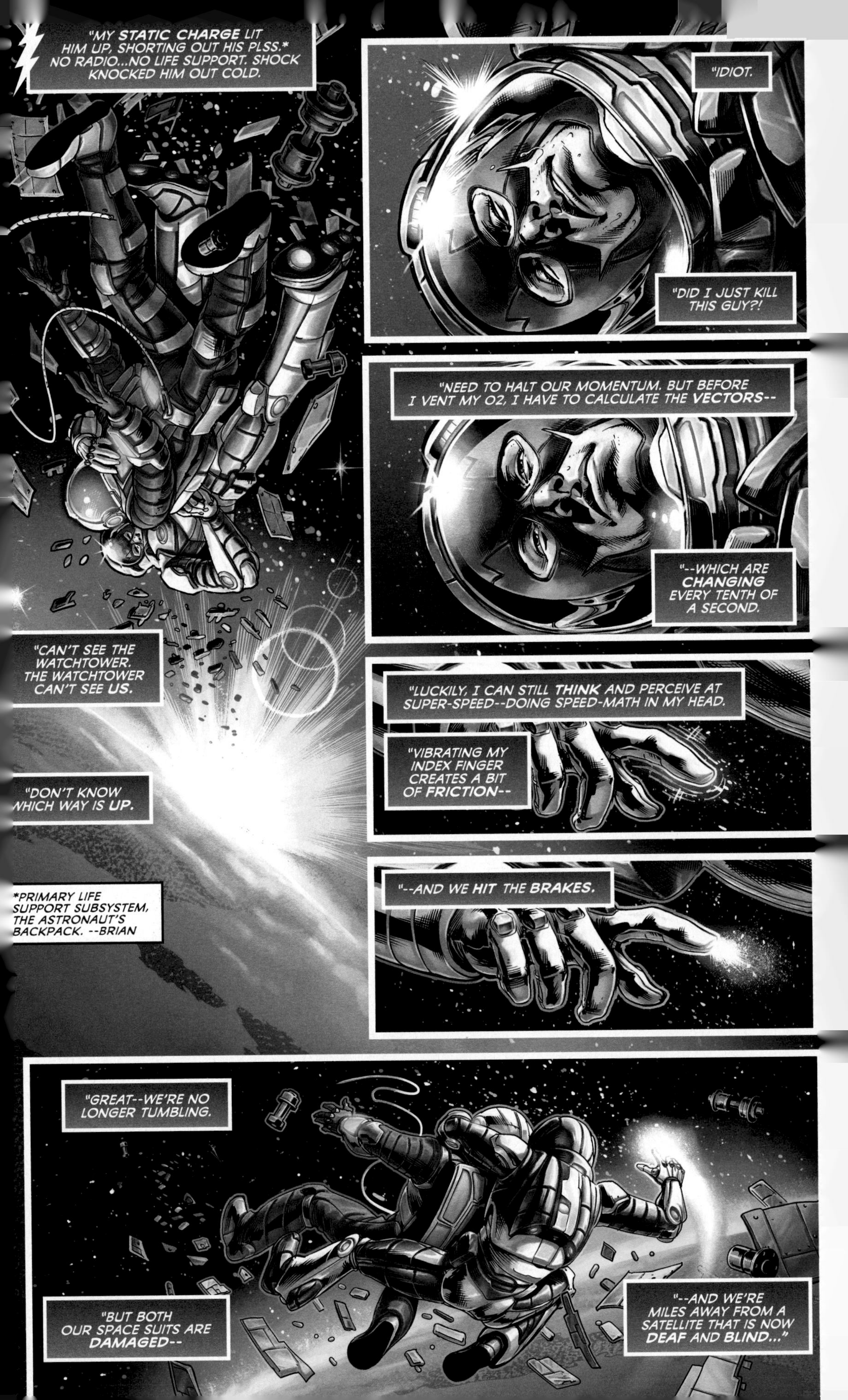
"MY STATIC CHARGE LIT HIM UP, SHORTING OUT HIS PLSS.* NO RADIO...NO LIFE SUPPORT. SHOCK KNOCKED HIM OUT COLD.
"CAN'T SEE THE WATCHTOWER. THE WATCHTOWER CAN'T SEE US.
"DON'T KNOW WHICH WAY IS UP.
*PRIMARY LIFE SUPPORT SUBSYSTEM, THE ASTRONAUT'S BACKPACK. --BRIAN
"IDIOT.
"DID I JUST KILL THIS GUY?!
"NEED TO HALT OUR MOMENTUM. BUT BEFORE I VENT MY O2, I HAVE TO CALCULATE THE VECTORS--
"--WHICH ARE CHANGING EVERY TENTH OF A SECOND.
"LUCKILY, I CAN STILL THINK AND PERCEIVE AT SUPER-SPEED--DOING SPEED-MATH IN MY HEAD.
"VIBRATING MY INDEX FINGER CREATES A BIT OF FRICTION--
"--AND WE HIT THE BRAKES.
"GREAT--WE'RE NO LONGER TUMBLING.
"BUT BOTH OUR SPACE SUITS ARE DAMAGED--
"--AND WE'RE MILES AWAY FROM A SATELLITE THAT IS NOW DEAF AND BLIND..."

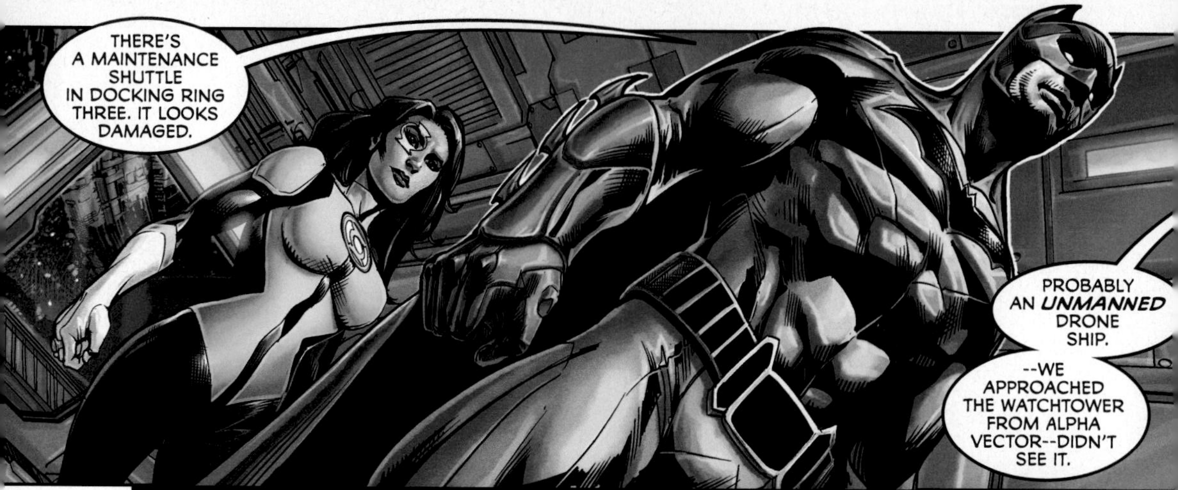
THERE'S A MAINTENANCE SHUTTLE IN DOCKING RING THREE. IT LOOKS DAMAGED.
PROBABLY AN *UNMANNED* DRONE SHIP.
--WE APPROACHED THE WATCHTOWER FROM ALPHA VECTOR--DIDN'T SEE IT.

"Come to Jesus"

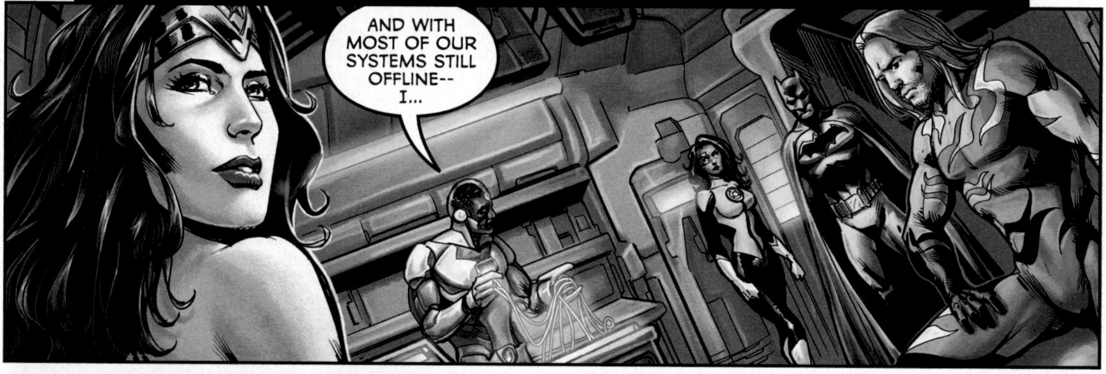
AND WITH MOST OF OUR SYSTEMS STILL OFFLINE-- I...

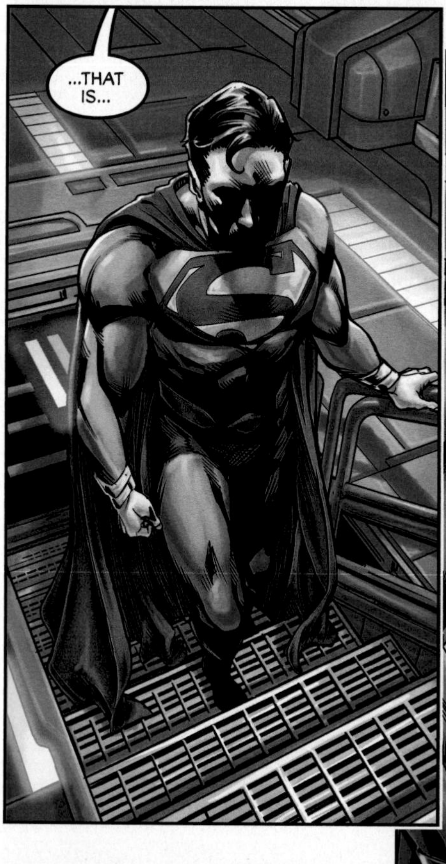
...THAT IS...

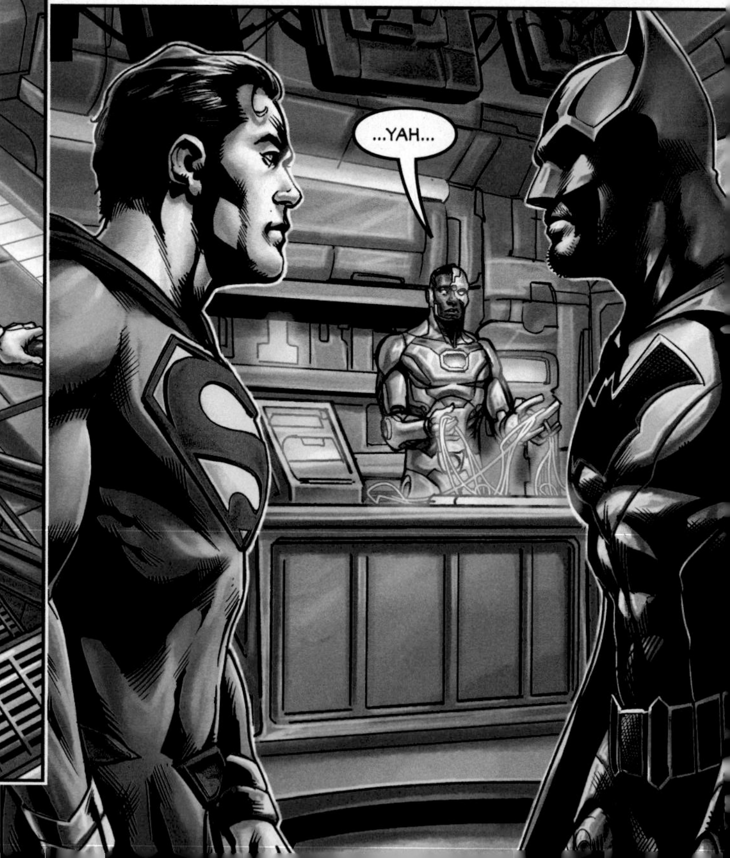
...YAH...

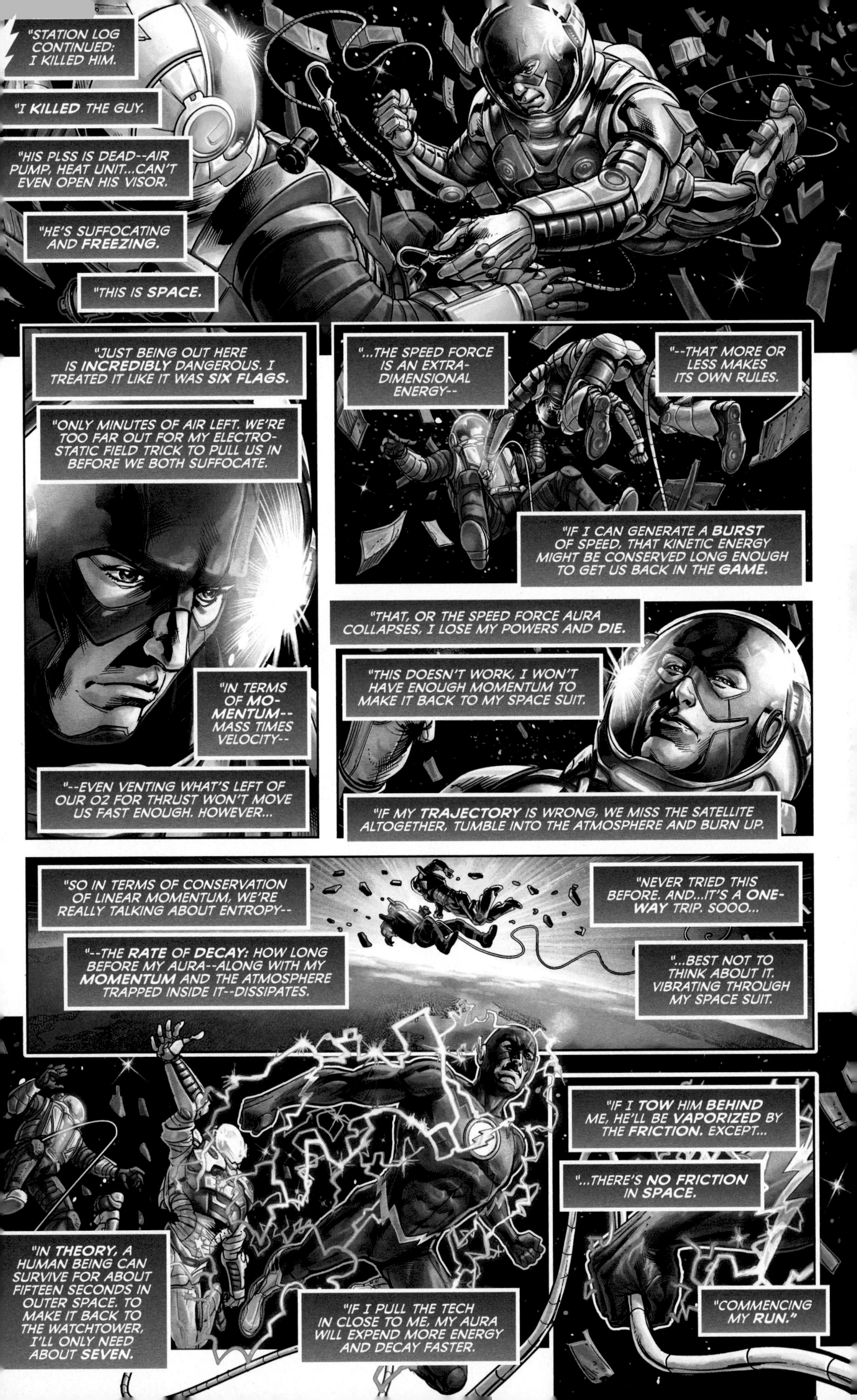
"STATION LOG CONTINUED: I KILLED HIM.
"I KILLED THE GUY.
"HIS PLSS IS DEAD--AIR PUMP, HEAT UNIT...CAN'T EVEN OPEN HIS VISOR.
"HE'S SUFFOCATING AND FREEZING.
"THIS IS SPACE.
"JUST BEING OUT HERE IS INCREDIBLY DANGEROUS. I TREATED IT LIKE IT WAS SIX FLAGS.
"ONLY MINUTES OF AIR LEFT. WE'RE TOO FAR OUT FOR MY ELECTRO-STATIC FIELD TRICK TO PULL US IN BEFORE WE BOTH SUFFOCATE.
"IN TERMS OF MO-MENTUM--MASS TIMES VELOCITY--
"--EVEN VENTING WHAT'S LEFT OF OUR O2 FOR THRUST WON'T MOVE US FAST ENOUGH. HOWEVER...
"...THE SPEED FORCE IS AN EXTRA-DIMENSIONAL ENERGY--
"--THAT MORE OR LESS MAKES ITS OWN RULES.
"IF I CAN GENERATE A BURST OF SPEED, THAT KINETIC ENERGY MIGHT BE CONSERVED LONG ENOUGH TO GET US BACK IN THE GAME.
"THAT, OR THE SPEED FORCE AURA COLLAPSES, I LOSE MY POWERS AND DIE.
"THIS DOESN'T WORK, I WON'T HAVE ENOUGH MOMENTUM TO MAKE IT BACK TO MY SPACE SUIT.
"IF MY TRAJECTORY IS WRONG, WE MISS THE SATELLITE ALTOGETHER, TUMBLE INTO THE ATMOSPHERE AND BURN UP.
"SO IN TERMS OF CONSERVATION OF LINEAR MOMENTUM, WE'RE REALLY TALKING ABOUT ENTROPY--
"--THE RATE OF DECAY: HOW LONG BEFORE MY AURA--ALONG WITH MY MOMENTUM AND THE ATMOSPHERE TRAPPED INSIDE IT--DISSIPATES.
"NEVER TRIED THIS BEFORE. AND...IT'S A ONE-WAY TRIP. SOOO...
"...BEST NOT TO THINK ABOUT IT. VIBRATING THROUGH MY SPACE SUIT.
"IN THEORY, A HUMAN BEING CAN SURVIVE FOR ABOUT FIFTEEN SECONDS IN OUTER SPACE. TO MAKE IT BACK TO THE WATCHTOWER, I'LL ONLY NEED ABOUT SEVEN.
"IF I PULL THE TECH IN CLOSE TO ME, MY AURA WILL EXPEND MORE ENERGY AND DECAY FASTER.
"IF I TOW HIM BEHIND ME, HE'LL BE VAPORIZED BY THE FRICTION. EXCEPT...
"...THERE'S NO FRICTION IN SPACE.
"COMMENCING MY RUN."

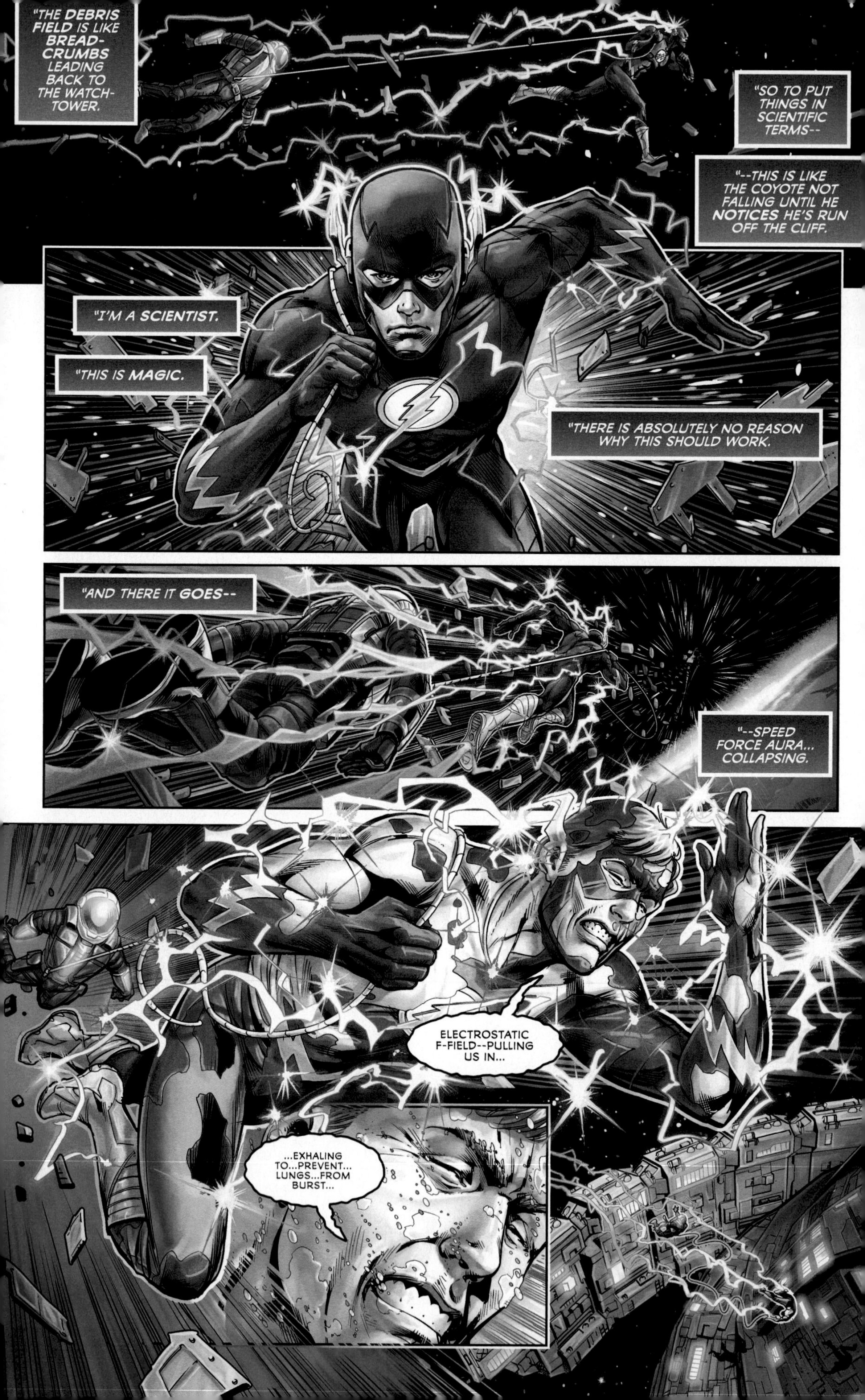
"THE DEBRIS FIELD IS LIKE BREAD-CRUMBS LEADING BACK TO THE WATCH-TOWER.
"SO TO PUT THINGS IN SCIENTIFIC TERMS--
"--THIS IS LIKE THE COYOTE NOT FALLING UNTIL HE NOTICES HE'S RUN OFF THE CLIFF.
"I'M A SCIENTIST.
"THIS IS MAGIC.
"THERE IS ABSOLUTELY NO REASON WHY THIS SHOULD WORK.
"AND THERE IT GOES--
"--SPEED FORCE AURA... COLLAPSING.
ELECTROSTATIC F-FIELD--PULLING US IN...
...EXHALING TO...PREVENT... LUNGS...FROM BURST...

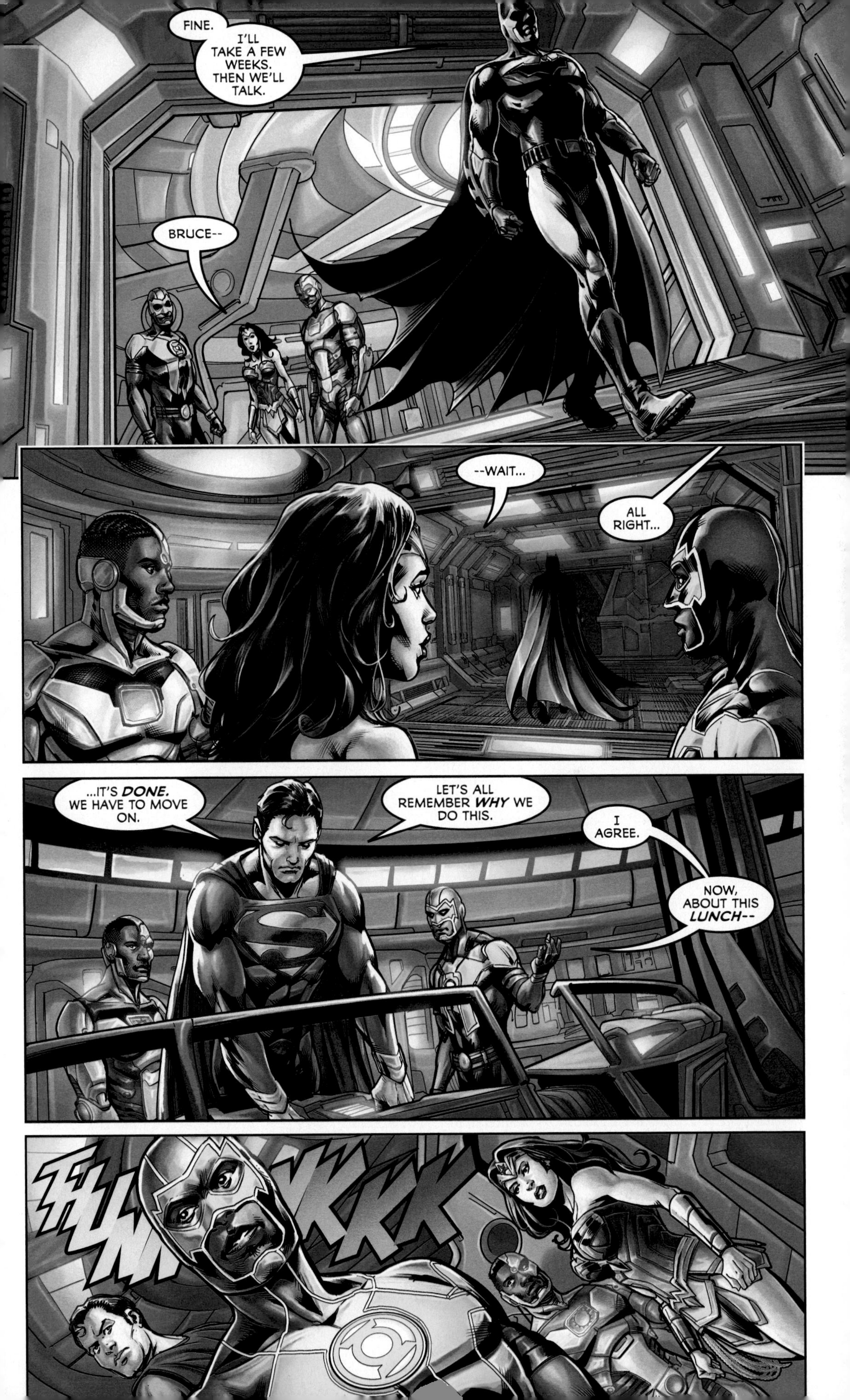
FINE.
I'LL TAKE A FEW WEEKS. THEN WE'LL TALK.
BRUCE--
--WAIT...
ALL RIGHT...
...IT'S *DONE.* WE HAVE TO MOVE ON.
LET'S ALL REMEMBER *WHY* WE DO THIS.
I AGREE.
NOW, ABOUT THIS *LUNCH--*

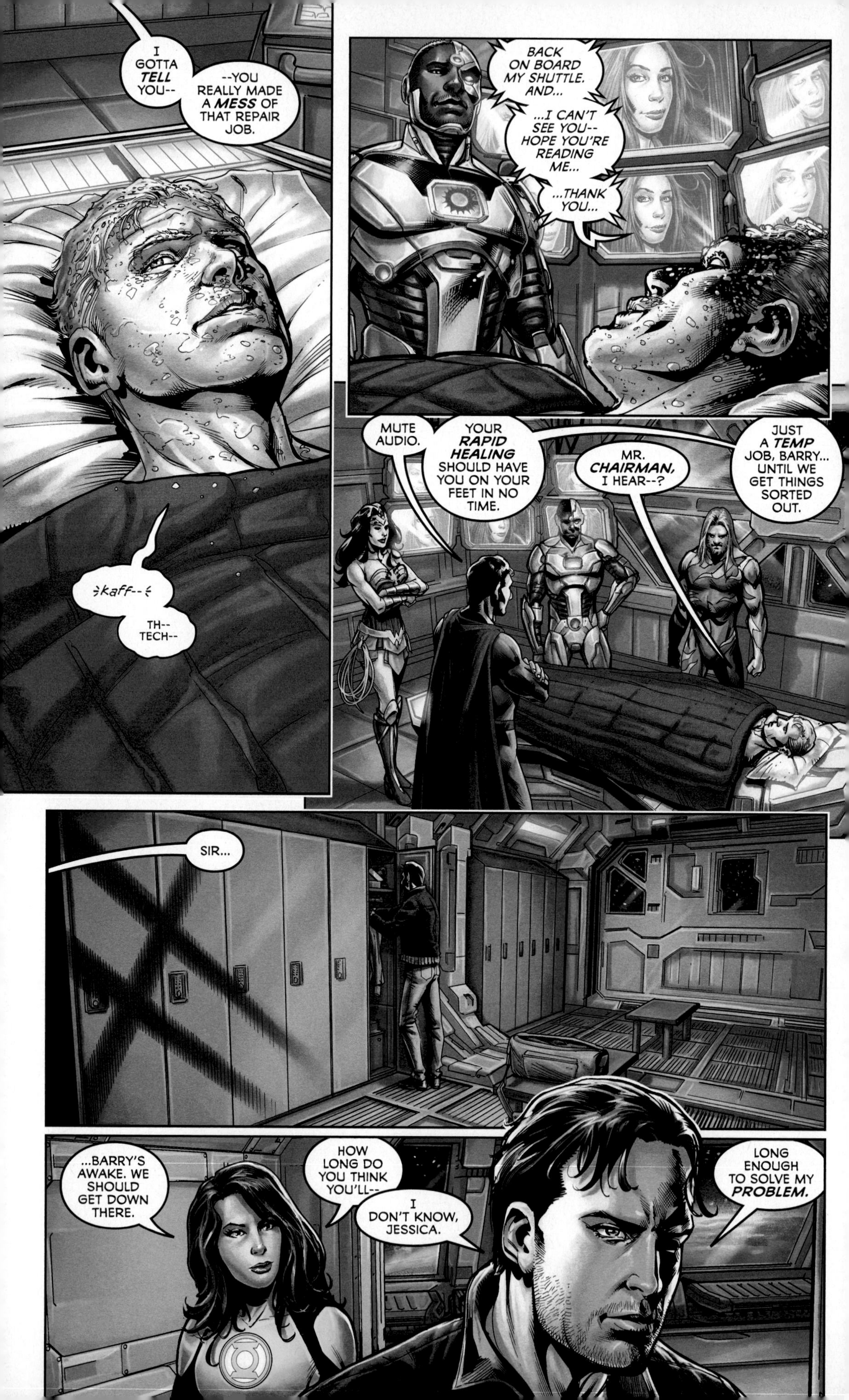

I GOTTA TELL YOU--
--YOU REALLY MADE A MESS OF THAT REPAIR JOB.
BACK ON BOARD MY SHUTTLE. AND...
...I CAN'T SEE YOU-- HOPE YOU'RE READING ME...
...THANK YOU...
-kaff--
TH-- TECH--
MUTE AUDIO.
YOUR RAPID HEALING SHOULD HAVE YOU ON YOUR FEET IN NO TIME.
MR. CHAIRMAN, I HEAR--?
JUST A TEMP JOB, BARRY... UNTIL WE GET THINGS SORTED OUT.
SIR...
...BARRY'S AWAKE. WE SHOULD GET DOWN THERE.
HOW LONG DO YOU THINK YOU'LL--
I DON'T KNOW, JESSICA.
LONG ENOUGH TO SOLVE MY PROBLEM.

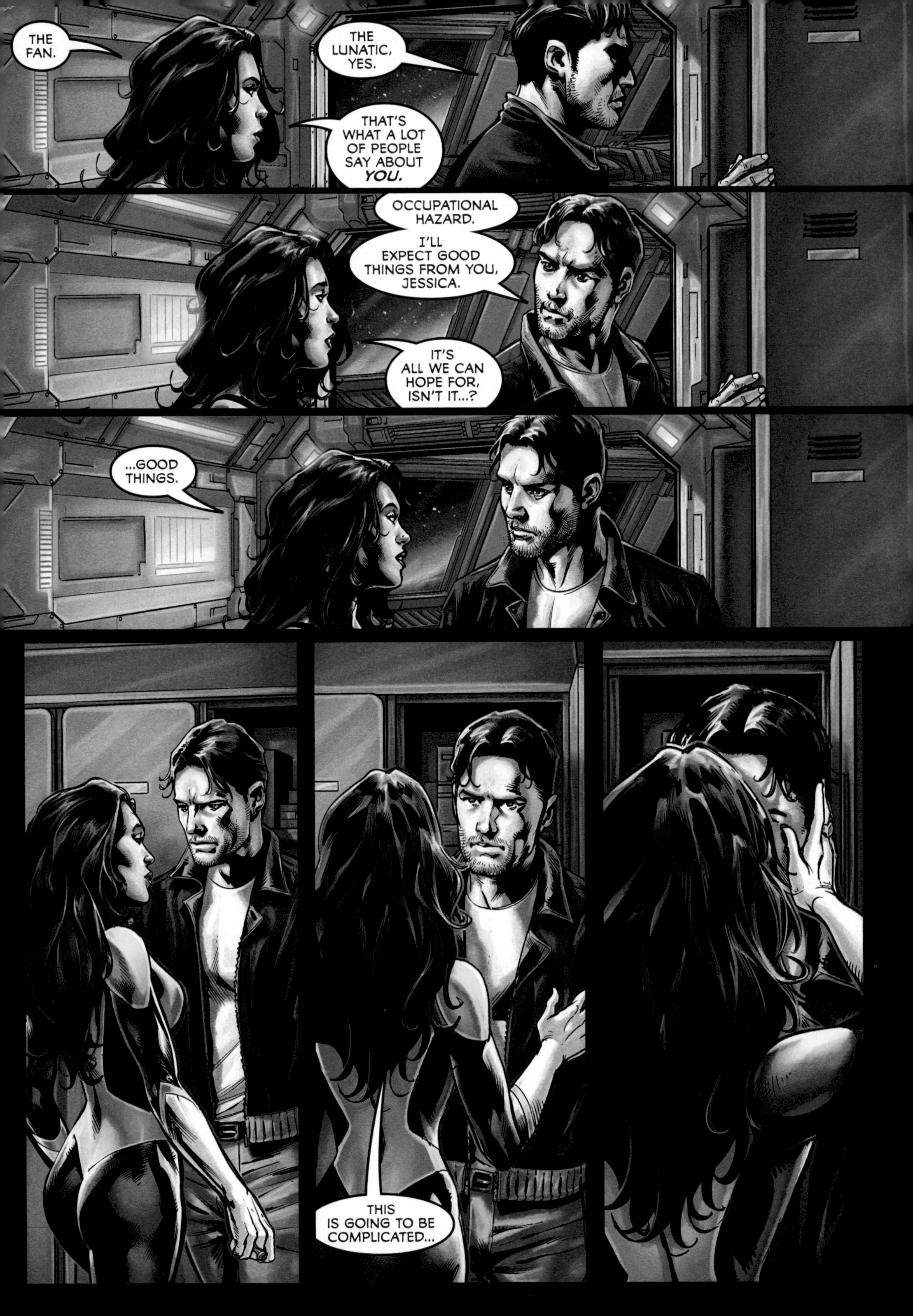
THE FAN.
THE LUNATIC, YES.
THAT'S WHAT A LOT OF PEOPLE SAY ABOUT *YOU.*
OCCUPATIONAL HAZARD.
I'LL EXPECT GOOD THINGS FROM YOU, JESSICA.
IT'S ALL WE CAN HOPE FOR, ISN'T IT...?
...GOOD THINGS.
THIS IS GOING TO BE COMPLICATED...

"Complications"

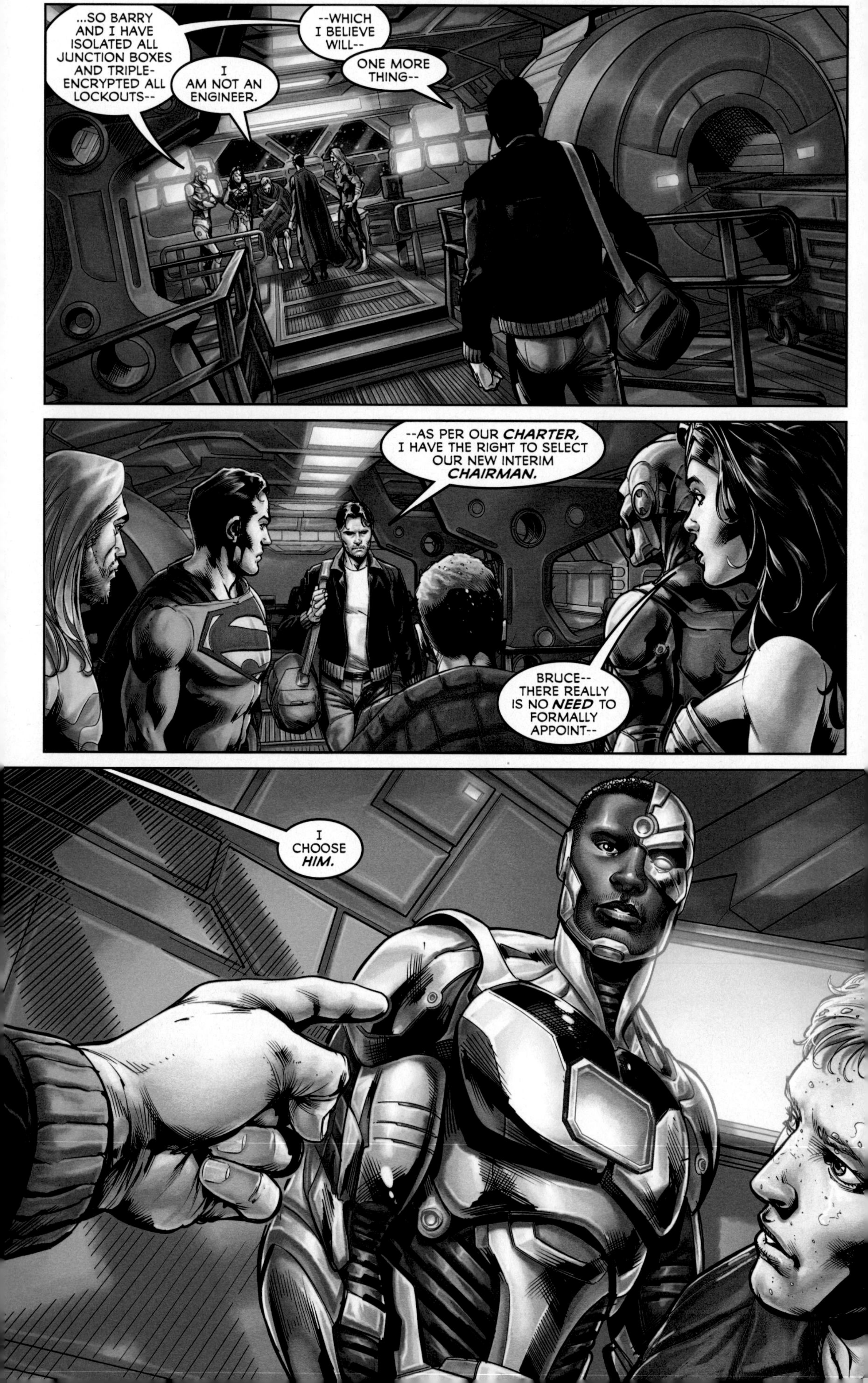
...SO BARRY AND I HAVE ISOLATED ALL JUNCTION BOXES AND TRIPLE-ENCRYPTED ALL LOCKOUTS--
--WHICH I BELIEVE WILL--
I AM NOT AN ENGINEER.
ONE MORE THING--
--AS PER OUR CHARTER, I HAVE THE RIGHT TO SELECT OUR NEW INTERIM CHAIRMAN.
BRUCE-- THERE REALLY IS NO NEED TO FORMALLY APPOINT--
I CHOOSE HIM.

JUSTICE LEAGUE

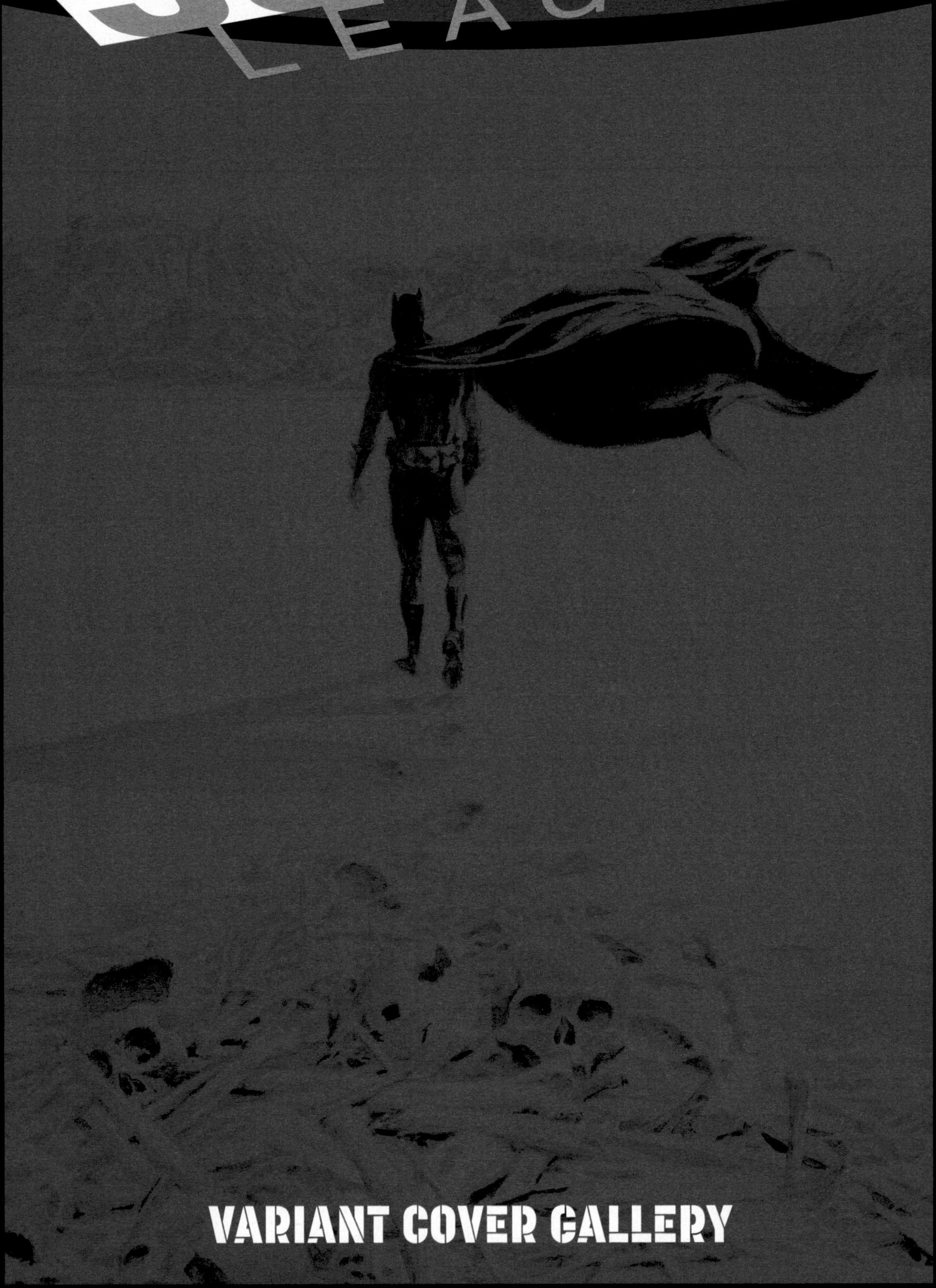

VARIANT COVER GALLERY

JUSTICE LEAGUE #34 variant cover by J.G. JONES

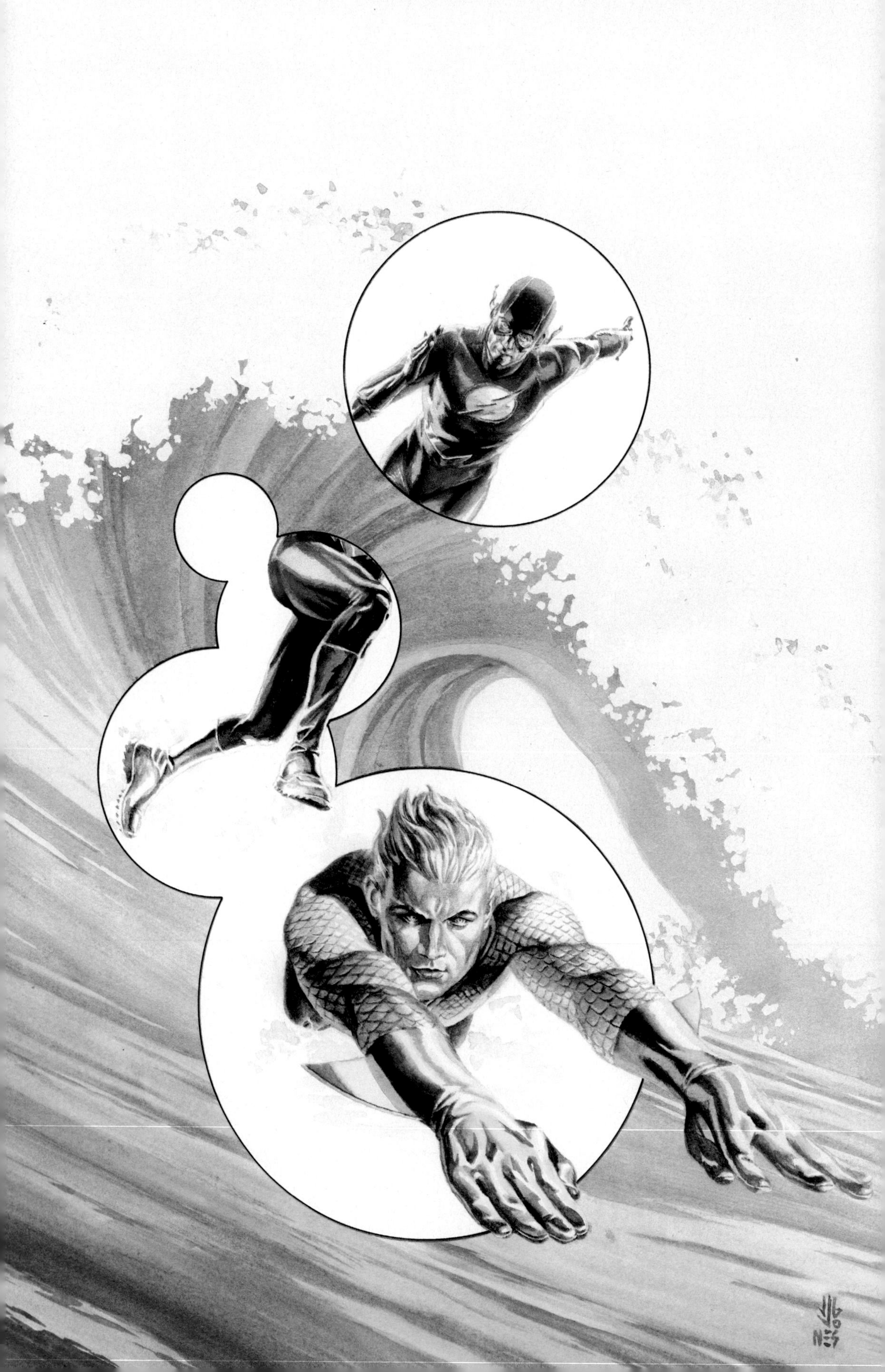

JUSTICE LEAGUE #35 variant cover by J.G. JONES

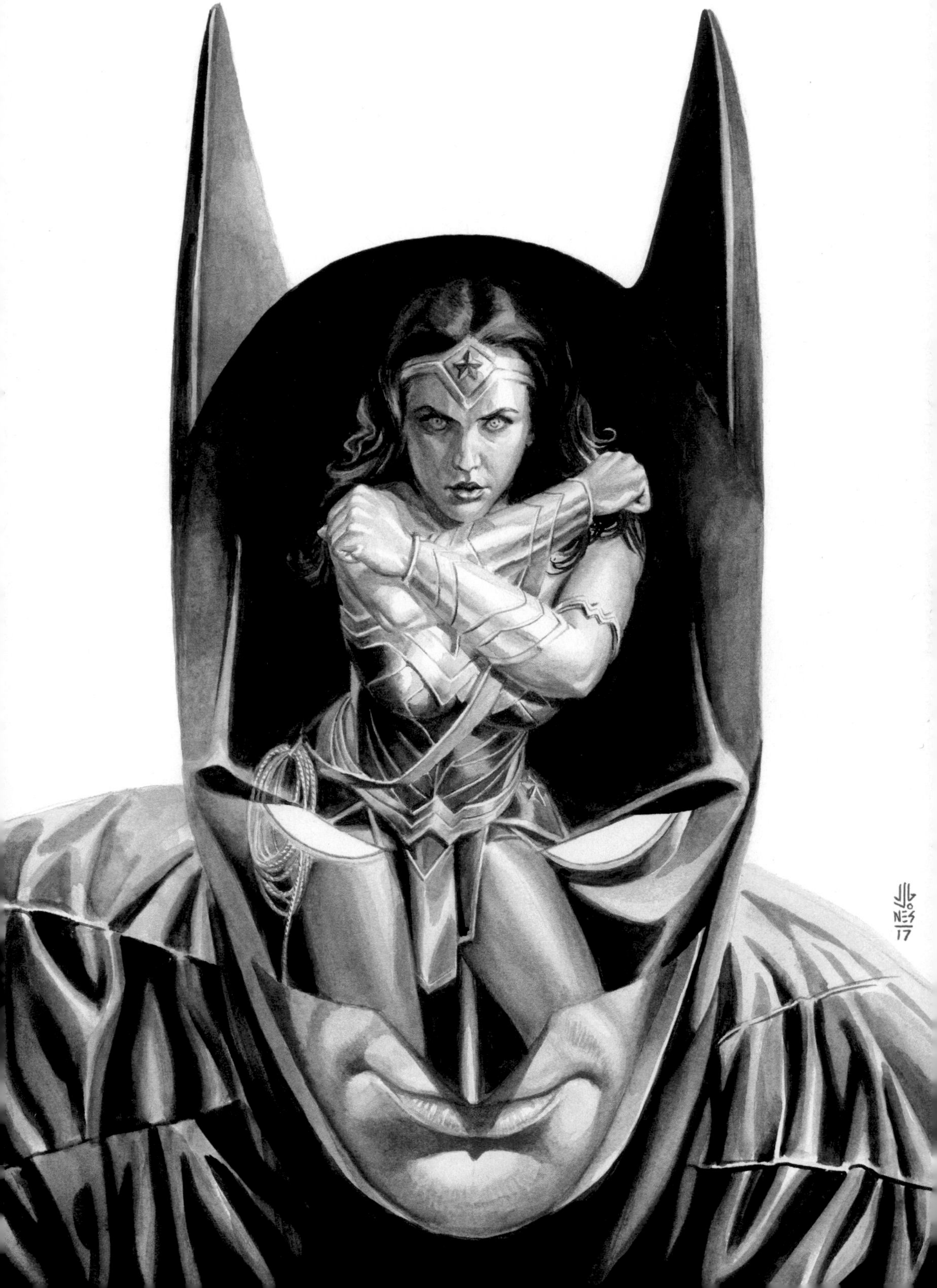

JUSTICE LEAGUE #36 variant cover by J.G. JONES

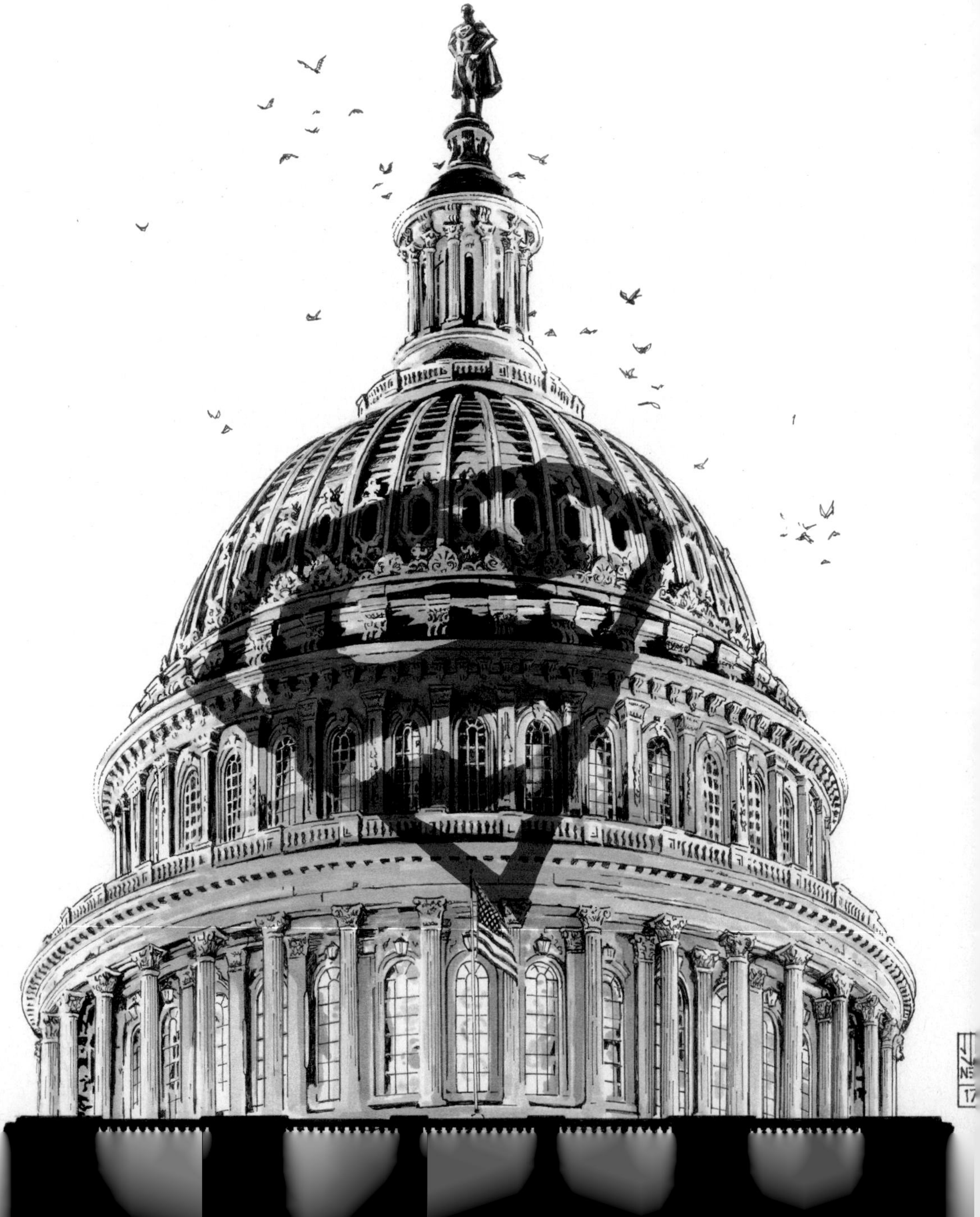

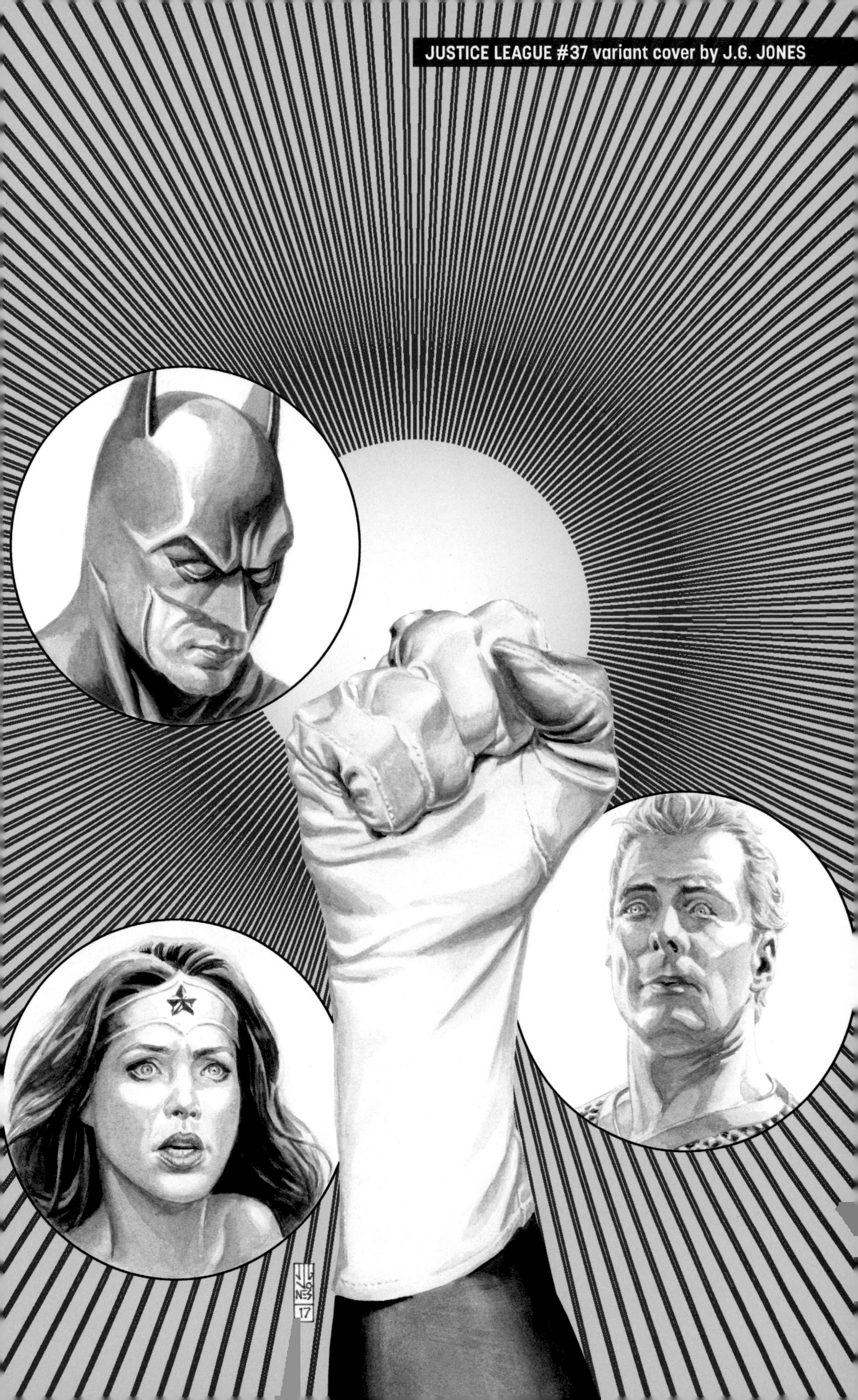

JUSTICE LEAGUE #37 variant cover by J.G. JONES

JUSTICE LEAGUE #38 variant cover by J.G. JONES

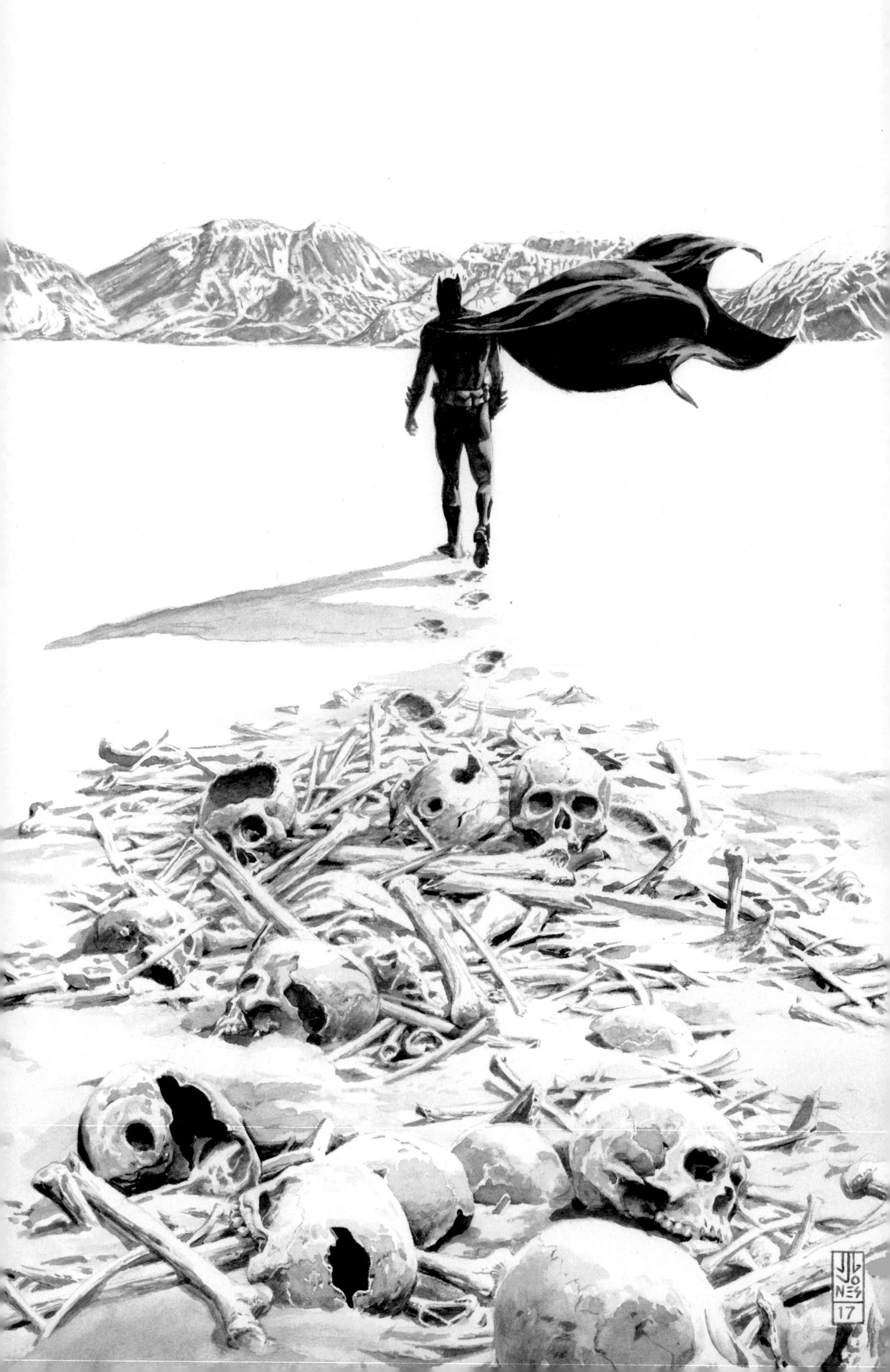

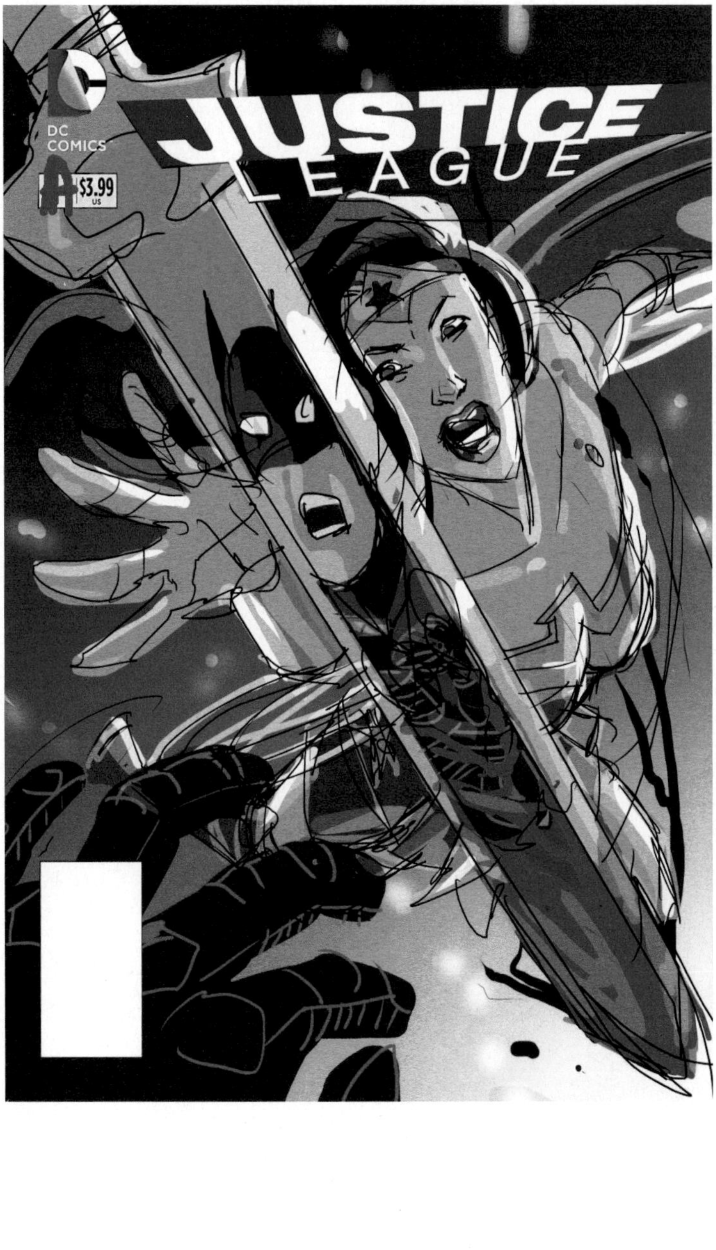
DC COMICS
JUSTICE LEAGUE
$3.99 US

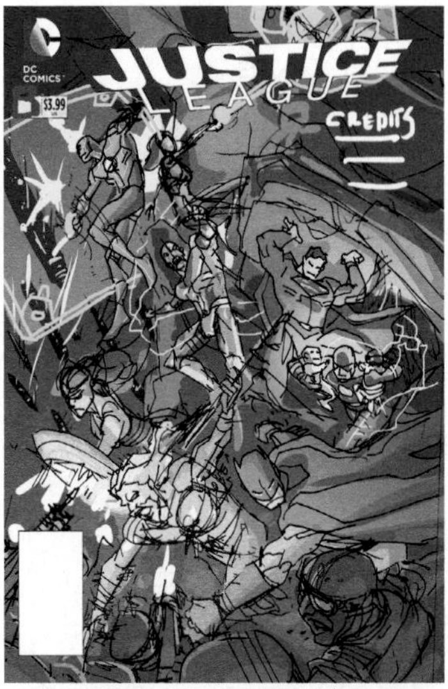
DC COMICS
JUSTICE LEAGUE
$3.99
CREDITS

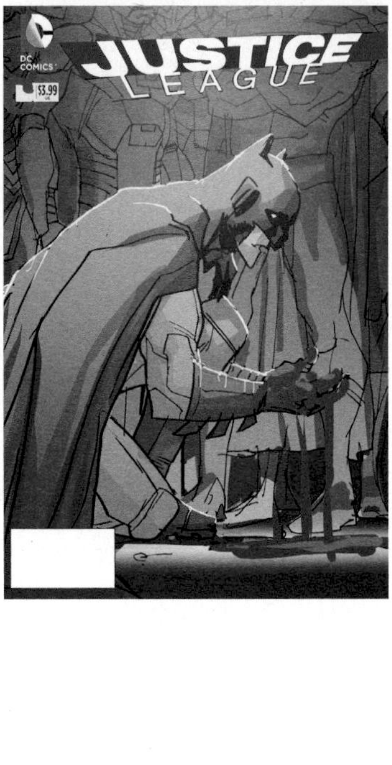
DC COMICS
JUSTICE LEAGUE
$3.99

JUSTICE LEAGUE #34 cover sketches by Pete Woods

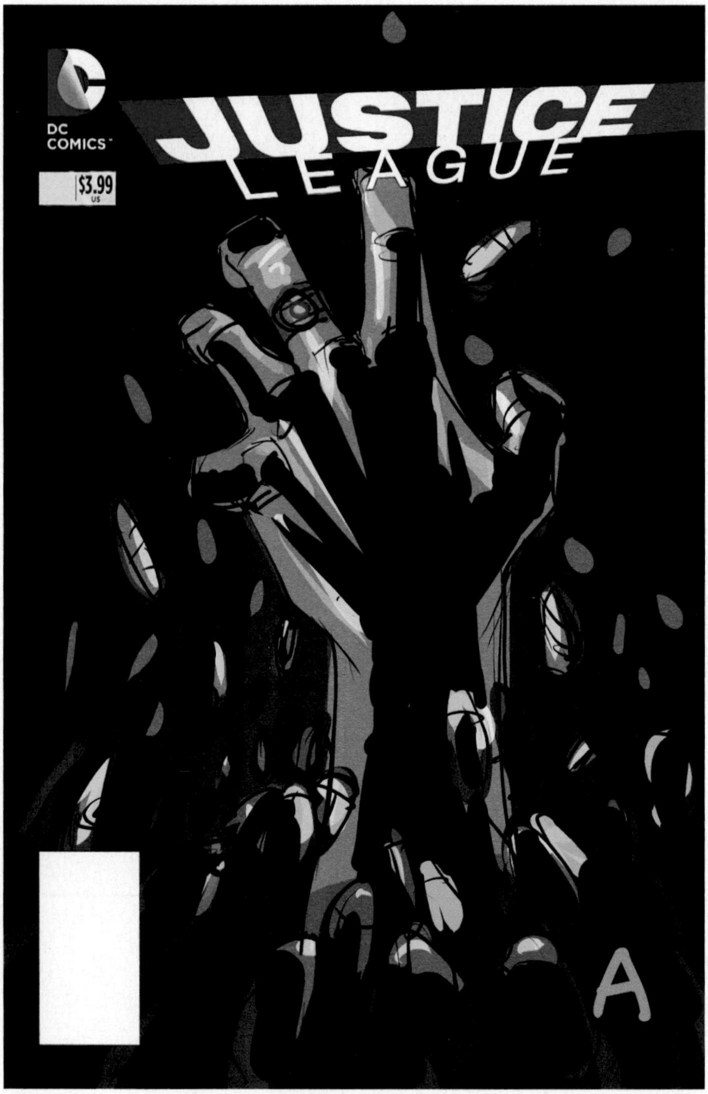
DC
COMICS
JUSTICE
LEAGUE
$3.99
US
A

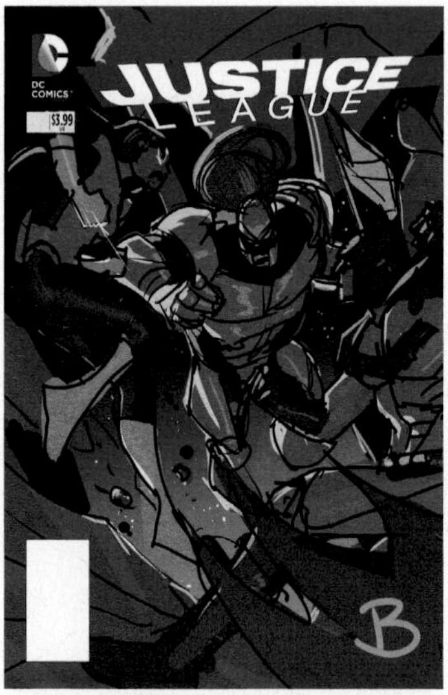
DC
COMICS
JUSTICE
LEAGUE
$3.99
B

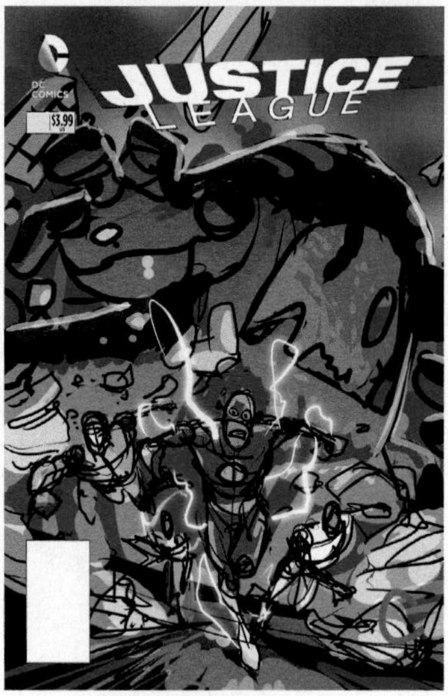
DC
COMICS
JUSTICE
LEAGUE
$3.99

JUSTICE LEAGUE #35 and #36 cover sketches by Pete Woods

SKETCH A
DC UNIVERSE
JUSTICE LEAGUE
88 $2.99
WRITER
PENCILER
INKER
COLORIST

SKETCH B
DC UNIVERSE
JUSTICE LEAGUE
88 $2.99
WRITER
PENCILER
INKER
COLORIST
WANTED FOR MURDER

SKETCH C
DC UNIVERSE
JUSTICE LEAGUE
88 $2.99
RATED T TEEN
WRITER
PENCILER
INKER
COLORIST

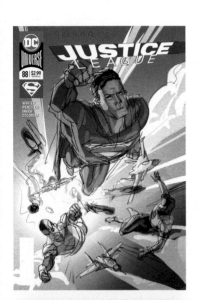

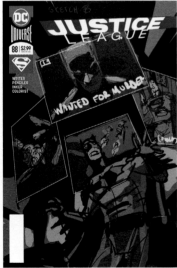

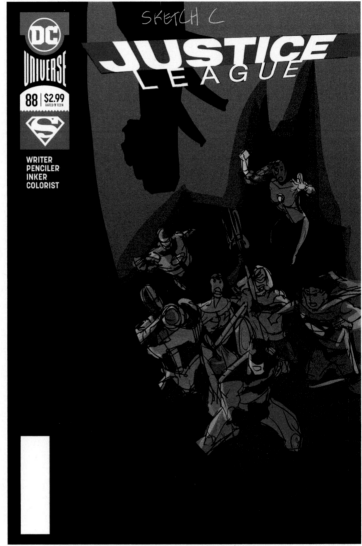

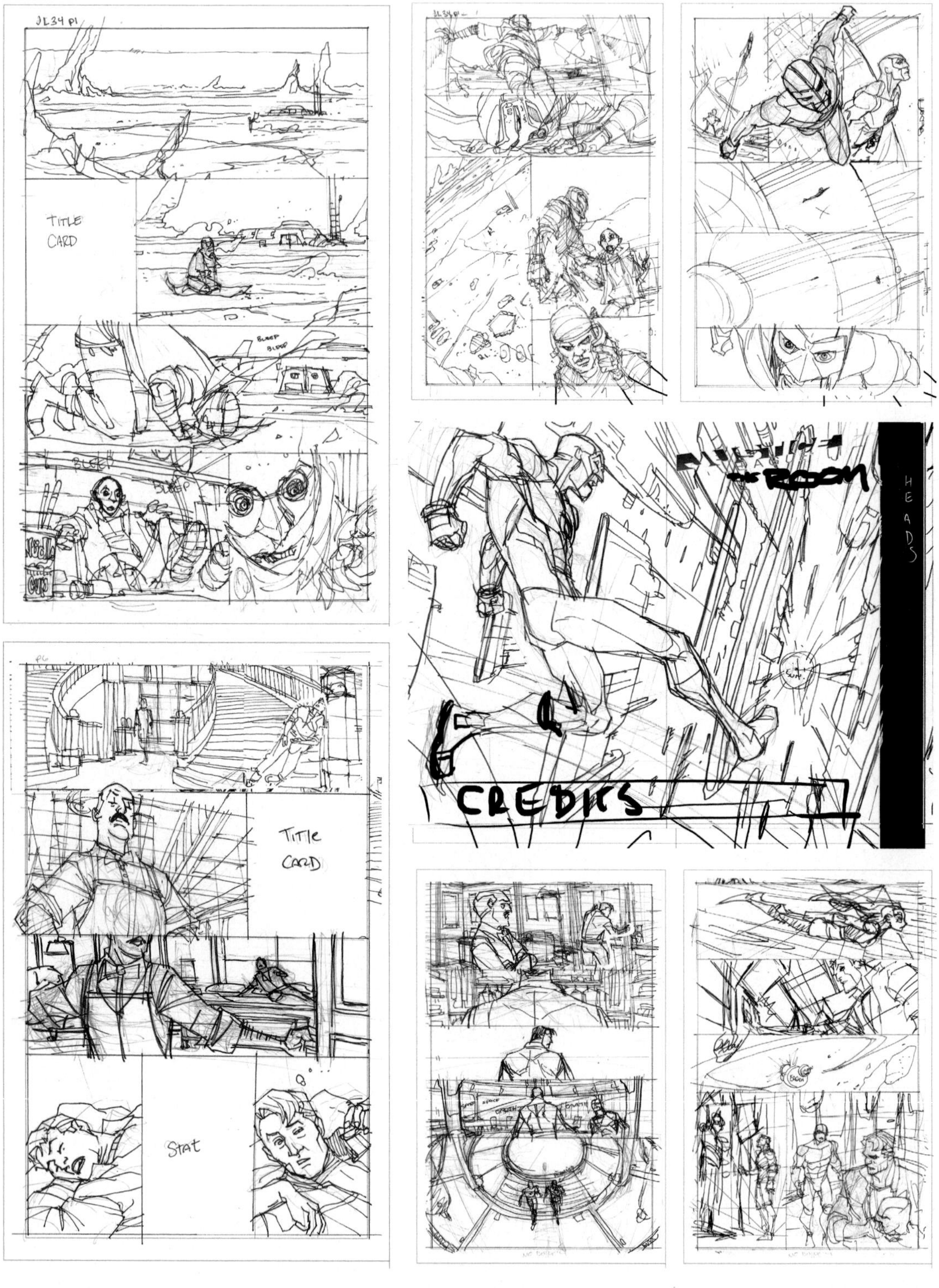
TITLE CARD
BLEEP BLEEP
ROOM
HEADS
CREDITS
Title CARD
Stat

JUSTICE LEAGUE #34 pencil thumbnails by Pete Woods

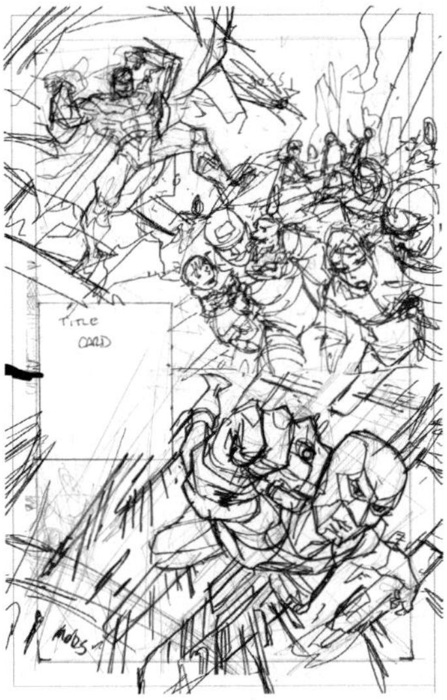
TITLE CARD

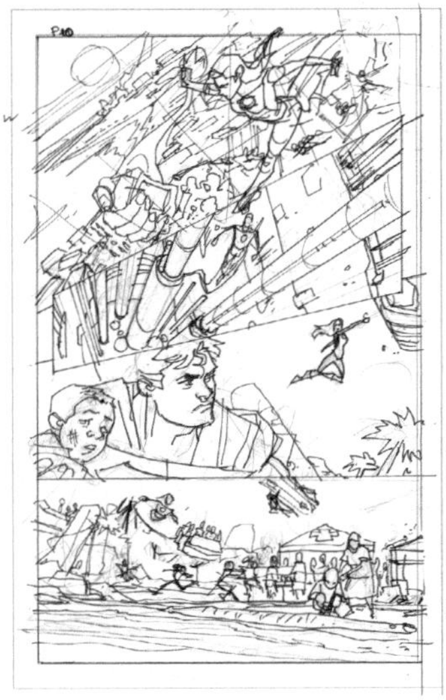
P10

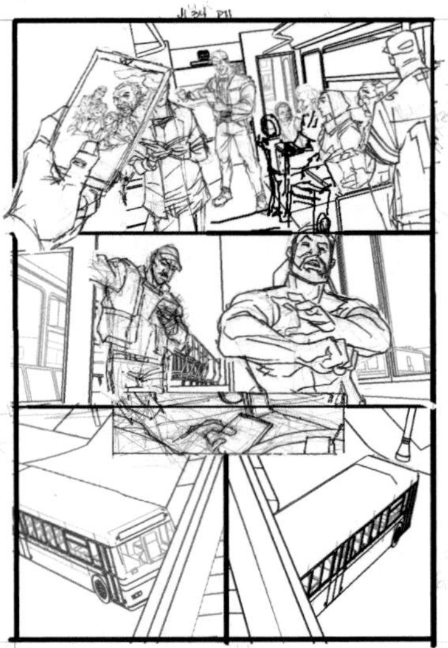
JL34 P11

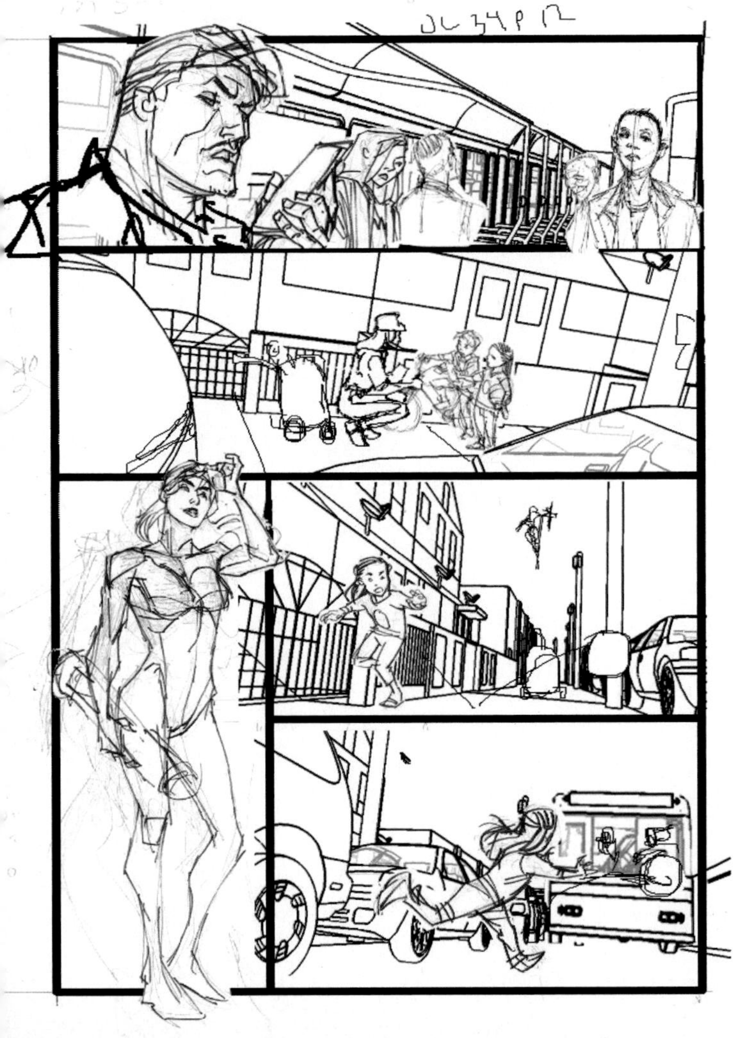
JL 34 P 12

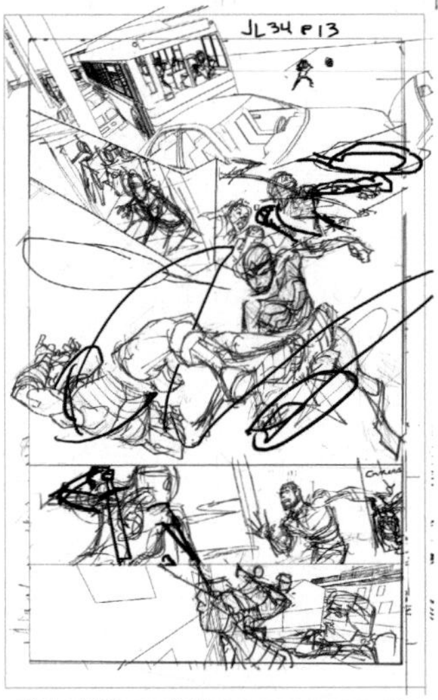
JL34 P13

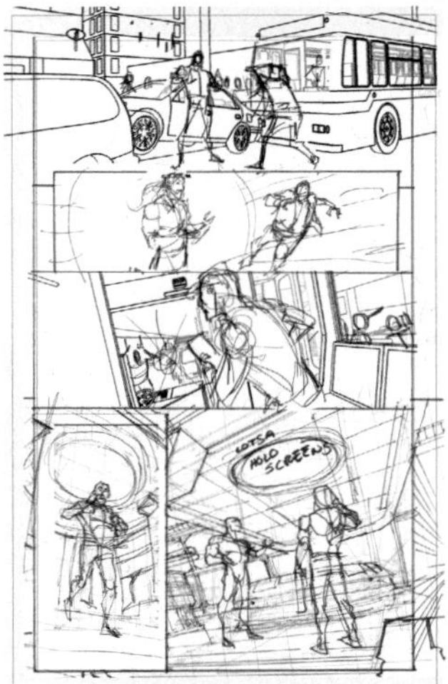
LOTSA HOLO SCREENS

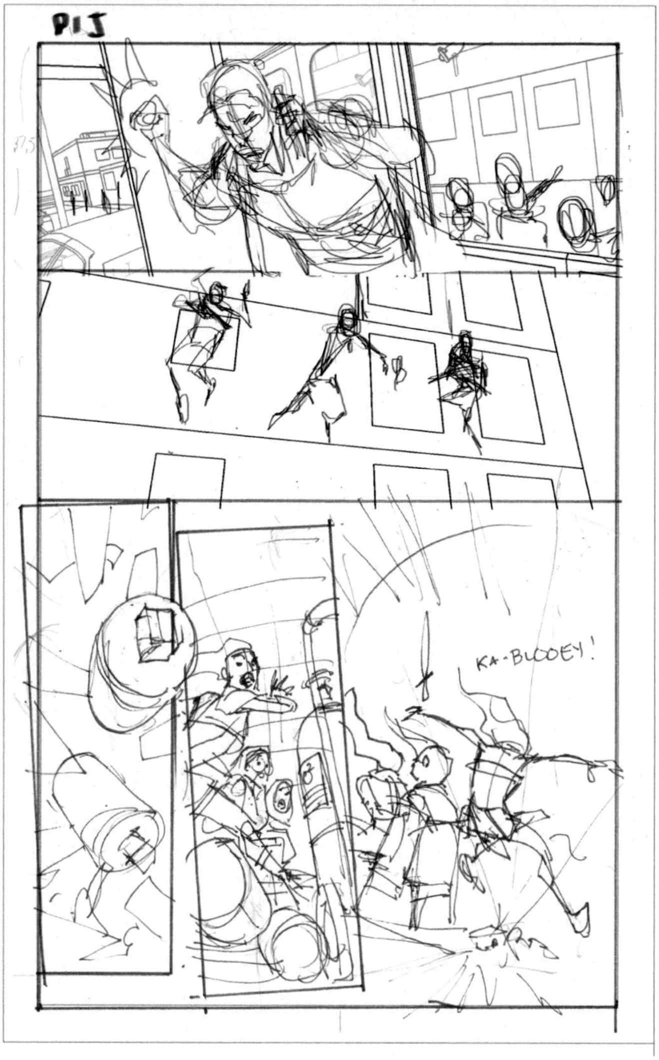
P15
KA-BLOOEY!

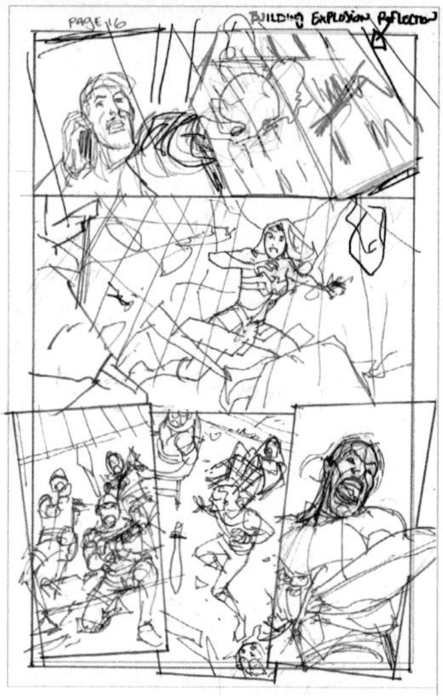
PAGE 16
BUILDING EXPLOSION REFLECTION

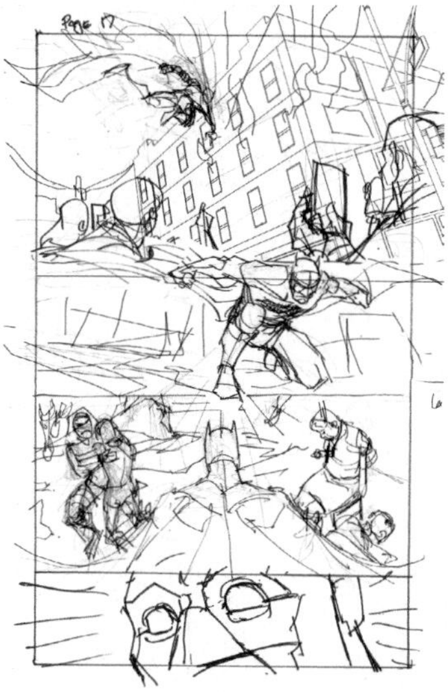
Page 17

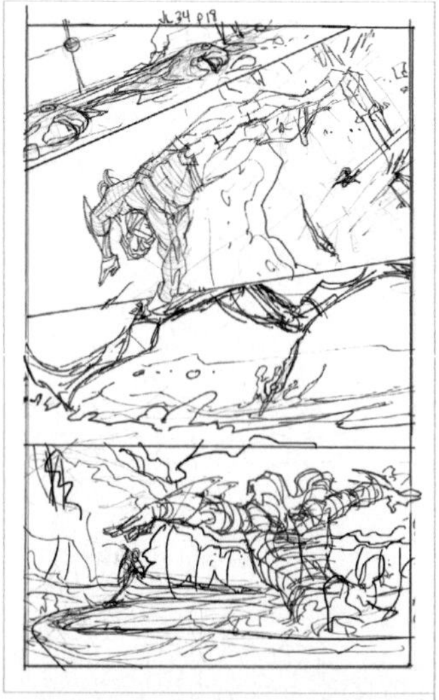
JL34 p19

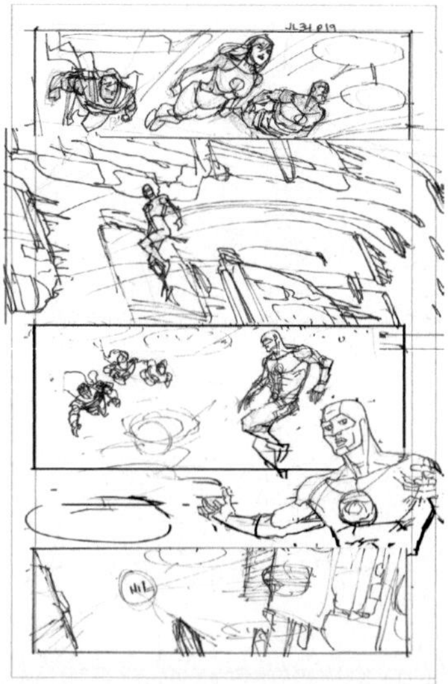
JL34 p19

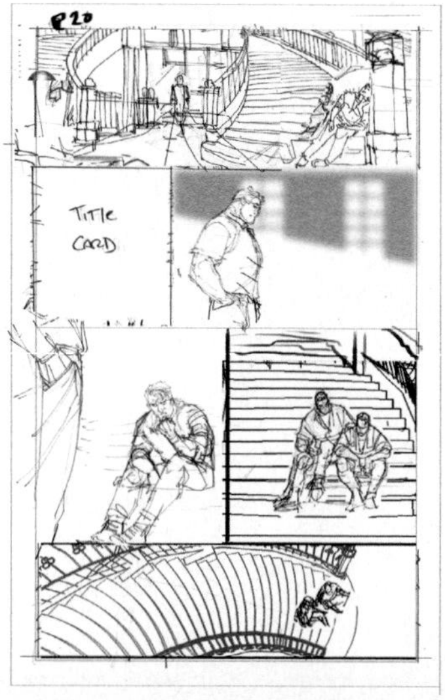
P20
TITLE CARD